Hey Ja.

Christian Govan

Hope you enjoy
the book.

Love
Christian

— ✗ —

Christian Govan

The Enemy with My Face

Olympia Publishers
London

www.olympiapublishers.com
OLYMPIA PAPERBACK EDITION

A CIP catalogue record for this title is
available from the British Library.

ISBN: 978-1-78830-837-3

This is a work of creative nonfiction. The events are portrayed to the
best of the author's memory. While all the stories in this book are
true, some names and identifying details have been changed to
protect the privacy of the people involved.

First Published in 2021

Olympia Publishers
Tallis House
2 Tallis Street
London
EC4Y 0AB

Printed in Great Britain

Dedication

I dedicate my book to my beautiful partner, Elizabeth Mary Houlihan. We recently celebrated our ten-year anniversary and I don't know how you made it this far with me. Lizzy, I couldn't see it at the time, but you are always there for me even when the chips are down; you never surrender, you never give up on me and you always have my six. There were times that all I wanted to do was give up; I didn't think I was going to make it through, no matter how hard I tried. I'm strong, but you make me stronger.

I also dedicate this book to my beautiful step-daughter, Shannon Elizabeth Spalding; I have watched you grow into such an amazing girl. You are always there quietly in the background showing me love and support; you never judge me and you are always understanding. You are unique and you impress me.

The road ahead is paved with uncertainty, but the one thing that has remained consistent in my life is both of you. I promise to be as dedicated to you as you are to me and if you ever fall, I will catch you. XX

Introduction

I am still at times my own worst enemy, but I will never face a bigger challenge than the enemy I found within my identical twin brother. In March 2019, I finished filming a documentary for Channel 5 called *Robbing Your Relatives* which aired on the 6th of November 2019.

Over 850,000 viewers watched this programme so you may already know a little bit about me. I now want to share with you the rest of my story and exactly what went on and why my twin brother, Richard, turned on me, things that you don't know about, some of which you will find hard to believe. This is a story of our lives growing up which later led to the rise and fall of identical twin brothers whose bond was meant to be unbreakable.

I have been making notes and writing my autobiography since 2016 and I can no longer put off wanting to share what I've been through, dealt with and still dealing with. I see and hear stories daily about mental health and suicide. There are a lot of broken people out there, I am one of them. I fight daily with OCD, severe anxiety and severe depression and I'm certainly no stranger to suicidal thoughts and feelings. You're not alone, I would like to reach out to you and give you hope that life is precious and worth holding onto. I struggle daily and have been to some very dark places, but hopefully I have made it through the worst of it, or I pray that I have as the daily demons are always there beckoning me back. Just hold onto the thought that everything is fixable.

I was brought down past my knees and I've been to hell and back dealing with wrongfully being arrested and sent to prison while fighting a European Arrest Warrant to extradite me to Germany. This led to my life spiralling out of control with cocaine, alcohol and gambling and then suffering the ultimate betrayal during this time by my twin brother, Richard, who was trying to bury me and take everything I own.

That was until I fought back and did some things quite extraordinary. Anyway, I'll get into all of that a little bit later on.

I'm currently in therapy and trying my best to write this, when most days all I want to do is hide under the duvet. I hope my story can at least help you face some of your demons or, at the very least, give you a little comfort that all is not lost. It does feel hopeless at times, but never give up because you never know what's around the next corner. If you're one of the lucky ones and your life is perfect then you'll still enjoy an amazing but truly shocking and unbelievable story.

There is so much going through my head right now and it's hard to know where to begin, you just couldn't write it, but I'm going to try. Okay, deep breath, let's start from the beginning.

Chapter 1
Gotta Start Somewhere

My name is Christian Govan and I have an identical twin brother called Richard; we were born at Mill Road Hospital in Cambridgeshire on the 30th of November 1977. I'm his big brother and the eldest by six minutes, even though Richard disputes this and will tell you we were muddled up at birth. I put him first, but he wasn't born first.

My earliest memory is living in a three bedroomed terraced house in a town called Biggleswade. We both went to Lawnside Lower School; this was a state school for children aged from 5–9 years old.

Richard and I were quite popular at school; we were carbon copies of each other: cute, cheeky and mischievous. We wore exactly the same outfits, even down to the same shoes and back packs; we had two of everything. Actually, if my mum could have had her way, we would still be wearing the same clothes. We were quite small in height and, with a flash of red hair, were like two highly charged Energizer Bunnies. We were inseparable and from the moment we were born, we were as close as two people could be.

We had separate bedrooms, but would always stay together and sleep in the same bed. Even at this age, we were popular with the girls and I remember being chased around the playground at break-time playing kiss chase. There is something intriguing with twins and you get used to the long stares and people trying to guess which one is which. When we were babies, Mum and Dad would even put our initials on the bottom of our shoes so that they didn't muddle us up.

Behind the scenes, Mum and Dad had a very volatile relationship. Dad was working away from home a lot and Mum's new love interest was for the two Afghan Hounds that she owned.

We were only 5 years old at the time; it was just another night alone in the house while Mum and Dad had gone down the pub. Both of us at the top of the stairs preparing to climb into our Formula One race car, which in reality was a sleeping bag. I climbed in and Richard sat behind me ready for take-off as we slid over the edge. Hurtling down the stairs at what felt like 100 miles per hour, we hit every step and glided along the skirting board, laughing and giggling as we went both trying to clamber on top of one another until Richard used my face to steer us out of trouble. With a large thud, we had made it to the bottom. 'Again,' Richard shouted as I burst into tears holding my mouth; it was throbbing as I realised one of my teeth had been knocked out. We would often try to hide any cuts and scrapes if we could so Mum and Dad would think we had just sat and watched TV all evening as instructed 'like good boys.'

It was a bit difficult to hide the fact that I'd knocked one of my teeth out and I knew we were in so much trouble when Mum and Dad finally got home. I ran around screaming asking Richard to help me while holding my face with blood everywhere. We were so used to the bumps and bruises that came with being left to our own devices and it just comes with the territory.

I recall another occasion when my auntie had dropped

round unannounced. If the door knocked, Mum and Dad had told us to hide and keep quiet. It was a game too us, like hide and seek. Mum and Dad were down the pub and my auntie had been knocking on the front door; with no answer, she was just about ready to leave until she heard a noise—it was Richard and I giggling at our latest hiding place. As my auntie peered through the letterbox, there we both were: Richard on top of one book shelf and me on top of another, practically touching the ceiling. 'Don't move,' she shouted fearing the cabinets could give way at any time and we would both come crashing down to the ground. I'm not sure of the conversations had between my auntie and my mum about us being left alone at such a young age, but it wasn't the first time we were left alone and it certainly wouldn't be the last.

Richard and I always seemed to be in trouble for something. Especially when Dad was away at work, 'You wait till your Dad gets home,' Mum would always say. It was just another dark cold evening, the rain tapping on the window outside as Richard and I hid under the bed waiting nervously for the front door to go. Suddenly, we would hear the sound of footsteps thundering up the stairs. A moment's silence, then bang as our bedroom door flew open; it sounded like it had come off its hinges. Holding my breath, with my eyes shut tightly, just hoping maybe today we won't be found. Then, suddenly, the bed was pulled away from the wall exposing me and Richard scrambling to get away and Dad grabbing both of us by our ankles and dragging us along the floor.

'That's it you're going to see Mrs Green,' said my dad as Mum shouted from the bottom of the stairs. 'She's coming to get you.'

'Please don't let her take us,' we both screamed, red faced

and so worked up still being dragged along the floor and out of the bedroom and down the stairs towards the parked car outside. Mum had already started the engine in readiness to take us away and had opened up all the doors of the car including the boot. 'We will, we'll send you to Mrs Green and you'll never come back,' Mum would say. 'Put them in the boot, David, let Mrs Green deal with them.'

Mrs Green was Mum and Dad's version of the bogey man. A scary character to frighten you into being good. The threat of Mrs Green felt like a daily occurrence and this was Mum and Dad's form of discipline if we'd been naughty or misbehaved—that was until we got a little older and they decided to take matters into their own hands. It didn't take much to earn a visit to see Mrs Green; so on the nights my Mum and Dad went to the pub or rowed with each other, it felt nice to have a break from it all. It didn't matter if my identical twin brother had misbehaved or if it was me. We were in it together and it was always just the two of us.

I remember the rows between my Mum and Dad gradually becoming worse. Dad would come home of an evening, the slamming of doors and the raised voices that got louder and louder. One particular occasion was a little different as Richard and I sat at the top of the stairs trying to listen to the muffled shouting. The sound of furniture moving was followed by the unmistakeable sound of glass breaking. 'What was that?' I thought as I gingerly tip toed down the stairs. I crept slowly to the bottom while Richard sat at the top watching me; the door on the left which led to the living room was shut. I summoned the courage to poke it with my finger, just an inch or so wide and peered in. I can feel the cold air on my face and the sound of the front door acting like a vacuum cleaner sucking everything in its path through it; the net curtains flowing in the wind like a flag. Dad had smashed the glass on the front door and had left. Mum was sat with her face in her hands—I can see blood; I don't know where it's come from or who it's come from. Thinking back, this was the start of a very turbulent and violent relationship between my Mum and Dad and later in life things became increasingly violent. I was no stranger to seeing my Mum with a knife in her pocket or wearing matching black eyes after a fight with my Dad. This worked both ways and I've been witness to my Dad wearing black eyes too. The pair of them were like two bare knuckle fighters and anything goes. Mum could deliver quite a nasty head butt considering how short she was.

I remember the neighbours didn't like us much and there were always crossed words between my Mum and the old lady next door. Whenever they crossed paths, they always shouted back and forth over the fence at each other. There was one particular occasion Richard and I were playing at the bottom of the garden. We had a green metal climbing frame which had a swing attached to it with a big bright yellow seat. Up and down, we would go trying to get higher and higher. 'Shut those dogs up,' I heard from over the fence. I was on the swing at the time so Richard scurried off down the garden path to tell Mum. Boom, with a massive bang, the back door swung open and my Mum came flying out of the house like a screaming banshee.

'What did you just say to my boys, Grotbags?' Mum said with a hyper aggressive raised voice.

'The dogs, it's the dogs, they're always howling,' I heard the neighbour say in a meek voice from behind the fence.

'Oh yeah, is that right Grotbags? Well, if you've got

something to say, I suggest you come round and say it to my face,' With that, Mum picked up the two toffee crisp wrappers that Richard and I had left on the garden bench and threw them both over the fence into her garden.

I heard the quick shuffling of feet from over the fence and the next-door neighbour's kitchen door quickly slam shut.

By now, my swing had almost come to a standstill. 'In you get, boys,' Mum said.

It wasn't long before there was a knock at the door. Richard and I were in our bedroom and ran to the window to see who it was. I could see a police car parked outside the house.

'Stay in your room until I call you down,' Mum shouted from the bottom of the stairs.

This wasn't the first time Richard and I had seen a police car outside the house; actually, this was quite normal to us.

Things had finally become too much for my mum and dad living in Biggleswade. The vicious cycle they were in had finally got the better of them; the constant rowing, fighting with the neighbours, visits from the police. I remember one evening specifically and being told by Mum that a very important man was coming to the house and it must be kept spotless. As Richard and I excitedly scurried around the house like a couple of worker bees, we were using up more energy than actually getting anywhere, but we tried our best. This was the time I got my first proper scar and I have a few. Determined to make Mum proud, I remember a loud knock at the front door. 'It was him the important man Mum was talking about,' I thought. On the floor, I'd spotted the smallest piece of paper, like the small piece of paper left behind when you rip a page out of a notebook. 'I must put it in the bin before the man sees it,' I thought and with that, I ran from the living room, across the hallway and into the dining room. The kitchen was at the back of the house and connected to the dining room and this was where the bin was hiding. It was dark, but I didn't have time to turn the light on in the dining room and without hesitation I charged as fast as I could towards the kitchen. Suddenly, and without warning, I was stopped in my tracks; I was totally dazed and confused—'why am I now on the floor and in so much pain? What's just happened to me?' I thought. Mum, hearing my screams, quickly ushered out our special guest—who was, in fact, an estate agent—and she came running back into the dining room and put the light on to see me covered in blood and crumpled on the floor. I had just run straight through the glass door that closes off the dining room from the kitchen. I was howling, 'Please, Mummy, don't let me die; don't let me die,' and I was actually still unsure what was going on, but I could see a large piece of skin flapping about and the whiteness of the bone underneath. My right hand was the first thing that had connected with the glass door while running and it took the brunt of the damage. This was the first time that I'd seriously hurt myself and the rest of the evening is a blur of syringes and stitches. It took 27 stitches to patch me up and sometimes I still get what feels like an electric shock through my hand even now, especially when it's cold.

At the time, I was too young to understand what an estate agent was, but what transpired is that Mum and Dad had decided to sell the house and move away from Biggleswade. Their relationship was suffering because they weren't spending enough time together so Dad quit his well-paid job and they decided to run their own pub. They had no experience of owning or running a pub, but it was perfect for them; they could spend more time together and they also had a continuous supply of alcohol within arm's reach. We moved from Biggleswade to a pub called The Gloucester Arms in Great Offley, Hertfordshire.

Chapter 2
Last Orders

A pub is a great place for adventure when you're young, so many rooms to explore and places to play and muck about in. Richard and I were between 6–7 years old and went to Offley Endowed Primary School. Mum and Dad seemed happier for a little while; it was a fresh start, but it wouldn't be long before the rows started again. As strange as it sounds, they were always so busy running the pub that it felt like I never saw them. Great Offley is a sleepy village and the pub itself was on the main road that cuts through it, leading to the major towns of Hitchin and Luton. On one side, you had the pub which faced directly into the main road and on the other side of the road was a small newsagent. On many occasions, Richard and I would have to traverse through the oncoming traffic to make our way across the road to get sweets; we used to love getting penny chews, pink shrimps, fizzy cola bottles, fried eggs and red laces.

We were making our way back from the shop one day when Richard had his face buried in his bag of sweets; we were laughing and teasing each other when he just walked straight out onto the road and in front of a car. I remember the sound of screeching tyres and the smell of burning rubber as the car had to swerve narrowly missing Richard by no more than an inch. The car snaked across the road and into the pub carpark while the driver was fighting to gain control. We both had our legs slapped so hard by Mum and Dad that day for not paying attention and they took our sweets away. The next time we were in school, we were both made to sit in front of everyone during the morning school assembly; we were both crying and felt so humiliated. We were paraded around in front of the entire school as the 'Naughtiest Boys' of Great Offley—'The Terrible Twins.'

After a couple of days or so when things had quietened down, Richard and I had free reign to pretty much come and go and do whatever we wanted again. As crazy as it sounds, there were many occasions where we would be roaming around at night time riding on our bikes all over the village. Just to the left of the pub was an old church which looked like it had been empty for years; it was a very eerie and creepy building to look at in the day time, so at night time when the darkness fell, I was terrified of the place. Its smashed windows and the strange noises that seemed to just jump out of it. A bit like waiting for that scary moment that makes you jump out of your seat in a horror film.

We watched our first horror film together at the pub. Mum and Dad were working downstairs in the bar and Richard and I were upstairs pawing through the videos that were stacked up on top of the TV cabinet. We came across a VHS tape called Salem's Lot; at the time, we had no idea what this film was about. We both ran to grab our duvets and we each had a paper bag full of sweets. We had been hoarding our sweets that we got from the newsagents' over the road. We had been hiding them just in case we had a similar incident like before so at least we could still eat sweets without Mum and Dad knowing.

We slid the tape into the video recorder and knew we

wouldn't be disturbed for hours as it was early evening and most nights, we didn't even see Mum and Dad until the pub closed, or sometimes it wasn't until the following morning. The film is about the residents of a small town being taken over by vampires and is an 18 certificate; certainly not something we should have been watching at such a young age. Thinking back now, the film still gives me the creeps and we were not prepared for something like that. We started off quite content rummaging through our sweet bags, giggling away and chomping through our treats ready for the movie to start, but it wasn't long before we were hiding under the duvet and clinging to one another absolutely terrified. I remember the last attempt I made at watching the movie and peeking through my fingers to see what was happening. That was it for me and I just couldn't take any more; there was this one particular scene and it sent me running off downstairs as fast I could. Down the stairs I went screaming at the top of my lungs and into the bar I flew while everyone in the bar stopped dead in their tracks to see what all the commotion was about. I still remember it vividly now: one of the vampires comes floating through the fog and starts to tap and scratch at the window of this boy's bedroom, 'Open the window, please let me in. Come on, open the window,' the vampire said trying to lure this young boy into opening the window to devour him. The music alone, like some rusty old violin playing, was enough to send you running for the hills. That night, I was too scared to go upstairs alone, so I lay on top of the chest freezer in the pub kitchen because that was as close to my mum and dad as I could get while they worked the bar. With a jacket on top of me for a duvet, the hard surface was difficult to sleep on, but I'd rather that then go back upstairs. That gave me nightmares for a long time. There was one other occasion we attempted to watch a video and this turned out to be an X-rated movie. Both of us traumatised, it's safe to say; we gave up watching videos for a while. Some things you shouldn't see and some things you can't unsee.

We had more space being at the pub, it was at this time Mums collection of dogs started to grow. We had the two Afghans from Biggleswade and Mum had got herself two new Dobermans: one called Luke and the other called Tiffany. I remember Luke and he was perhaps the only dog I have fond memories of. He had a problem with his back legs and would waddle around with his back legs swinging from side to side like the pendulum on a clock in overdrive. Richard and I would tease him and hide on top of the garage roof peering over the edge looking down at him; we would watch him wobble about looking for us. The other dog, Tiffany, was indoors a lot of the time while Mum used her as a breeding machine and would sell the puppies, often keeping a couple of back. Mum started keeping more puppies than she sold and it wasn't long before she had a collection of 7 dogs. The room itself where they were kept was in between the kitchen and the stair case, so you had to climb over a large wooden board to get up the stairs. The room was filthy and had a wretched smell about it: dog's excrement combined with a strong smell of bleach, creosote and iodine. Mum used this product called Jeyes fluid everywhere, inside and outside; you couldn't get away from it. Mum would fill up a bucket and splash it all over the place. I became very familiar of the smell throughout my childhood and teenage years. Living at the pub gave my mum enough space and free reign to do as she pleased; she even acquired a horse which was called Finny. Finny was huge, dapple grey in

20

colour and towered above Richard and I. On one occasion, Mum picked us up from school with Finny all saddled up. The school that we went to was next to the field where my Mum and Dad kept the horse and I guess my Mum thought it would be cool to pick us up in front of the other children. Finny was big and clumsy and as we walked alongside her, trotting along the road, we were half way between home and the school when Finny and all of her weight stood on my brother's foot. I laugh now, but at the time, Richard's foot was getting bigger by the second, almost twice the size and looked like a giant blueberry with toes. Richard was in so much pain that he could no longer walk so Mum put him in the saddle and we made our way home back to the pub. This was obviously Richard's fault and he was told off for putting his foot in the way.

Now that my Mum and Dad had a horse, they also had all the equipment to go with it, including riding crops. This was the first time Richard and I could now be threatened and hit with something, rather than either of them hurting their hands. Mum and Dad used to complain that we hurt their hands when they hit us because their rings dug into their fingers.

Roaming around the village as we did on one night, Richard and I decided to go into the local farmer's storage unit. We climbed all over the farmer's equipment and up a ladder and into a silo. A silo is a large round container that holds wheat grain and certainly not a place for two young boys to be mucking around in. Richard and I would army crawl across the surface and dare each other to get to the other side. It was dark and you could hardly see your hand in front of your face, but you could certainly hear us giggling and laughing while we rolled around in the grain; it was a bit like sinking sand—you had to stay flat or you'd start to sink down. After a while, we were soon tired out and it was time to head home; we were trying to be as quiet as we could, we knew it was really late and we had pushed our luck. We both went around to the back door of the pub kitchen and, opening the door quietly, we crept in not knowing that Mum had left a huge pile of clean washing on a pub stool by the door. Mum literally walked into the kitchen at the same time that we were creeping in. Richard and I were practically shoulder to shoulder and knocked over the biggest mountain of clean washing you've ever seen. In slow motion, all these clothes rained down falling to the ground like leaves from the trees in autumn. To make matters worse, Richard and I had no idea that we were absolutely filthy from head to toe. Both of us standing there antiqued in grain dust, Mum looking at us and us looking at her. This was the first time Richard and I were properly introduced to the riding crop.

Mum and Dad had all sorts of horse equipment dotted around the kitchen. 'You've had it now,' she screamed as she reached for one of the two riding crops that were lying on the kitchen work top; one was black and the other was red in colour. On this occasion, her weapon of choice was the red one. Grabbing my brother's arm, she pulled Richard towards her with a quick jolt, drew her arm back and swish. Mum wrapped the riding crop right across the back of Richard's legs with all she had. Richard let out a terrifying yelp and tried to pull away, lifting his leg up at the same time trying to deflect the second attack; it seemed to happen so fast and was over before Mum had really got started because on the second swipe the riding crop snapped across the back of his legs. The riding crop now looked like a broken flower with its head hanging on by a thread. Mum threw it down and used her hand a couple of times to finish the job which made her wince.

'Get up those stairs and get to bed, I don't want to see either of you again,' Mum shouted as Richard and I scampered away up the stairs. I was lucky to escape, getting hit this time, but I still had to see my little brother take the punishment. The red crop was useless now, but I was aware she still had the black riding crop and the way things are we'd be meeting that one soon enough or whatever item was close enough for Mum to pick up at the time. Like I said, Mum and Dad wore rings and they were hurting their own hands or fingers hitting us, perhaps because they were hitting us so hard. To combat this, they would just grab whatever item was closest at the time to finish the job.

There were times Richard and I got up to mischief and Mum and Dad never found out. The pub itself and the bar area was somewhere that was off bounds to me and Richard, but that didn't stop us on a couple of occasions creeping downstairs before Mum and Dad were out of bed. Like the time we crept down the stairs and emptied the till to play the fruit machine or a game that we invented using darts. One of us would hide on the bar side while the other was on the customer side; you weren't allowed to peek over the bar and had to crawl up and down while throwing darts over the bar at each other. Army crawling up and down, we would laugh and giggle which would actually let the other one know, roughly where you were. Keeping as quiet as I could, I crept along on my hands and knees while hearing the thud of darts landing in the floor behind me; I knew Richard was running out of darts so I prepared myself, took aim and chucked all of mine up into the air at once, like a bunch of spears raining down on your enemy. I hadn't noticed, while hugging the corner of the bar, that my leg was poking out, when I suddenly felt a sharp sting.

'Stop, stop,' I screamed. 'You got me,' Richard's head poked up from behind the bar, like you see in that game whack-a-mole. He was laughing and, through my tears, I started laughing too. Looking back, we played some really crazy games; we even invented a game where we would challenge each other to leap from the flat roof of the pub kitchen across to the garage roof which was covered in moss. There was about a meter gap and when it was wet the moss on the roof became extra slippery. So many times, we would leap across going from roof to roof and like a comedy sketch of someone slipping on a banana, we would land on the other side and both our feet would leave the floor as we crash-landed on the roof—it would strip the skin off our thighs.

Living at the pub eventually, and as expected, took a turn for the worse. Mum and Dad's volatile relationship was back and in full force and they were struggling to keep up with the bills or make any money, probably drinking more than they were selling was taking its toll.

Dad was drinking heavily when I experienced my first car crash. We owned a Volvo V40 Estate in the colour bottle green, this car was built like a tank. Dad was driving us back to the pub with his normal can of beer, Super Tenants, in between his legs as he drove. Richard and I in the back of the car, no seat belts on and mucking around as usual; suddenly, as we hit a sharp corner, we were no longer on the road and all I could see was grass as we drove straight into a lamp post.

'Are you okay boys?' Dad asked.

We were shaken, but all of us were okay. Dad reversed the car back to reveal the crumpled lamp post and got out to take a quick look. He didn't stay for long and jumped straight back in the car and sped off even faster than we were travelling before we first hit the lamp post.

'Whatever you do boys, don't tell you mother,' Dad whispered.

We both nodded and sat in silence until we got back to the pub. Dad drove the car round to the back of the pub and parked up as Mum came out to say, 'Hi.' Richard and I both leapt out of the car and, in unison, started shouting.

'Mum, Dad crashed the car! Dad crashed the car!' At the time, Richard and I thought it was funny watching Dad squirm and try to play it down.

'Don't worry, Marilyn, I just clipped it, that's all,' Dad said unconvincingly.

'Clipped it? You just clipped it?' Mum said while walking round to the front of the car to see the damage. The bumper was barely hanging on and the bonnet was all creased up. With that, Richard and I ran off and went to play in the garden.

It wasn't long before Mum and Dad's love for alcohol had finally got the better of them; they were drinking more than they were selling and the pub eventually failed and the doors of The Gloucester Arms finally closed.

Chapter 3
No Fixed Address

Mum and Dad were broke, and, to be honest, I can't remember a time that they weren't. The pub doors had finally closed and it felt like it happened overnight; one minute, we were at the pub and the following day, we were staying in a one bedroomed bedsit in a town called Hitchin with whatever furniture we had left all piled up in this one room. Richard and I were not going to school at this time and would hang out on the corner of the local newsagents' buying Garbage Pail Kids Trading Cards. All of the dogs were being kept at a local kennel, but it wasn't long before the dogs were gone and we went to a hostel for the homeless at Ridgeway in Royston, or 'Ridgeways' as it was called. If you said the word 'Ridgeways', everyone knew where you meant and there was a lot of stigma attached to it.

Welcome to the anti-social, social club. At Ridgeways, we had a two bedroom flat with a communal bathroom. We shared the bathroom with the people staying in the flat opposite. Ridgeways felt like it had blocks of flats scattered everywhere; there was a large concrete roundabout at the centre of the estate. Being young, it seemed so much bigger than it actually was—families from all walks of life struggling to get by or even get along; it wasn't long before Mum was fighting with the top dog of the estate. Her name was Bridget and I witnessed my Mum and her go toe to toe with each other a couple of times. Living here, it felt like nobody liked us and we didn't like anyone either. It was not a good environment to be in, everyone peacocking round the estate like they were better than you or you feeling you were better than them. The truth is we were all in the same boat and all struggling to get by.

I guess you could say we were at rock bottom; now, I'm not saying my entire childhood has been a complete disaster, but I just remember so much more bad than good. When it came to gifts, Richard and I always got one of each of everything, bikes, the latest Nintendo or Sega, but it was just a small plaster being used to cover up a much bigger cut. We had a couple of holidays, Butlins and Malta springs to mind, but that was just the same drunken fights in a different location. On the holiday at Butlins Richard and I would try and guide Mum and Dad back to our room while they staggered all over the place and would use Richard and I like walking sticks to prop themselves up. I just dreamt of some normality, a family home and just being able to have a friend over for dinner every now and again or a sleep over. At Ridgeways Richard and I had the smallest bedroom, with two single beds and base units all stacked up on top of one another; we were quite high up off the floor. The rest of the room was cramped with hardly any space to move while our racing bikes took up most of the space and were perched up against our bed.

In the pitch black, Richard and I would squabble for extra room trying to get to sleep tossing and turning; I was the unlucky one as Richard's side of the bed was up against the wall while I had to sleep dangling over the edge.

'Rich, move over, I'm falling out of the bed,' I protested.

'You've got loads of room,' he said while he put both of his feet and hands against the wall so that I couldn't push him across the bed anymore to try and create more room for me. Then, with a quick nudge, Richard pushed me out of the bed.

On the way down, I landed on the bikes and went face first onto one of the pedals—now, these pedals were solid metal with little rows of teeth like a piranha. Getting a mouthful of bike pedal, I was confused, dazed and in the dark. I started to feel hot and was aware that I'd just swallowed something. There was a quick patter of footsteps before the door flung open and Mum and Dad came bundling through the door, flicking on the light switch.

'What are you two playing at?' Mum said in a stern but angry voice. I just burst into tears, while touching my mouth and feeling that it was swollen and getting bigger every second.

'David, look at the state of him,' Mum said pointing her finger at me.

'Richard's hurt me, Mum,' I stuttered trying to catch my breath and just about squeezing the words out in between tears.

'No, I didn't; Christian did it,' Richard said protesting his innocence.

'You're both just as bad as each other,' Mum shouted.

Up until this point, Dad had remained quiet before he darted forward pulling back the duvet and slapping Richard on the back of the legs, while he lay in bed trying to move his legs frantically out of the way. Dad's arms were moving so fast, it looked like he was swimming the front crawl.

Being identical twins, and both being treated equally, meant we were both just as bad as one another, so Mum joined in and started slapping me round the back of the legs.

'Now get to bed,' she screamed. 'I don't want to hear another word from either of you,' and as quick as it had started, it was all over. The bedroom light was flicked off and the bedroom door slammed shut behind them.

I could tell something was wrong because I could feel the sharp edge of my tooth with my tongue, but it wasn't until the next morning while checking my face in the mirror that I saw that I was left with a perfect oval shaped gap at the bottom of my front tooth. It would have fitted exactly onto one of the metal teeth on the bike pedal. That's what I'd swallowed: it was a piece of my tooth.

During our time at Ridgeways, I would spend so many evenings perched on the worktop of this tiny kitchen looking out of the window waiting for Mum and Dad to come home; I didn't even know where they were most of the time. Richard and I, for a short period of time, were now going to a school called Icknield Walk Lower School and life ticked along really slowly while we were placed on the housing register waiting to be rehoused. When we were 9 years old, we started going to a school called Greneway Middle School. The days came and went until we were finally offered a house in a tiny village, just outside Royston called Therfield. After school, all of us went to go and view the property, potentially our new home and hopefully a new start.

All four of us got on our bikes and made the journey to Therfield. The trip itself is roughly 3.5 miles to get to, from Royston. Quite a tough journey for a nine-year-old, particularly having to navigate the hill on Royston Heath—to me and Richard that was like climbing Mount Everest, 'Well, at least we have the journey on the way down to enjoy,' I thought. It was a monster of a hill and we could come whizzing back down with our feet off the pedals and the wind in our faces; it would feel like we were flying. I was looking forward to that bit of the journey.

We arrived at the property, it was a long row of houses which all looked exactly the same and were all beige in colour. Our potential new home was house number 17 and the property itself was a semi-detached 2-bedroom house, with a kitchen, living room and the bathroom was located on the ground floor at the rear of the property. It had a long garden with a coal shed and a couple of out buildings. Richard and I went exploring, opening every door and cupboard and running off into the garden. As it was a semi-detached property, the house next door was identical and the neighbours who were sisters were keen to came out and investigate their potential new neighbours. They invited me and Richard in for tea and biscuits while Mum and Dad stayed at the property to look around.

We were excited about the possibility of change and the neighbours started asking Richard and I questions, like where we had come from, which one of us was the eldest—just your normal sort of conversation. During this time, they asked us if we had any other family or was it just the two of us and Mum and Dad.

'Do you have any pets?' One of them asked inquisitively.

'Mum loves dogs; we lost all our dogs when we had to move away,' I replied so innocently.

With that, the conversation moved on and Mum and Dad rang the doorbell to introduce themselves properly. The conversation was awkward and Mum and Dad were quite coy and were making the situation uncomfortable by keeping their cards close to their chest and not saying much.

Then one of the neighbours said 'Oh your boys were telling us you like animals and used to own a few dogs.'

'No not really,' Mum said while glaring over at Richard and me. 'We used to have a couple of dogs, but we aren't looking to get any more,' and with that, Mum and Dad made their excuses and we left very abruptly.

I could sense something was wrong as we got on our bikes and cycled far enough around the corner to be out of sight of the property and the neighbours who were waving us off.

'Get off your bikes, nowwwww!' Mum snarled and, in an instant, she erupted like a volcano; she was shouting in our faces demanding to know what had been said, what we had told the neighbours.

'Nothing, Mum,' we both replied nervously and in unison, 'You like dogs that's all we said.' By now, Mum was going berserk and I could hardly understand what she was saying anymore—she was shouting so loud and frothing at the mouth.

'I'll teach you not to talk about us,' Mum shouted.

To teach me and Richard a lesson, we had to walk the entire journey back home from Therfield to Ridgeways pushing our bikes along while Mum and Dad slowly cycled behind us. That was a long journey for us to walk on our little legs and I was still so confused by what we had done wrong. Richard and I were so tired and tearful and it felt like forever walking along the country roads in single file. I was so disappointed because I was excited at the thought of Richard and I riding back down the big hill together. 'Why are we being treated like this?' I thought. 'What have we done wrong?'

Unbeknownst to us, the reason for Mum's outburst was because she didn't want anyone to know about her possibly getting any more dogs. Mum was fearful of us losing this house if the neighbours decided to put in a bad word or make a complaint against us with the housing association or at Ridgeways.

Mum and Dad showed their interest in the property at Therfield and were accepted. This was to be our new home or the start of our new nightmare. Naively, I thought things were going to be okay. Why wouldn't they be? We were at a new school, we had moved into a new house, even though Richard and I were still sharing a bedroom, but this wasn't a big deal because we had shared a bedroom together for all of our lives.

It must have only been a matter of weeks living at Therfield before the first dog arrived and then the second and then the third and so on. Mum and Dad seemed intent on turning our new home into a giant-sized dog kennel; it was like a manufacturing plant spewing out one dog after another. We had a number of Dobermans, a couple of Irish Wolfhounds and some smaller dogs called Griffons. I lost track of each and every breed, but what had become really noticeable was the attention Mum and Dad were bringing to the neighbourhood. It was chaos inside this house, every day having to manoeuvre around all of the dogs, which at last count was 6 or so and some of these dogs weren't small either. Mum didn't care about how this was affecting Richard and me and, as long as Dad had his drink, he would just go along with whatever Mum dictated.

We were going to school and it was hard finding your feet and making new friends. Richard and I had each other and soon became a force to be reckoned with. Known as 'The Govan Twins'—we certainly didn't have it easy being twins—girls were fascinated by us, but a lot of the boys at school saw us as a problem and we were bullied quite a lot. Richard and I didn't take kindly to anyone being bullied, let alone anyone bullying us. We suffered all the names you can think of and, because we had red hair, that just made matters worse. However, Richard and I settled in quite quick and most of the friends I have today are the same friends I made back then. It wasn't long before I had my first fight at school; he was an older boy in the year above me. We used to play football at break-time in the tennis courts and I could sense that something was off on this particular day. A crowd had started gathering outside the gate of the tennis courts and the energy in the air felt different. Richard and I were tiny little boys and you wouldn't think much to look at us. I guess that was this older boy's biggest mistake; this boy thought he was going to intimidate me—he wanted to hurt and embarrass me and show off to his pals. By now, the crowd was quite large, with my friends on one side and this boy's friends on the other, almost joined together like a circle and there I was in the middle of it. This boy waded in with his hands up being goaded by his mates.

'Go on, Jack, let him have it,' they shouted. 'Smash his face in,' his mates kept repeating. They seemed so excited at the thought of me having my head kicked in.

Now the problem with these types of situations is that now neither of us can back down, even if we wanted to, you have to save face and are driven by a group of baying animals desperate for a show. My lads, to be honest, were relatively quiet and apprehensive; after all, this lad was older and bigger than me.

I remember it like it was yesterday, the sound of his feet shuffling through the grass towards me, the breeze in my face and how calm I felt. I'd shut out all of the background noise, but was completely aware of my surroundings and where Richard was positioned should I run into problems. I was not fazed at all by this inconvenience.

We were now face to face, this boy's hands were up in a boxing pose and my hands were down by my side. I knew he was about to hit me so I just stood there waiting, 'Wait, sit tight Christian, just a moment longer,' I said to myself. The crowd was shouting louder and then suddenly he swung at me with a right hook. 'Now,' I thought. It felt as though things were moving in slow motion as I ducked and was aware his punch had gone straight over my head and using all of the force in my legs on the way back up, I drove an upper cut straight into his face, I then went to work dismantling him bit by bit. That was the only punch he ever threw at me as I unleashed hell on him and I had no intention of stopping. This boy would get hit, take a step back and then he would come forward at me and then he would get hit again, then he would take a step back and then he would come forward at me and so on and so on until my friends finally pulled me away. I lost count of how many times I hit him in the face, but every hit was creating lumps, bumps and bruises and he was unrecognisable by the time I'd finished.

The group dispersed and I went straight to my next lesson as my right hand started to swell up and was bruised black and blue. The rumour mill had already started and this boy's friends were saying that Richard and I had both beat him up, which if funny considering they had all watched it happen. I received a visit from the police concerning the matter, but there was nothing they could do due to my age plus the fact that I was defending myself, although I was advised by the police that it would be a better idea to join a boxing club. This boy didn't come back to school for over six weeks and when I next saw him, he still had dark bags under his eyes. To this day, I do know that his parents still have a photo of him and the injuries he sustained that day, maybe as a reminder not to get involved next time. I realised quite quickly that I was wired differently to most people in those situations but, unfortunately after this fight, I had built up a bit of a reputation and it felt like Richard and I were fighting all the time while we were growing up. A lot of the time, we weren't fighting people our own age; the people we were up against were older and seemed to get bigger and bigger. For every person we took out, another older, bigger person replaced them. As twins, we were very protective of one another and if you had an issue with me then you had an issue with my brother and vice versa.

A twin is a best friend for life and that's awesome, or at least that's how it used to be. There is just no one that will have your back like a twin; they can move like you, think like you and fight like you, and do whatever is necessary to eliminate the problem at all costs—that's how Richard and I were designed.

Chapter 4
The House of Horrors

From around the age of 10 onwards, Richard and I floated through the next few years the best we could. Although we did start going to the pubs in and around the surrounding area quite a lot; well, the pub carparks should I say. Mum and Dad had started taking us to the pub with them and would leave us in the car while they both went into the pub until closing time. Dad would occasionally pop out to check on us and deliver a bag of crisps and a glass of coke each. We spent quite a bit of time in pub carparks and even though Richard was the only person I could rely on, we were both having a tough time getting along, both of us being stuck in the car like two caged animals for hours at a time will do that to a person. We would take out our frustrations on each other, it would drive anyone to despair being trapped in a car and we would end up fighting one another. It's not easy to fight in such a cramped environment, face up against the window or pinning each other up against the door with your feet. Richard wouldn't hesitate hitting me in the face, biting, pulling my hair whatever he needed to do to win he would do it. I was a little different and hitting my little brother in the face was a big 'No-no' for me. Of course I would give as good as I got, but would always hold back a little and when closing time arrived, we would both sit there pretending nothing had happened, even though we were out of breath, battered and bruised. I came off a lot worse growing up when we fought as he knew I wouldn't hit him in the face and this gave him a big advantage.

Mum was the driving force of the madness in our household and by the age of 16 years old Mum had acquired even more dogs. Richard and I were now working part-time jobs and saving all the money we could, I wanted to drive, buy nice things and go on holidays with my mates. Mum and Dad were not quite as quick to lash out at us as they used to be and I overheard a conversation between my Mum and Dad where Mum said, 'The boys are getting stronger, David. I hit Christian the other day and he hardly moved.' I knew the moment she was referring too. It was a couple of weeks back and Mum didn't like how I'd spoke to her; in an instant, with her fist clenched, Mum punched me straight in the face. I took it and looked at her dead in the face disgusted with what she just did—a look that said, 'I dare you to do that to me again.'

These days, Mum and Dad now resorted to throwing us out rather than anything physical. We were under threat of this daily and Richard and I were no strangers to sleeping rough on a couple of occasions.

It was difficult to socialise as we were so reliant on Mum and Dad driving us into Royston, as there wasn't much for us to do in Therfield. Apart from the general grind of going to school we played for the local football team, but it turns out we were both pretty decent at hockey. We started to become interested in girls and tried to have fun like most teenagers do. Richard and I were not allowed girlfriends, this was forbidden and Mum and Dad demanded we still dressed the same. Richard and I hated and resented the way we were being treated, and we would often put a change of clothes in a bag and throw it out of our bedroom window, we would then go outside to collect the bag and hide it in the car. Once we were dropped off in town we would then get changed in the public toilets. We were always under threat that they would throw us out, or Mum would wait until the last minute and then refuse to drop us down the town to meet our friends. I lost count how many times we would be ready to go out and meet our friends or go to a party and Mum would sink into the sofa with the dogs draped over her like a blanket while watching her soaps and she would say to us, 'You better start walking cos I'm not driving you.'

Our home life was always out of control, but things were gradually getting worse. Mum and Dad had more drink in the house and in their cars then an off licence, the daily rows, the violence, the state of the house, the number of dogs, the visits from the police, even the neighbours; the neighbours in every direction hated us.

We had grown up ever since I can remember in an unhealthy environment, but my Mum's infatuation with dogs had reached all new heights and the living conditions were deplorable. My mum and dad had now in excess of 28 dogs most of which lived inside the house. What was once a two-bedroom semi-detached house from the outside was, in fact, a giant-sized dog kennel on the inside. Most of the internal walls and door frames were gone, apart from the main walls which hold a house together. Not a single room in this property apart from the downstairs bathroom had a door. The plaster had been chipped off the walls and you could see the grey breeze blocks propping up the house. The house felt like one room downstairs and because there were no doors left it felt like one room upstairs. The house was littered with dog cages and metal fencing which compartmentalised certain batches of dogs. We had a kitchen and some cabinets, but the plinth was missing so some of the dogs would hide underneath the kitchen units, occasionally popping their heads out to bite your ankles. The corridor that led to the bathroom had four separate wooden boards separating each section of the corridor and in each section, a Doberman or larger dog would be in its own little square. It was like a scene from an Indiana Jones movie having to navigate all the booby traps just to get into the bathroom.

It was on one particular occasion that I had attempted to get a bath and moving like a hurdle jumper, I had made it to the bathroom door, using the knife which was hanging by a piece of string to open the door because there was no door handle, I walked in. The bathroom itself was damp and dirty, the toilet was broken and no longer worked, the bath was cracked and held together by super glue and the floor itself was just concrete with a wooden pallet to stand on by the sink.

Trying to organise myself, I stepped off the wooden pallet and felt a sharp shooting pain run through my foot and up my leg. In agony, I grabbed my foot and yelled out. Mum came rushing in to see what all the fuss was about. I hadn't noticed the dusty sharp dog bone lying on the floor; it was pointing upwards like a three pinned plug.

'I can't live like this anymore, Mum,' I shouted at her.

'What Christian? It's just a juicy bone,' Mum said.

'Ohhh that's all right then, as long as it's juicy,' I replied sarcastically.

The fact that my mum thinks it's okay to even have some dirty old bone lying in the bathroom was bad enough, but to excuse the bone because it was juicy was beyond me.

I have described the condition of the house to the best of my ability, but whatever images you have going through your head, trust me it's worse and one thing I can't describe was the smell.

It had got to a point that it was embarrassing for Richard and me because our clothes always smelt so bad from being inside the house. The garden wasn't in much better shape and looked like a chewed-up racecourse, but it did have a shed. Richard and I were left with no choice and moved all of our belongings into the garden shed. It was the best we could do with what we had. All of our clothes were in there, a mirror and hairdryer and the usual bits and pieces we needed to get by. Even in the cold winter months, we would get washed and then run down the garden path with just a towel wrapped around us. It wasn't ideal, but the space was ours. Richard and I were around 17 and just started learning to drive; we still had bunk beds and the daily alarm call was the usual sound of the dogs howling all desperate to be let out into the garden. It was winter and Mum was swishing around the garden with large buckets of bleach chucking this potent mixture all over the garden.

Even though the situation was dire, I still laugh thinking about one occasion when Richard was running down the garden path, naked, just wearing a skimpy towel and was bare foot. All of a sudden, Richard ran across a large puddle of frozen dog piss and ended up with both feet leaving the ground and landing on his back—the perfect comedy fall. Richard and I weren't in much of a position to change things at this stage, but we both agreed we were not going to live like this, put up with this, or carry on like this.

Richard and I both had girlfriends which we had kept a

secret from Mum and Dad for quite some time, until Mum and Dad started to relax about the girl situation. Although they never came to the house and we would always make excuses to go to their houses instead. I could never invite anyone into that environment. I was far too embarrassed and worried about people realising how bad things were and Richard and I becoming a laughing stock. Considering the circumstances, Richard and I were pretty cool lads, like most boys our age we were out for a good time and had the same circle of friends. We were not only protective of each other, but fiercely protective of our mates especially when trouble arose. We did the usual lads' holidays: Magaluf, Marbella, Kavos and Ibiza.

It was summer time and I was preparing for my driving test. I was desperate to pass my test and earn that extra bit of freedom so that I could get about on my own. My first test didn't go so well, everything was going to plan as I navigated my way around the roads in a town called Letchworth. Things were going well as I confidently moved through the gears and stopped at the traffic lights as instructed. Turning right, we entered into a housing estate and to my astonishment, I drove past a woman pruning her roses wearing nothing but an apron and her bare bottom was staring back at me as we cruised by. I stuck to the task at hand; well, it's not like I could stop to take a better look and I know the instructor had seen this too, but we both carried on as though nothing had happened. I think the instructor should have passed me there and then for not rubber necking and managing to keep my composure.

On the second time round, I passed my test with no distractions. Excited, I went straight back to school; I was in sixth form doing a two-year Advanced Business Course and Richard was studying A Level English and History. I was so excited and he was the first person I wanted to tell.

I walked across the school field and could see him from a distance. As I got closer, I was smiling and he stood up.

'Did you do it?' Richard asked me, he was smiling, I think he knew.

'Yeah, Bro; I got it this time,' I replied as he gave me a hug lifting me off the ground.

'Yes, bro, I had a feeling you would,' he said.

It was time to get the money that I'd been saving so hard and start looking for a car. Having a car was a necessity for me, a lifeline to be able to get out of Therfield. In the meantime, the only peace and quiet we got when we were at home was in the garden shed. That was until one day, during the summer time, Richard and I had gone out and unbeknown to us the shed was having a makeover. We got home to find Dad had ploughed through a good few cans, of Super Kestrel and was pretty drunk and, in his drunken state, he thought it would be a good idea to paint the shed in creosote. Now, if a 5-year-old had done this it would have been a work of art, but for my dad who was around forty years old, it was ridiculous. To just get hold of a paint brush and doodle all over the shed and slap it on thick everywhere and anywhere is unbelievable. Creosote has a strong smoky smell to it. We were livid because this was the only personal space that Richard and I had and now all of our clothes had been ruined by the smell of creosote. It just stuck to everything, all of our clothes, even our shoes, it was stuck in all of the fibres and the smell just lingered on for months.

Chapter 5
Heart-broken

My mum and dad's fights with the neighbours would carry on
for years to come and the next couple of years for Richard and
I was fairly chaotic before we were finally able to escape from
Therfield. There were more altercations between my mum and
dad and also from the neighbours in every direction. It was
generally a really hostile environment for everyone involved
and, to make matters worse, we shared the front gate and path
with our neighbour so confrontations were inevitable. To say
there was bad blood between my mum and dad and this
particular guy next door is an understatement.

Now I don't actually have an issue with the neighbours
and agree with their point of view, but Richard and I were
stuck in the epicentre of it. Let's face it, my mum and dad are
the neighbours from hell but Richard and I hadn't done
anything wrong and didn't choose this life, but that didn't
matter, we were guilty by association.

I mean apart from the state of the place and the dogs
escaping every other day, I forget how many times we would
have to scour the entire village looking for the runaways or the
amount of times I would come home to find that Mum had left
a stereo on in the garden; it was blasting away on full volume
while she went off to work as a carer, blaring out and playing
the same song all day long on repeat. I'm quite sure that this

was just the tip of the iceberg to what was really going on.

Mum would also encourage the Dobermans to get worked up when they were in the garden. It was a game to her and she would often get the dogs excited and yell the word, 'Attack.' The Dobermans would bounce around the garden, excited and worked up and they would literally go for anything that moved. On one occasion, Mum and Dad were out in the garden and Dad started to play fight with Mum.

'Attackkkkkk,' Mum yelled as though she was sending her soldiers into battle.

The dogs were on Dad quite quickly, they were super aggressive and snarling with all of their teeth showing as Dad frantically backed away, they engulfed him. My Dad had to scramble for the closest safe place which was of course our shed. He managed to back away and into the shed as the Dobermans went for him; one of them actually bit Dad on his arm as he was trying to close the shed door.

Mum, cackling away, shouted, 'I told you not to play with me, David.'

I just don't think my Mum realised the severity of it, like I said it was all a big game to her and she was the winner. Her attitude was, 'We're having fun, aren't we?'

The dog bite later turned septic and because of this my dad had a heart attack on the 29th of July 1995; he was only 44 years old.

I had actually fallen out with my Dad and we hadn't spoken for a couple of days before this happened or on the day it actually happened. I'd kept myself out of the way and was staying at my girlfriend's house for a couple of days when I received the call from my auntie later that evening explaining the situation and telling me I should get myself over to

Addenbrookes Hospital in Cambridge. Richard and Mum had followed the back of the ambulance all the way to the hospital and, when I turned up later on that night, I found my dad attached to all sorts of equipment; there were wires trailing everywhere and there were these square pads stuck to his body. My dad was lucky because my mum had called the doctor while he was struggling to breath and he recognised the signs early and called an ambulance to go straight to Therfield—this probably saved his life. When my dad was in the ambulance, they wired him up on route to Addenbrookes Hospital and radioed ahead to say he was having a heart attack. When they got to the hospital entrance, they injected him with Warfarin. Warfarin is a blood thinner.

Even as I write this now, I just don't feel I ever knew a lot about what happened that day and I struggle to recall the memory. I just didn't realise the seriousness of it all and felt like I was the last to know, maybe that's my fault. I actually had to call my dad while writing this to establish what had gone on so I could write this accurately. The good news is 'he survived.' Although I'm sure the neighbours would disagree with that.

When Dad was given the all clear and finally discharged from hospital, things returned back to normal; Dad was back home as though nothing had happened.

It wasn't long before I was able to buy my first car; it was a red Vauxhall Astra Mk1—not the prettiest looking vehicle and the front number plate was held on with a piece of string, but I was mobile and I loved being able to drive. Richard and I were out and about all the time—the less time we spent at home the better—we both had evening jobs from Monday to Thursday at a local factory and, even though the work was pretty mundane, we were earning pretty decent money and able to do the things we wanted. We lived for the weekend and always had something going on, or a party to go too. It was a Friday night and I'd opted for a movie night in with my girlfriend at the time.

I dropped my brother off in town and my girlfriend's house was just a short walk from the top of the high street in Royston.

'Rich, what are your plans tonight mate?' I asked him as he went to get out of the car.

'Meeting up with the lads, Bro. Start off with a few drinks down the Manor Club and take it from there; you know, just the usual,' Rich replied.

'Okay, Bro, take it easy, stay safe and any problems just shout me.' Richard got out of the car, shut my car door and tapped his hand on the roof as I drove away.

I'd only been at my girlfriend's for a couple of hours; it was around ten o' clock before the house-phone rang and I knew straight away something was up.

I answered the phone and heard my friend's voice say, 'Christian, it's Blake. Listen, mate, your brother's about to have a tear up in the park; we got quite a big group of people gathering and Rich shouted at me to call you.'

Blake had barely finished his sentence and I was already putting my trainers on; the problem was I'd had a few cans of cider by this point and I knew I was over the limit—not just over the limit, I was drunk. I had a decision to make, but my body was already making the moves. I grabbed my car keys ran out the door; my brother needed me and I know that time counts in these circumstances. If I ran it would take me 5 minutes to get there at full sprint and I needed to reserve my energy for whatever I was walking into. You can't roll up to a fight and ask your opponent, 'Do you mind if I catch my breath before we start.'

'In my car; I can be there in under a minute easy,' I thought. It was a snap decision, a really stupid thing to do. I pulled off the drive like a bat out of hell, accelerating as I flew down my girlfriend's private road; it was pitch black and large rain drops were falling from the trees onto my windscreen—it wasn't raining, but it had been and the roads looked slick and glistened in the moonlight. I had no other thought in my head than getting from here to that park and by my brother's side as fast as I could. Taking a left turn, I was now onto the main road which goes straight to the top of the high street. 'I should be there in 30 seconds,' I thought. Working through the gears and speeding down the main road, driving as fast as the car will let me, 'I'm almost there.' I never made it to the park that night because of the decision I made to drink and drive, I'd crashed my car. It was a write off and so was I.

There is a pub at the top of the high street in Royston called The Chequers and it sits on a really sharp bend that's almost at ninety degrees. The last thing I remember is the bang inside my head, like a grenade had gone off. It was loud and it hurt me; I'm trying to keep my eyes open, but can't as they keep trying to shut. I know I'm hurt, but I don't know why and, at the same time I'm thinking I need to get to my brother, I'm fading in and out until my eyes closed and the darkness came as I passed out.

I'd taken the sharp bend by The Chequers pub far too quickly. I had no chance of stopping even if it was dry, let alone when the road was wet and slippery. The car was now aimed directly at another pub which is on the other side of the road and I'm headed straight for it like a guided missile; I drove straight into a pub called The Boars Head. I could have taken out so many people that night as there is usually a large crowd of people standing out the front either having a cigarette or chatting away—there can be anything from a couple of people too as many as twenty people. The only thing protecting them or stopping me driving straight through the pub doors and directly into the pub was a 'No Entry' sign situated a couple of meters away from the front door. I hit the no entry sign and had taken it clean out of the ground. The impact of the car into this street pole smashed the car and me to bits as my head went through the driver's side window, which would explain the bump I ended up with on my right temple that was the size of a mango. The car on impact had adjusted its direction and had lost a lot of its momentum as it slid down the wall of the pub finally grinding to a halt and resting up against the front of the pub wall.

Opening my eyes, I now looked up at the sky, my head is in the lap of a woman who is sitting crossed legged with me on the road; I remember so many blurry images of faces looking down at me, flashing lights and the sound of so many different voices.

'I'm gonna be sick,' I murmured as the woman cupped my head in her hands and rolled me to her side.

'It's okay darling, I've got you. You're going to be okay,' the woman said with a really soft and tender voice.

I felt as though she had wrapped herself around me with her arms and legs like a protective cage, making sure no one could get near me as she suddenly started getting aggressive at these two dark shadows who were standing over us—it was the police.

'Stay away from him, you're not touching him; I don't care what you say, you stay away from us,' as she cradled me in her arms. No matter how much they tried to intervene, this lady would not let them near me.

Her voice then returned back to normal, the soft and caring voice that I first heard. 'The ambulance is here, darling; I've got to let you go, okay,' she said as she kissed me on my head and moved aside to let the paramedics attend to me.

There was so much background noise that I was still struggling to understand what had gone on and why am I now lying in the street. I don't remember much from that moment onwards until I reached the hospital. I was lying in a bland white-walled room with a blue curtain which quickly filled up with nurses and doctors all scurrying about attaching me to all sorts of machines and equipment. They were taking my clothes off and I was aware my jeans were soaking, I'd wet myself.

It wasn't until later that my friend Blake filled in a lot of the blanks that I had. Turns out that he had called me from a payphone which was directly opposite The Boars Head pub; he had seen me crash and ran off to the park to tell Richard what had happened—he saw people drag me through the driver's side window and that's why I ended up lying on the road with this woman. To this day, I still do not know who the woman is that showed me so much compassion and helped me that night. I've always wished I could give her a big hug. For that brief moment, I was connected to someone who I'd never met before, who put herself out for me. Thank you for helping me x

The police never followed up on my accident, I wasn't breathalysed and I never heard from them about the incident. I was, however, charged by the council to replace the 'No Entry' sign, plus the costs for my vehicle to be taken away to the scrap yard.

Battered and bruised, I'd also suffered quite a serious whiplash injury so had to wear a neck brace for a few weeks after I left the hospital.

I guess I did save my brother that night. When I crashed, it stopped whatever was going to happen that night in the park because everyone dispersed to see what all the fuss was about at The Boars Head. To this day, it's amazing to me that I never killed anyone or myself; I don't know what to say about it. I got it so wrong drink driving and I deserved what happened to me. I'm pleased no one else was hurt, but I just wanted to protect my brother. You protect the ones you love at all costs; that doesn't make it right, but that's just the way it is.

After my car accident, it took me a little while to get back on my feet. I was fragile and my confidence was knocked a bit, but I pushed myself to get out and about and, as soon as I could, I met the lads down the Manor Social Club for a pint on a Friday afternoon. We were playing pool, chatting away, laughing and just having normal lads' banter. Playing pool with my brother while wearing a neck brace wasn't easy, bending over to take my shot with about as much movement as a Lego character. I'm face down staring at the green cloth of the pool table and I'm not able to look up, it was tricky but I was happy. All that mattered to me was making sure that my brother was okay, we were both alive, we were together and all was fine; well, for now at least.

Chapter 6
I Don't Like Being Thrown Away

Richard and I had turned 18 and our difficult home lives still raged on. It was no longer a surprise to come home and see yet another modification to the house; we were at the mercy of Dad's DIY skills. Richard and I were sharing a bedroom and as I mentioned it was only a small two bed property. Dad also pulled all of the storage heaters from the walls in every room of the house leaving them freestanding and unusable, with the bare cables exposed. We never had any heating so when the winter came it was a nightmare for us having to deal with the cold. The arrival of yet another new dog was no great surprise either, it was like a conveyor belt of dogs, some would die along the way either through old age or needing to be put down due to some kind of injury, accident or illness but they would always be replaced by another one. Some of the bigger dogs Mum had would run over the little dogs while they were charging around the garden and on another occasion one of the Irish Wolfhounds died because it had swallowed a dog muzzle. The dog muzzle had wrapped itself around the dog's intestines causing it to starve to death.

Richard and I were so eager to move out and try to make something of ourselves. I'd completed and passed my Advanced Business Course in the Sixth Form at The Meridian School. I never saw the point of going to university; I figured getting a job in the real world and earning money far outweighed wasting a couple more years pissing a student loan up the wall. I felt I had the potential for something bigger, I didn't know what that was yet, but it was just a feeling. Richard and I were so determined to succeed and we were not going to go down like this or end up like Mum and Dad. We were better than that and set ourselves a target of having at least a million pounds between us at the age of 25. It was time to get out of this place, so Richard and I decided to both get jobs so that we could move out together. We knew it would take some time, as we had to save up for a deposit and have enough money to cover the bills and our day to day living expenses.

After leaving Sixth Form, both of us found jobs really quickly and were in full time employment. Richard worked for a company called Lightning Electronics Limited; Lightning was a small electronics trader that bought and sold electronic components. The type of components you find in all sorts of things these days, mobile phones, laptops, TVs and so on. I got a job for a company called Avnet EMG Limited. Avnet was the second largest electronics distributor in the world. Both companies essentially bought and sold electronic components.

Changing into our suits and ironing our shirts in the garden shed each morning was still really tough on both of us and we would walk into work like everything was normal. No one knew at work what we endured each and every day; we were just trying to look the best we could. We were older and the physical abuse we had suffered when we were younger had stopped; we were just too strong and both very able to defend ourselves that Mum and Dad just didn't even bother trying. Having said that, the very last time Dad did get physical with me was around Christmas time and I'd just turned 19. We were attempting to put up the Christmas decorations and the artificial Christmas tree, when a squabble broke out between me and my dad. I couldn't even tell you what it was about now, but I do remember the amount of blood spatter that came from the back of my head. During the argument, I turned my back on my Dad just for a second and he seized the opportunity to smash me over the head with the artificial Christmas tree pole—this pole was metal and had large thick metal hooks poking out of it; you would attach the artificial branches to these hooks. It was quite a nasty cut and I needed stitches; I still wear the scar which is about an inch long and in the shape of a fishing hook. Don't get me wrong, it hurt but it just came as part of the territory living there; I took it and moved on. Throwing us out or the threat of throwing us out was their last weapon of choice to try and get Richard and me to obey them; it was all about control. Mum and Dad were quick to demand rent as soon as we started earning a monthly wage, which was laughable considering our living conditions.

Mum would often say with a smug grin on her face, 'Well, you know what you can do if you don't like it.'

Now, I'm not saying we were complete angels; the truth is we're not and I'm sure there were times we were really difficult to deal with, but we didn't deserve to be thrown away so easily. I cannot accept and will never accept anyone giving up on me and discarding me like the wrapper from a McDonald's burger. On a number of occasions, Richard and I would come home and the front door would be locked. Mum would open the door and there would be about an inch gap. You could see just a bit of her face and my dad's head above hers, both staring out at us. 'What do you want?' She said menacingly as Richard and I both protested our innocence for whatever it was we were accused of this time.

'Please, Mum, come on let us in; what have we done now?' I asked and it was always me at the front trying to diffuse the situation.

'No, Christian! You're not coming in and using this place like a hotel, especially when you're not paying us any rent,' Mum said.

On this particular occasion, it was the rent money that Mum and Dad wanted from Richard and I—this was the problem. Mum and Dad had hatched a plan to throw us out without warning. The rent issue hadn't been resolved because Richard and I were arguing with them about what was reasonable, particularly considering the conditions we were living in and the fact that the other 28 guests were living there rent free. From memory, I think at the time they wanted £300.00 from both of us each month, which was way more than any of my friends were paying and some of my friends were not paying anything at all while their parents allowed them to find their feet. Now I wasn't opposed to paying something, but Richard and I had been dragging our heels on the matter.

The punishment of throwing us out was actually worse than the physical abuse, it was a tricky one to deal with at times and came with no warning. It was just so embarrassing for us to ask for help elsewhere, so Mum and Dad had us on this one. All doors locked and the lights out we would be staring up into the night sky in total darkness, cold and not knowing what to do or where to go, it was hard. We were defiant on a few occasions and not prepared to back down easily, but the reality was we were in a difficult position; we could just about handle it over a weekend, but we both had good jobs. I couldn't roll up to work on a Monday morning looking like 'Stig of the Dump.'

I recall Richard and I sleeping in the car for a couple of days a few times, on a number of different occasions, or both of us staying round my girlfriend's house for a couple of days; I appreciated her mum for helping us, but it wasn't ideal. It was awkward and I resented my mum and dad so much during these times; if I'm being honest, I hated them.

We never wanted to surrender, but with gritted teeth Richard and I would always go back after no more than a couple of days and bow down to them. With our tails between our legs, we would go home and beg to be let back in. They really made us work for it and we had to grovel and make all sorts of assurances. We gave them what they wanted and also started to pay the rent.

Whatever I said to them out loud was not how I felt on the inside. I eased my mind with the knowledge that there will be a day that I won't need them, I will be able to do what I like, when I like and, as long as I had my brother, I'm good so you carry on.

It was always going to be hostile at home but, once we were allowed back, we tried to keep it as calm as possible and focus on work. Richard and I did a little bit of business together while I was at Avnet, but it wasn't long before I was poached by another company called Ice Components Limited. It was a smaller firm which traded in the same way as the company Richard worked for and we were both buying and selling electronics components on the grey market. We were able to buy and sell products from all over the world cheaper and have them delivered quicker to our customers then most of the franchised distributors. We could undercut them on price and could deliver those hard to find products or products that had become obsolete. We both dealt with so many products from manufacturers such as Intel, Samsung, Motorola, Toshiba, Hitachi to name a few.

It wasn't long before Rich and I were crunching deals together, speaking daily on the phone; we had each other on speed dial. Most days, Richard and I were creating great opportunities and pulling together some amazing deals—it was fast and furious—trading in large quantities of stock and using different currencies daily. We were making the companies we worked for an incredible amount of money. We were also making good money for our ages and quickly got into a position to start looking for somewhere to rent. We were 19 years old when we were finally able to move out of 'The House of Horrors' and move in together.

It didn't take long before we found a two bedroom property to rent in Royston; we were childishly excited to have our own bedrooms and all of the things that came with it—the freedom to do what we wanted, when we wanted and, most importantly, we were able to live like normal people do. For the first time in our lives, we had the chance to try living a normal life—whatever that means—but it definitely meant NO more shed and NO more dogs.

On the day we were given the keys to our new home, we were so happy.

'We did it, Bro,' Richard said, smiling from ear to ear.

'Yes, Rich, indeed we did,' I replied looking away so he wouldn't see me welling up.

'What you crying for? Come on, man, give us a hug and don't be silly,' Rich said as he pulled me in and we hugged each other.

Once Richard and I had moved out, it wasn't long before Mum and Dad were at each other throats again, even more than usual. I was aware that their relationship was toxic at times and more off then on, but they seemed to thrive on these daily arguments and fights. More went on than perhaps I even knew about, but this time they would not be able to keep this fight behind closed doors. It was in the evening when I received a call from my auntie.

'Christian, hiya lovey, it's your Auntie. Listen, your mum and dad have been arguing; can you come to Therfield?'

Richard and I jumped in the car together and made our way to Mum and Dad's house. Pulling up outside the house, it was pitch black; there are no street lights in Therfield. We got out the car and made our way to the house. The closer we got to the house, the more I could recognise Mum's voice screaming and shouting. The front door was already open so we made our way in. It was hard to tell if the place had been wrecked or not as it looked like that on a normal day, but you could tell there had been something going on. Straight away, I looked at my mum; she was covered in blood, her face was swollen and I could see her nose was badly damaged. I was looking at my mum who just didn't look quite like my mum; her face was all over the place. She burst into tears and in between crying and trying to catch her breath, she was stumbling through her words.

'Your dad did this; he head-butted me' she said.

I'd noticed that since I'd got there, Mum's posture was quite rigid and she hadn't taken her hand out of her pocket; she was wearing a big tatty looking woollen cardigan.

'What's happened Mum and where's Dad?' Richard

asked.

'I don't know, Richard, ask your father; I didn't do anything—he left when I phoned the police.'

The police hadn't arrived yet, but were on the way. I put my hand into the pocket of my mum's cardigan and I could feel that she was holding onto something.

'What's in your pocket, Mum?' I asked, her pocket was bulging with bloodied tissues as I pulled her hand out, her fist clenched tightly, she was holding a kitchen knife.

'Jesus, Mum, what are you doing?' I said firmly.

In a moment of madness, Mum had grabbed the kitchen knife in order to protect herself and thankfully she never used it. This was only because she had grabbed it after the event, when Dad had left the house. I'm sure if she would have had it in her hand at the time, Dad would have been wearing it somewhere in his person. Only the two of them know what really went on that night, but when the police arrived, Mum acted like a naughty child; she was unwilling to talk or co-operate. The police were insisting that Mum make a statement, but she refused; she even refused to go to hospital for her injuries. It wasn't the first time the police had been called here and certainly wouldn't be the last and this played out exactly the same as it had every other time the police were called out. They would turn up and then had no option but to leave again. It's fair to say the police were familiar with us and our surname was well known to them; there are times in my life I have felt like my surname was a black marker. Richard and I were aware of how my parents acted towards each other and we didn't even bother to pick sides, even in circumstances which to most people would seem so severe or extreme. To us, it was fairly normal so we just let them get on with it. Give it a couple of days and they'd be acting like nothing had happened between them. It wasn't long before the Chinese whispers started in the village and people would stop and stare to look at Mum's broken face; a couple of guys at the company where my Dad worked had heard things about that night and would ask him what had happened to my mum. Hitting a woman, whatever the circumstances are, is unacceptable and they seemed ready to deliver their own form of justice on the woman beater, but my mum and dad between them had come up with the excuse that if anyone asked either of them then one of the Irish Wolfhounds had done it, which worked and was plausible as that had actually happened before to my mum. This kept any repercussions at bay.

I was used to seeing Mum and Dad getting physical with each other but, on this occasion, it was the most violent and by far the biggest fight they had ever had.

Chapter 7
I'm Not a Killer

Richard and I living away from home actually gave us the time we needed to think straight without the feeling that we were at a Mad Hatter's tea party every day. Our social lives were pretty hectic and we always had something going on. Richard and I would go for drinks together, discussing business and the deals we were doing together. We were sitting in a pub called The Jester—the pub was in one of the surrounding villages called Ashwell—we were chatting away as normal and amongst all the business chat it felt like we both went silent at the same time.

Richard was first to speak, 'Bro, we're making all these companies so much money and practically doing it all on our own, why don't we start a business together?' And it was as though he had just read my mind.

'Seriously, Rich, it's funny you just said that as I was literally just thinking the same thing.'

It's not something that we had to think twice about and almost instantly the idea took on a life of its own and our first company Fusion Electronics was created. We started off as a partnership and became incorporated as a Limited company on the 2nd of February 2000. We had the individual qualities and skills, plus a combination together which was unmatched to make this work. For me, there is a simple equation to business and it starts as an initial idea or a thought that just unravels and develops. Before you know it, you're just along for the ride—there are many times that I don't have all the answers, but I'll find someone who does. Don't get me wrong, there's an awful lot of hard work involved and you have to put the time in, but it just starts to transform into something real and grows while you nudge it and nurture it along, a bit like writing this book. We had one problem and the first thing we needed to do was make a sacrifice; we needed a base, somewhere that didn't come with a rental agreement or a six months tenancy agreement. We needed a fixed address, somewhere that wouldn't change until we could get ourselves into a better position and hopefully one day, we could have our own office. We were going to keep everything to a minimum until we could establish if our idea would actually work. It was a painful decision, but we decided to retreat: it was time to move back to 'The House of Horrors.' It really wasn't an easy decision and on the face of it seemed crazy to go back. There was a method to the madness—for us to be operational, we needed a dedicated, phone and fax line, but most importantly we needed somewhere that could accept deliveries from our suppliers. We would be expecting DHL and UPS to be turning up on a daily basis. For it to work, we needed to have everything set up in one location. Richard and I both had full-time jobs so wouldn't be around during the day, but most days either Mum or Dad would be at home to sign for parcels. Initially, we were only trading overseas and could take advantage of the time difference and would work when we got home in the evening. The thought behind it was to start off slowly and see how we got on. Being back at 'The House of Horrors' and sharing a small bedroom again was tough; it felt like we had never left—worse than that, it felt like we were going backwards. The only thing that had changed was the amount of dogs Mum and Dad now had. The dog population was on the increase and at the last count there were 32 dogs at this stage. Mum and Dad were clueless what we were up too and didn't really understand. I'd sometimes catch Dad hovering around watching what we were doing or listening into our conversations. We had this old PC monitor in the corner of the bedroom that Richard had pinched from the skip at his work. The screen was damaged and barely visible. In the daytime, you'd have to put a towel over the monitor and your head to be able to see anything on the screen and what you could see was all in dark green. We had covered the basics; our phone was attached to the wall and the fax machine was set up on the floor. We had arranged a couple of meetings in order to appoint an accountant and we also set up a company bank account. We started Fusion with nothing more than a £5,000.00 business credit card and now we were finally ready to start trading. Richard was really on point when it came to sourcing some of the harder to find products that everyone was looking for. We sourced a box of stock which had a large variety of different and expensive components in it, a lot of which were hard to find or had become obsolete. We sold a lot of these products overseas and, in particular, to a large number of American Companies; we were new kids on the block and Fusion had started to make a name for itself. We were able to trade and deliver products anywhere in the world. It had only been a couple of months and we had made in excess of £70,000.00, this was clear profit in the bank. We did not come from a wealthy or privileged background so we weren't used to seeing this kind of money, especially at such a young age, but we remained grounded and didn't let it go to our heads. We were taking everything in our stride; we were unfazed by what we were achieving: excited yes, surprised no.

Things were going well, Fusion was ticking along nicely and getting bigger every day; we were both still in full-time employment so by the time the weekends came, we were both eager to let our hair down and get out with the lads. It was around six months before my 21st birthday, Richard and I had arranged to go for a night out in Cambridge with some of our lads and the girlfriends were invited too. Everything for Richard and me was going great, but little did we know it was soon about to come crashing down around us. We had been out for dinner and finished the night dancing away in a club; there were around six of us still standing by the time the lights came on and the bouncers started kicking everyone out. Exiting the club, it was the early hours of the morning so we made our way to the nearest taxi rank which was right in the heart of Cambridge's City Centre. The taxi queue was long, loud and intimidating. This wasn't anything new, most taxi queues at the weekends in the early hours are; we joined the queue while taxis came and went picking people up. I watched a number of people, stumbling and falling all over the place; they were like drunken zombies ready to be delivered home or they'd end up sitting on the pavement shovelling food into their mouths from the nearest kebab van. In these types of situations, Richard and I have a tendency to switch on what we call our 'spidey senses,' it's become a habit for me and I rely on them. If I walk into a room, I'm always aware of my surroundings and aware of everyone around me and in particular anyone that could be a potential issue. Standing in the queue, I'd already spotted a problem; there's always someone who isn't prepared to queue like the rest of us and there he was this obnoxious, drunk giant of a man who had decided that he was not going to get in line like the rest of us; he was going to jump the queue and squeeze his massive body right in behind me and my girlfriend. At this point, he is practically leaning on my back and intimidating everyone in sight. He was a bully and, as far as he was concerned, he could do what he wanted and he could treat people how he wanted.

I looked across at my brother who at the time wasn't very far away from me and, before I'd even finished saying 'Bro, I ain't having this,' he was already by my side.

We both turned around and were now standing shoulder to shoulder, while this oaf of a man squared up to me aggressively shouting and raising his voice, flailing his arms around. Now there are times in life when the time for talking is over and this was one of them. I knew what was coming and my anger had got the better of me, I had to defend myself and everyone around me. I hit this guy straight in the face and I felt all the bones in my hand crunch, so I knew I'd hit him hard. We traded a couple of blows and none of his connected with me. Now I'm not a novice when it comes to a having a row and I should have known better than to think it would have been enough to stop him. This guy lunged forward falling on top of me and we both went down to the ground. At this point, I'm trapped underneath what feels like a human mattress. From a bird's-eye view, I'm sure you wouldn't have been able to see me underneath him; I was struggling to move with all of his weight on top of me, but it turns out I wasn't the only person disgruntled by this man's behaviour. A huge fight ensued and I can sense, kicking and punching, shadows of people coming in and out of the fracas to give me some help.

I'd managed to move just enough to get myself off the ground, brushed it off and went at him again. This guy was starting to topple and I could tell he was starting to think twice about continuing. I'd noticed his face was visibly swollen and he was looking beat. I would not back down and stood there solidly looking at him while he was looking at me. He then turned around and staggered away, I remember thinking I couldn't have done all that damage to his face. That should have been the end of it, all the commotion had died down and just as quickly as it had started it was over, with that a taxi pulled up. We all got in and went home. The journey home was quiet, my girlfriend suggested me and my brother stay at hers rather than go back to Therfield, so that's what we did.

It was Saturday morning when I received a phone call from my Dad, 'Christian, it's your dad; where are you, what have you and your brother done?' He sounded worried and I knew immediately something was wrong.

'What's up Dad, why do you ask?' I was still half asleep and feeling a little hungover.

'The police have been here really early this morning, they smashed through the front door and pushed me and your mother out of the way; they started pulling the place apart looking for you and your brother—they even had a police helicopter circling the house and the fields behind us. I'm not joking, Christian, there were loads of them; the helicopter had its lights on while the police went through the fields behind us,' Dad said.

It took me a while to take on board what had just been said. 'Okay, Dad, give me a minute; I need to chat with my bro,' Putting down the phone, I stood there for a moment thinking about what I'd just heard.

'Rich, I think we've got a problem,' I said with a deeply concerned look on my face.

'What's up, what's going on?' Rich asked.

'I don't know bro, I'm not sure yet but it doesn't sound good.' I then started to explain to Richard the conversation that I'd just had with Dad.

In the conversation, Dad had told me that they had left a calling card and we were to get in touch with the officer dealing with the case at the Parkside Police Station in Cambridge. This was worrying and we both needed a moment to mull things over. We spent the whole day considering our options; the bottom line is, we didn't have any and we would have to make that call. Common sense told me it was something to do with last night and what had happened in the taxi queue. Not knowing what was going on behind the scenes or what we were walking into was awful. Richard and I had agreed with each other that from the moment we walked into the police station we would make no comment until we knew what we were dealing with, no matter what and no matter how long it took. It wasn't until Sunday lunchtime that I made the call. The officer I spoke to, abruptly told me to come to the police station with Richard for questioning; they didn't give much away. The tone of the officer's voice had a feeling of urgency around it and I could sense this was serious, this felt bad, this felt really bad. Everything in my body was telling me not to go, but of course that wasn't an option. Richard and I organised ourselves and made our way to the Parkside Police Station in Cambridge. There are times being an identical twin, when you can say so much without saying anything at all. We hardly spoke to each other on the way there, but both knew what we had to do and how to handle ourselves. The moment we walked into the police station, officers popped up from everywhere, out of every door, all of them eager to manhandle us. We were arrested and then they dropped a bombshell.

'We are arresting you on suspicion of attempted murder,' said the officer who was in charge of dealing with our case.

He was excited and salivating as he said it because we were well known to the police. It was like the case he'd been waiting for. The big one, the case to finish on a high note. Maybe he'd receive the Queen's Police Medal and seek early retirement after this.

Being told you're arrested for attempted murder is not an easy thing to hear, it registers and you hear it but it just goes straight through you. The rest of what happened after has become a bit of a blur, perhaps the only way my brain can protect itself is to forget; if I forget then it didn't happen, but trust me it did. Richard and I were processed and all of our clothes and shoes were taken away. We were issued with dark blue tracksuits and flip flops and placed in the holding cells that Sunday afternoon and were not released until Wednesday afternoon. We were held in the cells at Parkside for three days. This was my first experience of being held for this amount of time; the structure of the cells and the process is all designed to stress you out and apply pressure to break you. The three days are a mixture of circling the cell, wondering how you ended up here and going in and out for questioning and I wouldn't recommend it to anyone.

I had picked up on certain facts during my three days of questioning and it transpires that this guy who had started the fight with me in the taxi queue had slipped into a coma and that Richard and I were the ones being accused of putting him there. Being twins, they were not entirely sure of who had done what at this stage. The police had received an anonymous telephone call from someone that night who told them we were the ones that had done it, which explains how they ended up on my door step so quickly. In the interview, all sorts of suggestions were made; they would drop in conversation that it was likely that we would be held on remand and go straight to prison. The situation was serious, it was scary and I just couldn't fathom how it had come to this. I couldn't go to prison, 'What about the business we'd just started?' I thought.

Due to the fact that this guy was still in a coma and was yet to make a statement, providing that he woke up at all, enquiries were still ongoing.

The police pushed for us to be sent to prison, but we were granted bail and the charges were eventually downgraded by the CPS from attempted murder to GBH. The main condition of bail was that we were not allowed to go into or visit Cambridge.

Seeing my brother again after being apart and locked up for three days was a great feeling, an instant re-charge under such horrendous circumstances. We were far from okay and had a lot to deal with, but we hugged each other and then started to discuss between us certain aspects of the case— compare notes if you will. At this stage, it felt as though we had no control of what was happening to us, both of us trapped, our fate was now in the hands of someone else.

Chapter 8
The Brains and the Nose Behind the Operation

After three days of not being able to have a shower or wash properly, even the bathroom at home looked appealing. Washing away the drama, I was sombre and thoughtful. We had a number of missed calls and messages for Fusion and no one at work knew where I was, everything had stopped since my arrest and it was like I'd vanished off the face of the earth. It took a day or so to get things back on track and Richard and I carried on like nothing had happened, chucking ourselves back into work and more importantly our company. After a few weeks, I decided to quit my job at Ice Components Limited. I felt a bit lost and just needed to do my own thing so I slowed things down a bit and dealt with Fusion during the day.

After being arrested, it wasn't long before it started to weigh me down; I knew what we were facing was serious. In my eyes, I hadn't done anything wrong; I felt that I had no choice and had used reasonable force in the circumstances. As far as I was concerned, dare I say it: 'This guy got what he deserved.' I kept thinking back to that night and images of his face and thinking that I couldn't have done all that damage. During the next few weeks and months information was drip fed about our current position. The guy had come out of his coma, was awake and ready to make a formal statement. I'd seen this guy's statement and he'd bragged about doing twenty shots and multiple spirits and that he'd had a good night. He wasn't aware how he'd received the shoe prints to his face, but recalls an altercation. For all I know, when this guy staggered off from the taxi queue, he had gone on to make a nuisance of himself elsewhere in Cambridge and started another fight. I can tell you this I wear a size 7 shoe and not the size 13 boot print that he ended up wearing on his face. The signs were looking positive and, from my understanding, our clothes and shoes had offered up very little in the way of evidence, although to this day they have never returned them. Things had gone very quiet for a while, it was my 21st birthday and Richard and I had gone to a local pub in Royston called The Post Office. All of our lads had gone to Cambridge that night which to me seemed harsh as they knew Richard and I were out on bail and were not allowed into Cambridge. We celebrated our birthday together the best we could, still with a dark cloud hanging over us. Little did we know at the time that a letter had been sent dated 10 days before my birthday dropping the case in its entirety. Turns out, we could have actually gone into Cambridge that night to celebrate our birthday with the lads had Royal Mail been more efficient. That didn't matter to me, the point was it was over and we were free.

During this time, things had become a bit stagnant; we had been existing rather than flourishing. It was time to start making new opportunities again, make a fresh start. It was time to step things up so Richard and I decided to get ourselves an office to push Fusion forward. Fusion was also becoming too big to keep as a part time secret and it wasn't long before Richard's boss at Lightning became aware of 'Fusion.' Richard was practically running Lightning so, when he left, he took all his existing clients with him.

It didn't take us long to find an office; it was in Royston and used to be an old police station that had been renovated into offices. It was built in 1883, the building itself had so much character and the last court case was heard there in 1990. There was an Old Magistrates Court and the cells branched off from the main courtroom and this was where the offenders were held. There were two other buildings attached; the building in the middle was used by the police to park their vehicles in and the building on the right was the police officers' headquarters. Our office was on the top floor in the police officers' headquarters, it was large enough for two desks and storage for our products, it was perfect. Richard essentially was operating the business at this point. We were cautious about not diving straight in and draining the company resources by both of us taking a salary. This was fine by me and I'd come up with an idea during one of our chats down the pub.

We were at The Jester in Ashwell, which was starting to be our office away from our office, when I came up with an idea.

'Rich, I've been thinking; what are your thoughts on me getting a job as a purchaser? If I can get a job doing that, I could purchase products from Fusion and we supply them to the company I work for.'

'Yes, bro, that could work; I love the idea, but you would have to be careful how you go about it—although if you think you can pull it off, why not—but the last thing we need is any more hassle after what we just went through,' Rich said as his eyes lit up.

'Yeah, I know; to be honest, Rich, the whole nightmare in

Cambridge has knocked me back a bit,' I said.

'As long as we've got each other, we'll be all right; we always get through it,' Rich said.

I agreed, but couldn't help feeling everything always seemed to fall on my shoulders and, as always, I shrugged it off and pushed forward; I was starting to develop a view that everything is fixable—if it can be fixed, I'll fix it.

The idea of getting a job as a purchaser was very simple, but even in its simplicity, it was very clever. Basically, I would put myself in a position to buy products for the company I worked for and supply them from the company I owned. This could be seen as a conflict of interest, but it isn't illegal providing you do it right. Slightly naughty maybe, if I wasn't considerate, and I had to think about every move I made, but I didn't need convincing; after all, it was my idea and I knew the risk to reward was worth a shot. I'd thought about how I was going to do this and I would try to be as transparent as I could for the company I worked for without actually saying to my potential employer that I owned 'Fusion,' my intention was not to get myself into trouble, but if there was an opportunity there I was going to take it. I would weigh it up as I went along, until I found the right match.

I was quite sought after in the electronics industry, I was young and had a decent background in electronics so it wouldn't take me long to find another job. It needed to be in purchasing, so I would have control of large lists of products that I would need to source. Essentially, this meant I was at the end of the supply chain; I am the company who would physically use the electronic components. Fusion had clients that built all sorts of products including the finger touch tills that you would find in all pubs these days and we even had customers as far afield as Israel that used our components to build complex laser measurement tools.

It took no time for me to find the right place to work and I got the job as an assistant buyer for a company called TS Electronics Services Limited. My main role was to purchase components cheaper than the previous buyer had purchased them for. This couldn't have been easier due to the fact that the previous purchaser had been so lazy and was only buying products from one place. This was a company called Farnell and they are based in the UK. The prices that TS Electronics were paying for components was absolutely staggering, I could not believe how expensive they were and what they had previously been paying.

It wasn't long before I decided to arrange a meeting with the two owners of TS Electronics. I showed up at the meeting with a list of all of their components that they needed and the prices that they had been paying. I then showed them what I could buy them for and introduced them to a new supplier called 'Fusion.' Not forgetting Fusion could purchase products from all over the world and we could beat most prices and most competitors in the UK.

When I worked for TS Electronics, I never ever purchased any products for more money than this company had paid previously and I actually was saving them money, although I appreciate how it looks. I made sure that the owner signed off every single purchase order that was ever placed with Fusion by TS Electronics and I also showed the owner the saving that I made his company.

On one particular day, the boss was so pleased with me he made this noise like a police siren and pointed his finger at the actual purchasing manager in front of everyone in the office.

'Be careful; this boy is going to take your job,' he shouted while making this high-pitched whirring noise.

'I'll break his ankles,' the purchasing manager said meekly, under his breath, trying to save face.

It felt a bit awkward and I was aware he felt threatened by me. I had only been there a couple of months before they increased my salary. There was a note attached to my payslip showing me that I had received the highest pay rise in percentage terms than any other employee in the company.

It wasn't long before things were starting to take their toll on me working for TS Electronics; it was like I was living as two different people. The person I wanted them to see and the person I really was. I was really struggling with who I was and made a couple of foolish mistakes, perhaps the most obvious mistake was being only 22 years old when I pulled up to work in a new MG Sports car. It was a nicer vehicle than anyone else had in the carpark; actually, it was more expensive than the cars the actual owners had. The truth was I didn't care anymore and felt as though I was taking all the risks while Richard was sat in the office enjoying his day. This car I pulled up in had raised big red flags.

It was a really awkward conversation the day I got called into the office by the two owners. It wasn't long before everything came to light and it was inevitable that I would get the sack. I had made Fusion a lot of money and I'd done enough, so it was time for me to move on and join Rich.

'Let's see what Fusion can really do,' I thought.

We were finally running our business together—things were going really well—that was until we had our first argument in the office. We had just purchased a new software package called Quickbooks and this would help us run the business much more effectively. Richard and I both have severe OCD which is not surprising considering our backgrounds and what we have been put through growing up. We are particular about how things need to be run and everything has to be perfect. Our home lives were still as chaotic as ever and that would never change, but the business is one thing that we did have control of and it was ours. Inevitably, this would cause Richard and I to clash at times over the silliest of things.

On this particular day, Richard was sitting at his desk ignoring all of my suggestions on how we should set things up with Quickbooks. I ended up standing over his shoulder looking at his computer screen to try and give my input, which was ignored. Looking back now, perhaps I should have just let him get on with it, but I couldn't help myself as I leaned over and pressed delete on his keyboard undoing the last entry that he'd made.

'If you do that again, Christian… I'm serious, I swear to God I'll fucking kill you,' Richard's voice was raised and defiant; I could sense this could go sideways, but I wouldn't be ignored. I had as much right as him to discuss how things should be.

'Rich, you can't just fucking bulldoze your way through everything and have it your way without hearing me out too,' I said—I was equally as loud as Richard.

He wasn't listening to me and just went onto repeat himself, 'Go on, do it again; you touch my keyboard one more fucking time and we'll see what happens,' he said.

With that, I leant over his shoulder and pressed delete again and in a split-second Richard was out of his chair and on his feet. Being identical twins, when we love each other we really look after one another, but when we fight each other there is no bigger enemy on this earth. If you remember: hitting my little brother in the face was a big 'No-no'. This was my weakness and Richard knew it; it gave him free reign to do what he wanted and I had a huge disadvantage. What had started off as a silly squabble over the layout of our invoices quickly escalated into a full-scale battle that spilled out of our office and onto the staircase, and as quick as it had started, it was over. Richard was backing away from me and I could feel blood dripping down the bridge of my nose; suddenly, droplets of blood started to fall faster and faster onto the floor. I'm feeling dizzy, stunned and really disorientated while Richard turned and ran off down the stairs and out the front door. I'm weak on my feet and walked into the upstairs toilet to look in the mirror. I was pretty startled with what I saw. I was hoping the mirror was broken or wished it was a carnival mirror because my reflection looked so bad. Richard had punched me in the face and broken my nose. I was horrified; my face was a mess and I couldn't really tell what went where—a banana would look straight in comparison to my nose.

I had been looking at myself for about five minutes before I heard the front door of the main building open and a voice shouted up, 'Christian, it's Carl; are you okay mate?' He said, sounding worried. Carl is a really close friend of mine.

'I don't know, mate, I don't think I am,' I replied; I was still in shock.

By now, Carl had come to the top of the stairs, 'Jesus, mate, that don't look good; your brother just called me and said you were hurt and I should come and help you. You're going to need to go to hospital,' he said looking really concerned.

I was on autopilot, Carl was doing his best to try and help me, but I asked him to leave; I wanted to be alone and didn't want to be seen by anyone looking like this. I left the office, got in my car and drove myself to hospital; I remember pulling up at the Lister Hospital in Stevenage. The pain was really kicking in as I opened my car door, and I was sick on the road.

I was eventually seen by a doctor and my nose was broken. I had a deviated septum and bigger black eyes than a panda. I had to go back to hospital a week later once the swelling had gone down for an operation and I was scheduled in for a rhinoplasty, which is carried out under general anaesthesia.

This wouldn't be the last time I'd have a rhinoplasty operation. The damage Richard caused was extensive and I lost count after the fourth operation, so I don't know exactly how many nose jobs I've had in total, but I've spent a lot of money privately trying to fix it and get it right. This is an injury that I have suffered with throughout my life and still do even to this day.

Up to this point, I had never hit Richard in the face and he had taken advantage of this weakness; this had given him a false sense of security. Richard had relied on this through the years when we fought each other. I was, in a sense, submissive to him; deep down, I knew I was in control, but I allowed him to act like the boss of us. I guess, in a way, I was happy to go along with things, looking for his approval; we were so close, but there were times I felt like I wasn't good enough in my brother's eyes.

After Richard broke my nose, I would stare in the mirror for hours at a time and I didn't like what I saw. I spent most days feeling self-conscious with how I looked and I made the decision that I will do everything I can in the future to protect myself and the gloves were off. I didn't want to fight him or anyone, but if someone was brave enough to touch my face, then do yourself a favour and please run for cover.

Chapter 9
It Doesn't Matter What She Did

I think it was around 5–6 weeks before I showed up at work again; I had to get myself sorted out and recover after my operation so I had left Richard to carry on running the business. It had taken me this long to heal and calm down for what he had done to me. This fight was over and it was time to get back on track.

I walked up the stairs and into the office as Richard looked up at me from his desk. There was a small exchange of words. Richard asked if I wanted a cup of tea, which felt like he was extending a small olive branch; Richard isn't the type of person to ever say sorry even if he is in the wrong.

'Yeah, sure, Rich; I'll have one, so what have I missed?' I said.

'Let's go downstairs and I'll bring you up to speed with what's been going on,' he replied.

I'd noticed that there was a blood stain on the bannister as we both went down the stairs and into the kitchen. For a brief moment, it crossed my mind that the last time I went down these stairs I'd ended up in hospital.

'The company accounts have gone in and are currently being dealt with,' Rich said to me with a smile.

This got my attention as my mind was wandering elsewhere and I had started to gaze blankly out of the kitchen window.

'Okay, so how we doing? Any idea on the figures,' I replied.

'I know the accountant has to finalise everything, but I've already checked it all myself. You're gonna like this: we have turned over around £287,000.00. We've got about £140,000.00 in the bank once all our customers pay,' Richard said and, by now, he was grinning.

I stayed straight faced; I was secretly pleased, but didn't want to show it. The whole day was quiet and felt a little frosty but it only took a couple of days before we were chatting away like normal and as though nothing had happened; I hadn't forgotten, but I was just getting on with it. Richard and I could have the biggest battles and arguments that most people would see as unrepairable and no coming back from but somehow, we would always work it out.

A few days later, I was at home in the evening and Dad started asking me questions about 'Fusion.' I knew he wanted to know how much we were making, but was just dancing around the subject.

After a few beers, he just blurted it out, 'So how much money did you and your brother make this year then?' Dad slurred.

I was upfront about it and I told him the figures and I knew it would shock him.

'I asked you a simple question, I don't expect you to lie to me,' Dad snapped back at me.

'Seriously, Dad, I'm telling you that's exactly what we've made; why would I lie about it?' I said.

He mumbled something about being interested to see our finalised accounts and didn't speak to me for the rest of the night. 'I wasn't showing him my books, why couldn't he just be pleased for both of us,' I thought. The truth was that I knew I'd get that reaction—I didn't expect anything less. 'Why would he be pleased?' I was only 23 and earning treble what he was.

Anyway, it wouldn't be long before we could leave 'The House of Horrors' once and for all. There was a new housing development being built in Royston by a developer called Twigden Homes. At the weekend, Richard and I turned up at the showroom and started looking at the show homes. I stood there with Richard thinking how strange it felt that we could actually buy a brand-new house, but that's what we did. We bought a brand new three bedroomed home; it wasn't actually built yet so we purchased it off plan. We had a few months before it was completed so I moved in with a couple of really close friends of mine called Kirk and Tasha; I've got a real soft spot for these two. They married quite young and their hearts are in the right place even if they can be a bit clumsy sometimes. Richard moved in with his girlfriend at the time, a girl called Chelsea; she's such a lovely girl and to this day still a great friend of mine, as for my brother… hmmm, not so much.

Richard and I would laugh together that the builders must hate us because we would go on-site every single day until the day it was built; we were excited that we would own a brand-new home and we moved into our new house on the 7th of September 2001—we were only 23 years old.

On the day of completion, Richard and I stood on the doorstep wearing only the clothes that we had on. We woke up early the following day and went out to buy everything brand new and, to go with the new house, came new cars: a brand-new BMW 330CI and a Porsche Boxster.

We wanted a totally fresh start because everything we owned previously felt tarnished or ruined by the dogs and the living conditions at Therfield. I have no doubt that Richard and I suffer from severe OCD because of what we went through. Mum and Dad had a choice and they chose this life we didn't. Every single item I have ever bought since has to be brand new; Richard and I both strive for perfection and will not compromise. The damaging side of OCD for me is the non-stop pursuit to be perfect or waiting for the perfect moment and it just doesn't exist. What you don't see is the incessant rituals that I have. So many lost hours switching lights on and off a certain number of times, continuously straightening things, repetitive behaviour that takes me forever just to leave the house. Meanwhile, I have to hold my breath while I complete these tasks and if it doesn't feel right, I have to start all over again and I end up breaking a lot of things because of it. I'm anxious before I've even woken up.

Something I noticed when I walked into our new house that you wouldn't usually think about is the carpet. The feeling of carpet under my feet was amazing; it was really alien to me at first. Therfield had nothing but concrete floors and exposed wooden floor boards while you daily had to navigate and traverse a minefield of dog shit.

Richard and I had finally left 'The House of Horrors' and would never live there again. At this stage, we were in no way turning our backs on Mum and Dad, but what had gone on was not okay and that's an understatement. For us that was in the past and from now on and in the future, everything would be on our terms.

Our relationship with Mum and Dad improved almost

overnight once we moved out. It was December and it was nearly Christmas; Richard and I were looking forward to spending the Christmas Holidays in our new place, business was good and things were going well. Trouble always felt like it was just around the corner but, for the first time in a while, the coast was clear. We'd arranged to go down the town to a pub called the Banyers for Christmas Eve. Getting in the Christmas spirit, we'd bought ourselves a real Christmas tree with all the decorations and we took the time to put it up together. It was the Christmas tree of Christmas trees.

'It wouldn't look out of place in the shop window at Harrods,' I thought as I stood back to admire it.

It was so green and covered in gold glittery decorations and red and gold beads that we used instead of tinsel.

'Rich, I know it's not ideal, but shall we ask Mum and Dad round for Boxing Day? We can get some food and drinks in,' I was a little anxious when I asked him as I was unsure how he would react.

My intention was to get Mum and Dad out of their house so they could put their feet up at ours and just sit back and have a nice day.

Richard scrunched up his face at me, 'Really? Seriously, Bro, I get where you're coming from but it's not ideal. Think about it, they'll stink of the dogs and have to sit on the sofa.' He then paused for a moment to think about it, 'Ahhhh I hate the idea but go on then,' he replied.

'Yeah I know, Bro, but it's Christmas and I think they'll enjoy it; any problems, I'll sort it out,' I said while at the same time picking up my phone to give Mum a call.

'Hey Mum, it's Christian; do you and Dad fancy coming over on Boxing Day? Me and Rich will look after you. You don't need to bring anything, just yourselves.'

'Hiya, Christian, it's your mum; you all right lovey?' she replied.

'I know it's you, Mum, I called you; who else would it be?' I said cheekily down the phone.

'Oooh that would be lovely, I'll tell your father; he will be pleased. I'll bring a bottle of my wicky and my baileys,' Mum said cackling down the phone.

'All right, Mum, no worries; catch you later, darling,' I said and I hung up.

My mum calls whisky, wicky; it's her favourite tipple and is a concoction of two large measures of whisky and one large measure of baileys both poured together into a tumbler. She would always have a litre bottle of each in stock somewhere in the house and in the boot of her car. Mum named her drink a 'wicky and baileys,' like it was some mysterious cocktail that no one would be able to ever figure out the secret ingredients. It's all in the name.

It was Christmas Eve, and Richard and I had cleaned the office; it was spotless. This was one of our weekly rituals and when we locked the office door everything with Fusion was perfect. Leaving around midday, we headed to The Jester for a few drinks, just the two of us. It was like a mini celebration and to recap how we were doing and where we were at.

I couldn't have imagined at the time what was about to happen that night. Leaving the pub, we went home in good spirits to get changed and made our way to the Banyers. The pub was crowded and all of our lads were there, most of which had brought their girlfriends with them; it felt like everyone in Royston was squeezed into the pub and I knew most but not all of the people there. Everything was going great, drinking, laughing and just generally having a good time. I hadn't noticed the tense atmosphere between my brother and his girlfriend, Chelsea, and wasn't aware they had started to argue. I was standing with the lads joking about and they were both at the bar; they couldn't have been anymore central, slap bang in the middle of it. I'd left for a moment to go to the toilet. I was walking down the corridor and as I placed my hand on the door of the gents and started to push it open, suddenly and out of nowhere, I heard this almighty roar of voices coming from the bar's direction. I could tell from the sound whatever was going on; it wasn't good, this wasn't people cheering. Even though I was drunk, I was quick on my feet and back in the bar in a few seconds. I took a moment to scan the room, tables and chairs are moving and falling over in the wave of people pushing and shoving each other while drinks are being spilt and glasses are smashing everywhere. I didn't know why this was happening, but my first thought was: where's Rich? Glancing over and in the centre of the commotion, I could see him. Rich is drowning in people, they are grabbing him and trying to restrain him. Everything was happening so fast I didn't have the time to ask what had happened, so I just waded in.

Rich had wriggled free and was in amongst the crowd, I'd got to him quickly and we were both now in the mix. This, no doubt, confused some people as being identical twins they didn't know which one was which. 'Too many people, too much confusion; we need to get ourselves out of here,' I thought.

I'm guarding Rich and trying to pull us both out of the pub. I needed to get us out and into the carpark to separate who's fighting and who's just stuck in the commotion. This is all happening in seconds, although it feels like forever and in slow motion—then, boom, I'm hit. It was like I went straight into a human brick wall as I came up against this burly fella who had just hit me in the face, catching me on the cheek; I knew he was handy and had a reputation. Okay, time to back up as I pulled Rich by the scruff of his neck into the carpark, people are still coming as we backed up across the road and stood in the church directly opposite. Richard and I were about a metre apart with four guys circling, it was a standoff. I'm still thinking, 'What the hell's going on?' and by now, it is obvious whatever it is involves Rich. I've got to try and diffuse this situation; I didn't want to fight, but had no choice but to be aggressive.

'Okay, who's fighting?' I shouted as I raised my arm and pointed my finger at them. Richard hadn't said a word and he was surprisingly quiet.

'Which one of you is the fucking woman beater?' One of them shouted back.

This came as a complete shock to me, I hadn't misheard him but thought, 'Who's he calling a woman beater?' as I stepped forward towards them. I wanted this to end and I think they did too, it was Christmas after all; they wanted to get back to their pints and I wanted to keep us safe and get to the bottom of what had gone on. It went quiet as they backed up and they slowly dispersed making their way back into the pub while Richard and I stood there outside, on our own and in the cold.

'Rich, do you wanna tell me what just happened there? What the fuck was that?' I said to him firmly.

Rich was looking down at the ground and wouldn't look me in the face. His mannerisms were like that of a naughty child. He was just staring down at his feet when he murmured.

'I punched Chelsea in the face,' he said, as he looked up at me; he looked really sad.

'What? For fuck sake, Rich; what have you done? Why have you done that?' I said to him and the tone of my voice was one of total disappointment.

I was in shock; this is one of the worst things you could ever to do to a girl. Disappointed was an understatement; we were meant to be going to her house tomorrow for Christmas dinner with her and her parents.

'I can't fucking believe you've done this; what were you thinking?' I shouted at him.

I was fuming, but at the same time a feeling of sadness came over me. 'Why had my brother done this? What had gone on for him to react like that?' I thought. I walked off and made my way home leaving him to think about what he'd done.

To this day, Richard has never told me why he did it; he just wouldn't open up to me about it. It wasn't long before the rumour mill started and people were saying all sorts around town. I actually heard about a year later from a close friend of mine that they had been arguing at the bar and Chelsea had apparently leant into his ear and, out of spite, whispered that she'd had a threesome which caused Richard to just lash out in anger. I don't believe that's true and anyway whatever the reason is, you never hit a girl, not under any circumstances, whatever she has done.

It doesn't sit right with me. I would always protect a girl from being hit or hurt by a guy whether it's my girlfriend, a friend that's a girl or even a girl that's a stranger. Whatever the circumstances, I'm stepping in and I'm all in, so I don't blame anyone in the pub for how they reacted.

Chapter 10
Send in the Clown

It was Christmas Day and I could feel the negative energy before I'd even got out of bed. The house was quiet. Stepping onto the landing, Richard's bedroom door was shut so I thought I'd go downstairs, put the kettle on and have a cigarette. I was mulling over last night and the possible aftermath. It was one of those moments when you just want it to go away, but you just have to face it and start damage limitation. This was going to be so, so difficult. For starters, Rich had just hit a girl and it was done spectacularly in front of everyone. There was no rock big enough to hide under this nightmare so dealing with it head on was the only approach. There wasn't much I could do as I didn't do it, but I carried my brother's burdens too. I sent a text to Chelsea checking she was okay… what a stupid question, of course she wasn't okay, her boyfriend, my brother had just punched her in the face. I said something along the lines of 'Hi, Chey, I can't believe what happened last night and what happened to you. I hope you're okay and I'm here if you need me; just tell me what you need me to do and I'll do it.'

I stood on the backdoor step of the kitchen and lit a cigarette. As the cigarette crackled and sparked up, I heard movement from upstairs. I could hear Rich moving about and I'm just waiting for the footsteps to patter down the stairs.

'What's taking so long?' I thought then, straining my ear, I could hear his voice; he was talking on the phone.

It wasn't long before I heard the creak of his bedroom door and he came down the stairs and into the kitchen; he walked straight at me and put his arms around me for a hug.

Hugging me tightly, I could tell he was waiting for me to respond. I gave it a moment and said, 'It'll be all right, Bro, we'll get through it; you're an idiot though and it's not all right any day of the year, but today of all days.'

'I know,' he said solemnly.

I could tell he was close to breaking and for Rich that would be unusual.

'Okay, so what's the plan? What we doing today?' I said.

'I've just spoken to Chelsea; she still wants us to go round for Christmas dinner—she doesn't want her mum and dad to know anything is wrong,' Richard replied.

'Have you noticed my face? They're going to see something is wrong,' my face on one side was a bit abnormal looking and swollen where I'd been hit in the cheek. 'What about Chelsea? How's she looking?' I asked.

'She has a slight black eye, but Chelsea is going to do her best to cover it up with makeup and wear her hair down,' Richard replied.

'Well, Bro, let me tell you that's fine and we'll get through today but you've got a lot of making up to do; you've got to fucking own this and put it right the best you can,' I said firmly. I wasn't convinced about Chelsea using her make up like a mask to cover up what Richard had done.

'I know I do; I can't believe I hit my girlfriend,' his voice was starting to tremor so I interrupted him.

'All right bro. Come on, let's get ourselves organised,' I

said.

'Okay,' he replied as he let go of me and went upstairs.

I shouted up after him, 'Rich,' but he was already in the shower. I went upstairs and could hear the water running so shouted through the door, 'Happy Christmas, okay.'

The water stopped and he replied back, 'Happy Christmas,' and then the water started again as he went back to having a shower.

We made our way over to Chelsea's parents' house and knocked on the front door; I was feeling a little apprehensive standing there. The front door opened and we were greeted by her mum and dad and they were bang in the mood for a Christmas knees up. Christmas songs were blaring from the TV and the song 'Happy Xmas (War is Over)' by John Lennon was playing. With a big sigh and putting on my bravest face, Richard and I walked in. 'This is going to be a long day,' I thought.

Chelsea was still upstairs getting ready so we made our way into the kitchen while Chelsea's dad had nominated himself as the resident bartender.

'What you drinking boys?' He said.

'I'll have a beer, thanks, Neil,' I replied.

'Yeah, me too; I'll have one as well thanks,' Richard said.

Richard was standing behind me, being a bit sheepish; neither of us had seen Chelsea yet and I guess we were both a little apprehensive. I had no idea how she was going to look. Chelsea was now downstairs and it caught me off guard as I'd been listening out for her, but she'd managed to sneak up on me. My mind was elsewhere as Richard was so quiet that I was trying to keep the conversations flowing.

'Chelsea, hey babe. Happy Christmas; you all right?' I

said, giving her a big cuddle and trying not to make it obvious that I was trying to get a good look at her face.

'Happy Christmas, Christian,' she replied as we kissed each other on the cheek.

The reception Richard got was frosty to say the least as they gave each other a peck on the lips. There was an atmosphere between them which I was expecting, but to be standing in the middle of it while her mum, Kath, was in the kitchen preparing this huge feast for Christmas dinner and Neil was now in the background singing along with the TV, oblivious to what had happened; made it even more uncomfortable. It was harder on me as I suffer with anxiety; sometimes I'll just talk for the sake of talking to fill in any awkward silences.

Sitting down at the dinner table, it was the first time that I got a proper look at Chelsea's face. Chelsea had done a good job covering up her bruise, but I could still see it; she had a black eye and her face was swollen. I felt for her and it upset me to see her like this. This was a tough day and not how I was expecting to spend Christmas.

We all sat round the table having Christmas dinner and Chelsea was looking at me with a black eye and I was looking at Chelsea with a swollen face, while Richard… well, he didn't know where to look.

We were not going to shift this dark cloud that was hanging over all of us today so I took on the role of Richard's dancing monkey, entertaining everyone and holding the fort. I was trying to keep most of the attention on me until it was time to call it a night and get home. I stayed for as long as I could, but it wasn't long after Christmas dinner that I decided to call it a day. I said my goodbyes and I left Chelsea's house alone—

I was exhausted.

I was walking along the road and it was peaceful on the way back home until I reached our housing estate. I walked past other people's houses and stopped to stare at the Christmas lights that were flickering and flashing through the windows; occasionally, I could hear cheering and laughter coming from some of the houses—they sounded like they were having the best time and were enjoying the Christmas celebrations. I couldn't help but think, 'That should have been us, but Richard's gone and fucked it up; he reminds me of our Mum.' Both of them would just lash out with no control and would destroy everything and anything insight regardless of the consequences. This was something for me to keep an eye on. When I finally got home, I threw my keys on the kitchen work top and made my way upstairs to bed.

It was Boxing Day and Mum and Dad were due over; Christmas had turned into something I just wanted to get through rather than appreciate and just enjoy the moment.

In the morning, Richard had told me that he had called Mum and Dad to tell them what had happened with Chelsea and apparently, they were okay about it; they had a 'Well it happens' kind of attitude. This didn't surprise me as this behaviour was normal to them. It was later on in the afternoon when Mum and Dad finally came over as they had the dogs to sort out first. I was determined to have a nice time so I organised the food that Richard and I had bought. Stepping back from the dining room table, I took a moment to admire my creation; it was an assortment of all sorts of food, cold cuts of meat, prawns, dips, cheeses, snacks, a black forest gateau and a Christmas cake, 'A feast fit for a king,' I thought.

I heard the doorbell ring so went to open the door as

Richard came down the stairs at the same time to join us.

'Ding Dong,' Mum said loudly in my face as I opened the door.

'Oh, Jesus,' I thought as Mum stood there in front of us wearing this huge dark green, fake fur coat and long matching gloves.

'Your father bought it for me for Christmas; what do you think?' As Mum strutted through the front door with Dad trailing closely behind her, the putrid smell of the dogs and their house floated in behind them. The smell is so distinctive yet I can't describe it—it's unbearable. Mum reminded me of a shit looking Cruella de Vil from the film 101 Dalmatians; as Richard looked over at me and rolled his eyes, I tried not to laugh.

'It's nice, Mum, looks warm,' I said still trying not to burst out laughing.

I could tell they were both already drunk. With Dad, it was obvious as his eyes always gave him away then he'd speak and that definitely gave him away. Mum could hide it better, but the half-empty litre bottles of whisky and baileys in her hands was a good indicator; they didn't eat very much as they were both in drink mode and it wasn't long before they were both asleep on the sofa, drinks in hand.

I can hardly remember most of the Christmases that have come and gone, but this one ended up memorable for all the wrong reasons, perhaps that's why I don't like Christmas very much.

In the next few days that followed, Richard was doing his best to make things right with Chelsea and he wasn't about very much for the rest of the Christmas holidays. Richard spent a lot of time going from house to house apologising directly to our friends for what he had done, which was quite a task considering the size of our group of friends. I know this was tough on him; what he did was wrong and I was pleased to see that he was trying to do something about it.

I had started to think about the ramifications of what had happened that night, but could only deal with things as and when it happened. Even though I had done nothing wrong, to some people, that didn't matter; we were twins and I'd experienced it all my life that it was easier for people to put us both in the same pot. I've heard it a million times before people asking me, 'Which one of you is the good twin and which one of you is the bad twin?' The things is, when things go wrong, there is no such thing as a good twin; in most people's eyes, we are both just as bad as each other.

Over the next few months, Fusion was going from strength to strength. Richard was still licking his wounds and wasn't out as much; I think Chelsea had got him on a tight leash. It was the weekend and I decided to go down the Banyers for a couple of drinks with the lads.

I hadn't been in the pub very long and I ordered a pint and went outside to have a cigarette. On the way out, I was passed in the corridor by someone that I had seen a few times around town and he was in the pub most weekends propping up the bar, but I couldn't remember his name. He was a local and well-known for doing cocaine—him and his partner. He spent more time in the toilets then out of them.

I remembered him for some snide remark he'd made about me a while back. He'd said it to his mate, but he said it loud enough for me to hear him, something about me being the skinniest fucker in the pub. I didn't show it at the time, but this hurt my feelings as I'd always struggled to put weight on. I am really muscular and Richard and I aren't strangers to the gym, but as much as I tried, I could never put any size on. At my lowest, I only weighed 8 St 12 lbs and I hated it; I think this made people think I was an easy target and not much to worry about.

Finishing my cigarette, I made my way back into the pub where this guy was partially blocking the entrance to the bar. He had deliberately positioned himself there and the only way to the bar was to go past him.

'Sorry, mate, can I just get through?' I asked him politely.

'All right, woman beater,' he said under his breath as I squeezed past him.

I was taken by surprise and questioned myself; 'Did he really just say that to me?' I thought.

Later on in the evening, and after a few more drinks, it felt as though this guy was working his way across the pub so that he could get himself closer to me. He was bouncing from one group of people to another making small talk; I was aware of him and he was making me feel uncomfortable. Now, I would normally react to someone like this in a heartbeat, but my heart just wasn't in it today. I was on my best behaviour; I didn't need the hassle or the grief after what had happened here on Christmas Eve. Peeking over the top of his pint glass, he was staring at me and was now easily within arm's reach.

Fuelled by coke and alcohol, he had enough Dutch courage to lean in and say to me;

'You love it, don't ya? Love to give a woman a good slap and shag it in the mouth,' he said with this Joker style grin on his face and his eyes were bulging.

I looked at him straight in the face and wanted to rip him to bits, but something was stopping me; my body stalled and wasn't doing what I wanted it too. I hadn't fought anyone since Richard had broken my nose and back then I'd told myself, 'If anyone was brave enough to touch my face, then they should run for cover.' I did allow the burly fella on Christmas Eve to hit me in the cheek but I let that slide considering the circumstances, but now I was face to face with this guy and it was actually me that was running for cover.

This guy was excitable and getting a kick out of what he had said to me and he wanted me to react, but I didn't. I walked over to the bar and put my drink down to get some space between me and him and to consider what I was going to do next. I felt like leaving, but I didn't want him to think that I was running away so I walked to the gents to take a moment and gather my thoughts.

I was washing my hands as the door of the gents swung open, this guy had waited for his opportunity and had followed me into the toilets. I knew it was coming, but I froze; there were no words exchanged as he smiled and then punched me in the face catching me on the left side of my jaw and then he walked out. I looked up to take a look at myself in the mirror, he hadn't done any damage and it didn't even hurt. The only thing that he had knocked was my confidence. I shook it off and walked back into the bar.

'You're a fucking joke, mate, is that the best you've got?' I shouted at him.

He looked so pleased with himself as he stood there with his drink, he'd slotted himself into a group of four or five people who were standing at the bar. When I shouted at him everyone in the bar looked over at me and I stood there for a moment and could feel myself welling up so I walked out of the pub. I was so mad and annoyed with myself for allowing someone to do that to me. 'How could I let that happen?' I thought as I started to walk home.

This wasn't a one off either, every time I went to the Banyers and he was in there something would happen; I remember on two other separate occasions that he hit me in the face. The problem was we both frequented the Banyers, it's where me and my mates went most weekends. This was my local and I had no intention of going somewhere else.

Chapter 11
Stand up to Bullying

I'm 24 and I was being bullied. My bully had been hiding in plain sight, parading around the pub like a true gentleman. With one arm resting behind his back, he was putting on a display of fearlessness and superiority while he sucked on his cigarette. Being an adult, I hadn't even realised at the time that I was being bullied. I've since learnt that bullying exists in all walks of life and doesn't just stop at the school playground. My bully, in reality, was just an average looking guy: 6 feet tall, medium build and his face was all squished up like a pug—he wasn't much to look at. I've certainly faced off with some scary looking people and he wasn't one of them. I'd heard through the grapevine that this guy had a bit of a reputation for being pretty tough and whispers in the pub were 'Oh yeah, he can handle himself; I wouldn't mess with him.'

That meant fuck all to me, I've heard it all before, someone who's apparently really tough yet no one's ever seen them fight.

The problem I had and it's hard to describe, but there was a combination of things going on in my head that had brought me to this point. My nose had been broken and this affected me more than I realised; it was severely knocking my confidence. Chelsea being hit had affected me; for some reason, I felt guilty about it, like I should suffer and take on any backlash to get my brother through it or take a kicking on his behalf. When I got hit the first time and didn't respond, this gave my bully all the power; the more he did, the more I would shy away. His confidence was growing safe in the thought I was afraid of him. I wasn't afraid of him I was just stuck in a mind-set that was holding me back.

The more he did to me, the bigger he got and the more I allowed him to treat me this way the smaller I became.

I've never told anyone this before but, on one occasion, I'd walked into the pub and he was at the bar standing there with a few friends and he grabbed hold of me, pulling me towards him and stuck his tongue in my mouth as brazen as anything while him and his friends started laughing like it was just lad's banter.

He might have thought it was a bit of lad's banter but, as far as I was concerned, it was sexual assault—his way of asserting control over me, 'I'll do what I want to you,' sort of attitude.

Everyone has a breaking point and I'd just about reached mine. Rich and I were at the office, and I was mulling over the situation. I hadn't done anything wrong and not only that 'I'm the last person you would choose to have a row with let alone want to bully,' I thought. People around town knew who the twins were and we had a reputation; we weren't the bad guys and never went looking for trouble, but if it came looking for us then we'd deal with it. I was speaking to Rich about it and explaining what had been going on.

'This isn't like you, Bro; what is going on with you? If I'd have been there, I'd have knocked him out,' Richard said.

I stood there listening to Richard's bravado and thought, 'Hmmm, yeah… well, that's easy for you to say, you've not been around lately; you weren't there and, as usual, you're leaving big brother to pick up the pieces.' Richard never really suffered any backlash for hitting Chelsea. I hadn't done anything wrong and this was happening to me because of what Richard had done; this guy wanted to fight for the sake of fighting and was using the Chelsea thing as an excuse to pick on someone he thought was an easy target.

Richard was always quick to get over his actions and, as far as he was concerned, he'd gone round apologising to everyone for hitting Chelsea and that was the end of it; he acted like me being hit was not connected and it was a separate matter. His attitude was like, 'You know how to deal with it, so deal with it.'

'I'm just nipping out, Rich, I'll be back later,' I said as I left the office.

I wanted to find out a bit more about this guy so went to see one of my close friends who knew him; he'd worked for my mate Kirk a couple of times. I wouldn't usually care enough to do homework on someone, but I was interested to know my enemy a little better.

Pulling up in town, Kirk was working locally on a house he was renovating.

'Kirk, hello, mate; how's it going?' I said as I leant in and gave him a hug.

That's how I greet people. I'm more of a hugger than a shake hands type of person.

'Hey, Crystal, I'm good mate, you?' Kirk replied.

Crystal is my nickname and a lot of the lads call me this.

'Listen, man, what's the crack with that fucking idiot the other night who hit me in the face and what's his name?' I asked.

'His name's Craig, mate. Just ignore him, he's a prick when he's drunk and coked out of his head; he was saying stuff about you the other day and we all ignored him. He's an embarrassment,' Kirk replied.

'Oh yeah, what's he been saying?' I asked Kirk.

'He was saying stuff about you, like bringing up when you came to live with me and Tasha. He was saying shit like, I bet when me and Tash were out of the house, you were sniffing Tasha's knickers. I just ignored him, mate, he was being a pest and bothering everyone in the pub; honestly, Crystal, don't worry about it. Fucking hell, mate, he's a fine one to talk—it wasn't that long ago he was dragging his own wife, Val, along the floor by her hair at the Banyers,' Kirk said.

It was fucking unbelievable to me that this arsehole was going around saying to people that I was sniffing my best mate's wife's knickers. I was raging because not only had this guy taken it upon himself to act like the hero and protector of woman, he was also on a crusade to get the woman beater— which was me, the wrong person—but what was really pissing me off were the things that he was saying about me behind my back. I'd found what I'd been waiting for: something to trigger a response big enough to set me off and what he'd been saying behind my back was it. I was mad and the anger inside me was building. I was not only starting to feel warmed up, but I could sense I was firing on all cylinders; I was vexed and ready to face my bully.

It was laughable to me and the irony of it was he was a woman beater himself. I've never hit a woman in my life and I've got a guy who's been hitting me and is also regularly knocking his own wife about.

I thought to myself, 'For fuck sake, I'm a nice guy. I have

a big heart and would do anything for anyone and every time I see this guy, he gets physical with me and now he's going behind my back and saying all sorts of horrible shit; I'm not having it.' His character assassination of me was over.

In between dealing with this fucking clown, Fusion was growing and had turned over this financial year £321,000.00. I'd met a girl called Abby who I'd just started dating and I also decided to buy my own house. This guy Craig was a thorn in my side; he was holding me back and it was time to take control.

I called Rich and asked him to meet me down the Banyers. I'd made a few calls and found out where Craig lived and what time he finished work. Rich pulled up in the car and wandered over to me and I got up to give him a hug. It was late afternoon and Richard and I were outside in the pub garden sitting on a bench.

'What's up? You all right?' Richard asked me.

'Yeah, I'm all right. I need you to do me a favour, I've found out where that guy lives and I'm going round to his house after I've finished my coffee,' I replied.

'Nice, it's about time we sorted that out,' said Rich.

'Listen, Bro, I don't want you to do anything, leave it to me; it would just be nice to have some back up as I don't know what I'm walking into,' I told him.

'That's cool, whatever you need.'

I wanted to chuck myself in at the deep end; I felt like I will only test myself if I do this sober and put myself in a position that makes me feel uncomfortable. Let's face it; no one likes to fight if they don't have to. It's one thing fighting drunk and letting the alcohol do the talking, but it's a completely different thing doing it sober. I wanted to prove to myself that I could do it. I was going to dish out some polite violence and give him a chance.

'Can you drive, Rich? I'll tell you where to go, it's not far.'

'Not a problem, are you sure you want to do this?' Rich asked me.

'Oh, fuck yeah, I'm sure. Let's hope for his sake he's not in,' I replied confidently.

I was very calm on the way to Craig's house. My bully lived in a rough looking house at the end of the road in a cul-de-sac. I loved that Rich was there with me as it gave me that extra boost I needed, to deal with it, even though I wanted to do this alone. Rich pulled up a couple of houses back and we both got out of the car; I could see the number of the house I was looking for and made my way to the gate with Rich right behind me.

'Stay there; this shouldn't take long,' I said as I walked down the path.

My adrenalin had kicked in as I raised my hand and knocked on the front door. Taking one step back, I waited. I took a step back to give me enough space to react to whatever came from behind that door. The front door was dark blue with two strips of blurred glass; I could see movement through the glass: it's him, I knew it was.

The front door opened and the look on Craig's face was one of fright and confusion; he definitely wasn't expecting to see me on the other side of the door. Craig just had a pair of jeans on and no top. Like a dear caught in headlights and I could see his heart beating. I'm not kidding; I don't know if it was his adrenaline or pure fear, but his heart was beating so fast that I could see it bouncing back and forth out of his chest like a cartoon character and his breathing was fast and shallow.

At this point, I'd not said a word as things for a moment went into slow motion. It was the look on his face, a look of complete bewilderment. His body language and his reactions were all over the place as I calmly stood there.

He just couldn't get to grips with me being on his door step; he wasn't the cocky arrogant guy that I'd seen in the pub on so many occasions. He looked pathetic while his body stuttered all over the place. He stepped out onto the door step and then rushed back in and reached for something from behind his front door. I was at least expecting a baseball bat, but it looked like a cricket stump that had shrunk in the wash— hardly my weapon of choice and it didn't look like it could do a lot.

I didn't flinch and wasn't bothered at all as he raised it above his head making these grunting noises; he was struggling to get his words out.

'C-c-c-come on then, son,' he said frantically waving his stick above his head.

'Listen to me, Craig, you fucking idiot; if you hit me with that, you better make it count because if you get it wrong, trust me, I won't,' I said to him calmly.

He was taken aback and remained on his doorstep, darting backwards and forwards unsure whether or not to engage so I said to him.

'I'm being nice to you and I'm gonna leave you to it, but I know where you live and if you carry on with any more of your shit, I won't give you another chance.'

With that I turned around and walked up the path and out of his front gate.

He was scared and I felt like I'd turned the tables on him.

Whatever the glitch was, that caused me to hold back, was gone. 'If I see him again and he leaves me alone, that's fine—but, if not, we'll see what happens,' I thought.

A few days later, I heard through the grapevine that after I left his house, he had turned up at the Banyers with a socket wrench in his pocket. I gave the bully an opportunity, but clearly, he didn't want to play when it wasn't on his terms. Apparently, he sat outside all night, slowly getting drunk and doing a few lines of coke thinking I might turn up at some point. I'd taken away his control showing up at his house unannounced; the place where he should feel safest. He was out of his comfort zone and it didn't surprise me that he'd gone straight to the Banyers to load up on Dutch courage and to save face. It reminded me of the final scene in a horror film when the monster always crawls back to its lair to recover just before the final fight. This wasn't over yet but, overall, I was feeling pretty good about myself. This wasn't going to continue on his terms anymore.

Things went quiet for a while, I focused on Fusion and buying a new house; it was a bit of a snap decision to buy this house. It was on the same development as the first house that Richard and I had bought and owned together. It was a brand new three-bedroom detached house just around the corner. I can't say Rich was that pleased about my decision and he wouldn't say it, but I think he was going to miss me.

I moved into this house on the 20th of December 2002 and for the next 6 months, I owned two houses. Richard certainly didn't make it easy for me dividing up our first house and I can relate to anyone that has suffered through a divorce. What Richard couldn't see at the time is that I was enabling both of us to get on the property ladder while we were making money.

I knew it was impressive being only 25 years old, owning our own business and both of us having our own houses.

We hadn't forgotten where we had come from which pushed Richard and I to keep going, to keep pushing and see what else we can achieve. I'd noticed that Richard was becoming more ruthless, even greedy and unforgiving; failure, for us, was not an option.

Chapter 12
Love thy Neighbour as Thyself

Since Richard and I left 'The House of Horrors', we weren't aware just how severe the rows and disputes had become between Mum and Dad and their neighbours.

Mum and Dad had been keeping most of what was going on in Therfield a secret. Occasionally, I'd hear snippets of information but, to be honest, Rich and I didn't care and weren't interested. We had left that life as far behind us as we could. There was physical and verbal abuse occurring daily between my Mum and Dad and the neighbours in all directions; I'm sure the police and the council were on every neighbours' speed dial. Mum and Dad had chosen to live this way and inflict this upon their neighbours—this was Mum and Dad's mess and we wanted nothing to do with it.

I cannot express this in strong enough terms that I do not believe anyone should have to suffer what the neighbours suffered living next door to my Mum and Dad and I should know I lived right in the centre of it.

I was in town after work and had stopped to grab some milk in the local Somerfield. On the other side of the road as I pulled up in my car, I thought I saw my mum and dad's neighbour, Andy. I hadn't seen him for a while so was looking at him thinking, 'Is that him or someone that looks like him?' I was unsure. It wasn't until he started running across the road towards me, that I realised, it was him. I was a bit bewildered watching him run towards me until he got close enough for me to think, 'Oh shit, I think I'm about to have a fight,' so I threw my car keys through the driver's side window and prepared myself. He skidded to a stop right in front of me; we were now face to face.

'You wanna go, you little fuck? Come on, let's go round the corner,' he said aggressively at me.

'What the fuck are you doing?' I asked him; I could see his adrenaline was going and he was really hyped up.

'Come on; let's go round the corner, round the corner,' he repeated tripping over his words.

'Are you fucking stupid mate? I'm not going anywhere with you and if we're having a fight I'll do it right here,' I said to him; he was starting to get my back up.

'Gonna do me are ya? Come on then, yeah didn't think so,' he said without pausing for breath and, as quick as he'd charged across the road at me, he was gone again walking away at pace and muttering to himself. He kept looking back at me over his shoulder, until he got in his car and sped off.

I stood there for a moment thinking, 'What the fuck was that, what just happened there?'

Getting back into my car, I called Rich.

'Hey, Bro, you'll never guess what just happened to me,' I said.

'What's up, mate?' Rich asked.

'Just had that fucking idiot who lives next door to Mum and Dad rare up on me.'

I proceeded to explain to Rich what had gone on.

'What the fucks that about I wonder. Bro give Dad a shout and see what he says,' Rich said.

'Yeah, no worries, Rich; I'll shout you back.'

I pulled up outside my house, parked up in the drive, had a cigarette and then I called Dad.

'Hey, Dad, how's it going? Listen, I've just squared up with your neighbour… what's that about?' I asked him.

'Oh, nothing Christian, don't worry about it. It's just your mother,' he replied sheepishly.

'No, no hang on a minute, Dad. Don't say to me don't worry about it. What's gone on?'

'You know how your mum gets. It's all right,' Dad replied; he was being evasive.

'Well it ain't all right, Dad, is it? so you tell me what the fucks going on.'

'Your mum and next door just had a row and he grabbed her and spat in your mum's face,' Dad replied.

'Really, why did he do that? What did you do?' I asked knowing full well that there was more to the story.

'Well, while I was sorting out the dogs, your mother and next door were having words out the front,' Dad said.

'Right, Dad, I want to know everything and exactly what's been said. Dad put Mum on the phone,' I demanded.

Mum came on the phone sobbing and, in these situations, she would always start off by saying what had happened to her and how wounded she was and none of it was her fault and that she hadn't done anything. The truth of the matter was, on most occasions, Mum was the instigator and would say or do whatever it took in the heat of the moment to win, even if it hurt herself. Maximum devastation and fuck everyone else; she couldn't give a shit about any casualties or who she hurt along the way. 'This is where Rich gets it from,' I thought.

It took me a while to get it out of her, but Mum and Andy

had crossed each other on the shared path at the front of the house and Mum was goading him and a fight ensued. Her exact words before they started wrestling with each other were, 'Come on then, Muncho Man, we'll see, won't we? That's right, Muncho Man, I've spoken to my sons and they've said they are gonna sort you out.'

There are two things wrong with this statement; firstly my mum has never been able to say the word 'Macho' correctly and kept calling the neighbour 'Muncho Man' and, secondly, Richard and I have never said anything of the sort and we never wanted to be involved or have anything to do with the feud that Mum and Dad were having with Andy or any of the other neighbours for that matter.

It all made sense now. The neighbour had just had a row with my Mum; she basically told him we were going to kick his head in and he's driven down town, seen me and seen red.

Mum and Dad were out of their depth and were now using us to fight their battles. That was bad enough, but it was about to get a lot worse when the weekend arrived. I had been out for the night and stayed over at my girlfriend's house. It was early Sunday morning when my phone rang and it was Rich. I nearly ignored the call as I was still half asleep.

'Hey, Rich, how you doing?' I asked him.

'Bro, I've got four car loads of people outside the house and that wanker next door to Mum and Dad is walking up and down the street.'

'Hang on, Rich, say that again. Tell me exactly what you see,' nobody knows Richard better than me and I could tell he was really worried.

'There are four cars parked outside the front of my house; there must be at least twelve men in total that I can see and

Andy is slowly walking up and down the street. I think he has a bar or something metal up his sleeve; it's hard to tell, but his movements are really stiff. He's now leaning on one of the cars staring straight at the house.'

'Okay, Bro, sit tight and don't move. I'm on my way,' I put the phone down and started chucking on my clothes as quickly as I could.

'Abby, I've got to go babe, Rich needs me; I'll explain later,' I said to my girlfriend as I dashed out of her house and jumped in my car.

I hadn't even thought far enough ahead, to consider what I was walking into. All I knew was I'm about to go round the corner to Richard's house and drive straight into all of the action; my attitude was I'll have to deal with it, as I deal with it. It was only a couple of minutes to get there, I was fucking livid on the way there, 'Intimidate my little brother, is that fucking right?' I thought to myself as I drove onto the estate. I was switched on and alert, Richard's house was a couple of turnings away and once you get round that last corner, his house is directly in front of you—there's no escape. As I turned the last corner, I was expecting to see the road blocked with cars and a bunch of guys baying for blood. To my surprise, the estate was dead with no one in sight: no cars, nothing; it was so, so quiet. Not what I was expecting at all. I parked on Richards drive, got out and, as I approached his house, Richard opened his front door.

'What the fuck?' I said as I walked into his house and gave him a hug.

'They all just left a moment ago, literally just before you got here,' he replied.

'Okay, well I can't imagine what would have happened

had it all kicked off. Fucking hell, Bro, we could do without that. I'm more bothered that he thinks it's all right to rock up with a bunch of people to intimidate us—the bloke's a pussy.'

'Yeah, tell me about it; what's really wound me up is he was walking up and down with this fucking grin on his face. This is Mum and Dad's fault, I'm fucking calling Dad up; we have done our best to get away from all this shit and I'm not having it,' Rich said.

Richard was more rattled than me by what had just happened as he went upstairs to phone Dad, which was understandable. I stood in the kitchen and was wondering how Andy knew where we lived and then I remembered Richard saying that he saw Andy recently laying turf down on one of the neighbouring houses and he had seen Rich coming out of his house and get into his Porsche. Apparently, Andy looked dumfounded and he stared at Rich as he drove by. No doubt, there was some jealousy involved; Richard and I had gone from living at 'The House of Horrors' in Therfield to owning our own houses in one of the nicest estates in Royston. He probably couldn't understand how we'd gone from living like that to now living like this. One thing I knew for sure is that they now knew where we lived and could get to us whenever they wanted; we were going to have to do something about this.

Richard was still upstairs and I could hear his voice was raised; after a couple of minutes, it went quiet and then he came downstairs.

'Right Christian this is the situation, we're not going to have anything more to do with Mum and Dad, that's it, I hope you're with me on this.' Richard said to me firmly.

'Okay, Rich, what was said? What did Dad say?'

'Dad basically said it's got nothing to do with them and that I was talking rubbish and that I was out of order blaming them for Andy turning up at my house and there's nothing they can do. Dad said we're going to have to deal with it.'

That sounded really harsh to me, it sounded like Dad had bottled it and left us to deal with it. I took what Richard said on face value and supported him whole-heartedly. If Richard needed me, I'd be there; it's always been that way. My loyalty towards Richard never wavered.

There and then we made the decision to cut Mum and Dad from our lives; they had brought us nothing but trouble. Next on the agenda, we had to deal with what had just happened with Andy. Richard and I wouldn't let something like this slip. Going to the police wasn't our thing because Mum and Dad had taught us from an early age to treat the police as the enemy. It was wrong of Mum and Dad to teach us this, but then again what did they ever teach us that was right?

This was serious, what were we supposed to do? Richard had four car loads of people turn up on his door step and I'd rather deal with it head on then one of us get caught out on our own one day. We spoke long and hard about this and our attitude was if you want to bring trouble to my door step then I'm going to bring trouble to yours. As stated in the Old Testament, 'Do unto others as you would have them do unto you.'

'This fucking thug needs to stay in his lane. Why do we have to deal with Mum and Dad's shit? This was their fault and we'd tried hard to get away from all this,' I thought.

We were going to have to fight fire with fire. We drove to Toys 'R' Us in Stevenage that night and picked up a couple of baseball bats.

Richard and I were quiet as we drove from Stevenage to

Andy's house in Therfield; we didn't actually have a plan and would deal with things as they unfolded. The baseball bats weren't for show and we were prepared to use them. I kept running things through my head from this morning and pictured this group of animals in their cars intimidating my brother and thinking about what could have happened if they had got hold of him. This was not okay and Andy turning up the way he did had to be met with a different level of violence.

It was pitch black when we pulled up in the car, the only light that we had was coming from the inside of the car when we opened the boot. The boot light shined across the aluminium baseball bats; they were electric blue in colour and the handles had a black rubber grip. We picked up one each and made our way in the dark to my Mum and Dad's neighbour's house. As we approached, I could hear dogs barking. This racket was coming from my Mum and Dad's house.

Walking through the front gate and down the path, we veered left to the front door of Andy's house. It was eerily silent as we both stood there. I raised my hand and knocked firmly on his front door and waited. There were no lights on in the house, but I was anticipating the porch light going on at any moment; we waited a minute and still nothing. I knocked again, this time for longer and much harder, and waited a minute. Still nothing, he wasn't in.

Richard and I started having a conversation on his door step.

'Fucking hell, Rich, how lucky for him is that? What do you want to do now?' I asked him.

'I want to deal with this, this is not something I want to do again,' Rich replied.

'Well I can't do fucking much if he's not here; gimme a

minute, I'll get this guy's home phone number.'

I sent out a few texts and it wasn't long before I had his landline number. We had probably been standing on his doorstep for around five to ten minutes by now and there was still no sign of him. I called the number and I could hear Andy's phone ringing from inside the house and, after a few rings, it went through to his answering machine. Listening to his answering machine message, I pondered quickly what I should say. I didn't go in all Liam Neeson with the classic line 'I will look for you, I will find you, and I will kill you.' I was a bit more delicate with my approach because I was thinking we could have the same impact with words without actually having to have the fight.

Slowly and calmly, I said, 'Andy it's Christian, one of the twins. I only just missed you today when you came around my brother's house this morning. It looks like you're not at home either and I know this because I'm standing on your doorstep. If you carry this on so will we; whatever it takes. I really hope you understand what that means.'

Hanging up the phone, we made our way back to the car; we chucked our baseball bats in the boot and went home. Rich seemed instantly happier that something had been done about it. I was relieved for Andy's sake that he wasn't in. Only God knows what would have happened had he answered the door that night.

I know that the war raged on between Andy and my Mum and Dad and all of the surrounding neighbours, but after we went round his house that night, Richard and I never heard from him again—he was a ghost.

Practically all of our family and relatives have fallen out over the years. It was now just Richard and I and we were totally okay with that; just me and him against the world.

Chapter 13
Red Mist

Getting back to business, we put all of our efforts into Fusion. Recently, it felt like we'd been dealing with all sorts of hassle and I sometimes wondered if it was our success that was bringing some of the drama; people had taken notice that we were making money and they either wanted it, wanted to be part of it, or resented you for having it.

Richard had his core business and a constant set of customers so we were making good money, but I was struggling a little bit and my customer base wasn't so solid. I was a little bit lost, sometimes wondering where my next orders were coming from and how I was going to make money each month. Some months, I wasn't earning what I should be, but I didn't panic as something would always come my way. I started to focus on some different products, components that we hadn't sold before. It just takes me a little longer but, when I get it right, I really get it right. I can be a bit clumsy and a bit reckless when it comes to business; the problem is I'm too trusting. I'm a risk-taker and the paperwork side of things, like the book-keeping and raising invoices and delivery notes, wasn't my thing—that's what my brother and the accountant were there for. I don't consider myself academically smart, more street smart, and I have a knack for spotting an opportunity, but the problem was I never knew when it would happen. Sometimes Richard would nag me and make me feel like I wasn't good enough because he was consistent each month and always made a profit; it wasn't unusual for him to make as much as £14,000.00 in profit in one month on his own. During this time, Rich certainly let me know it and I'd sometimes feel more like his employee then his equal business partner. I'm a team player and always thought, 'What's the point of crossing the finishing line and clinking champagne on your own, when we can do it together?' Whereas Richard was more inclined to trip you over and cross the finishing line on his own. That was okay with me and I was submissive waiting for the time I would feel like his equal and make him proud of me. After Richard breaking my nose, I took a softer approach and would rein him in subtly when I thought he was acting wrong while, at the same time, still letting him think he was the boss. Putting aside our different approaches to business, our chemistry together was formidable.

Fusion sold a variety of electronic components. In particular, an electronic component called a semiconductor and inside some of these chips is a product called silicon. I'd been reading a few trade magazines for a while and I managed to find a supplier in Wales for silicon wafer.

It was just one of those moments when I thought, 'Why can't I try and sell this product?'

So that's exactly what I did, my contact in Wales was a girl called Angela and we hit it off straight away; we spoke most days and did some great deals together and I sold this product to a customer in Hong Kong. I was turning over some pretty big figures and making really good money. From memory, I made around £40,000.00 profit in only a couple of months and this had got Richards attention that maybe I was onto something; unfortunately, it was quite short-lived and the product became obsolete and was no longer required by my customer. This wasn't unusual in the electronics industry and happened all the time, but it did get me thinking. 'If only I'd have got there sooner, but there must be other products like this that I can take a look at?' It's now Halloween on the 31st of October 2003, this is my favourite time of year and I remember it well. It was Friday evening and Abby, who was living with me, was getting ready for work; Abby occasionally worked at her mum's friend's pub, in one of the nearby villages. There was a fancy-dress party being held at the Banyers and Richard and I had arranged to go together for a night out in Royston.

'See you later, darling, be good,' Abby said as she kissed me and left for work.

'Yeah, of course I will,' I replied sarcastically.

The thing is I already had a feeling about tonight and sensed something may happen and I think Abby had sensed it too, that's why she told me to be good. It had been a while since I'd been down the Banyers and it had been even longer for Richard and I to both be down there together. Perhaps it was obvious, there was a party at the Banyers and it was going to be really busy with a lot of people there. I was aware that Craig could also be there tonight and I hadn't seen him since I'd rolled up on his doorstep.

I was listening to 50 Cents' album, 'Get Rich or Die Tryin' and it was blaring out of my TV while I got ready. I certainly wasn't looking for trouble but, because of what had happened to me, I think subconsciously I was preparing for it. The last thing I told Craig on his own doorstep was, 'He won't get another chance,' and I meant it.

'If he is there tonight and he's okay with me, that's cool, then I'll be okay with him,' I thought.

Switching off the TV and trying to make my way to the front door, I performed one of my many OCD rituals that I have. I'm running late as usual because it takes me forever to leave the house, while I flip light switches and run up and down the stairs checking each room and banging the door handles.

Stressing myself out, I'd finally made it out the front door and could breathe a sigh of relief.

'Right, I'm ready,' I thought as I walked round to my brother's house, which only takes me a couple of minutes.

Walking along it was cold, but I loved seeing all the decorations dotted around the estate: the carved pumpkins, the fake cobwebs, the skeletons and paper bats all glowing in the windows. I wasn't dressed up this year and it happens to me every time. I always say, 'This year, I'm definitely going to dress up,' and then I leave it too late and end up going to a party and feel like the odd one out because everyone else has a costume on.

I walked along the path and on the next corner Richard's front door came into view. Richard opened his front door and came to meet me; I knew he wouldn't be dressed up either— that just wasn't his thing—he wouldn't be seen dead in a costume.

'What the fuck took you so long? I've been looking out the window waiting for you for ages,' he said.

'Yeah, sorry Bro. I was just sorting myself out; it took me longer than I thought,' I replied as we shook hands and hugged.

I don't mean that we actually shook hands, but we had this signature handshake that we'd started doing; it was like our own little greeting, only for me and him.

On the way to the pub, we chatted and laughed and had a brief conversation about any potential issues that could arise tonight. We both agreed that we would just look out for each other and it wasn't a big deal.

Walking into the pub, it was packed as we made our way to the back of the bar. There were groups of people, some dressed up, some not, but a lot of our lads had made the effort. I'd already scanned the room as I walked in and there he was: Craig was in his usual spot propping up the corner of the bar. I held my gaze for a moment to see if he looked at me, but he didn't and if he had noticed me, he certainly wasn't showing it. It was something to keep an eye on, but I wasn't concerned, everyone was getting drunk and there was just a generally good vibe in the pub. I knew Richard had spotted Craig too and, as the night went on, I'd noticed Richard had placed himself next to him at the bar. No one else would have noticed the slightest movements Richard was making, but my brother's body language was very obvious to me. I know all of his facial expressions and the one he was currently wearing told me something was about to happen. I'm standing in the bar area about four metres away from the bar itself chatting with the lads and keeping one eye on Rich. I was just about to shout over to him and call him over to me but, before I could, I watched his face change again; he's in fight mode. I've seen that face so many times as Richard placed his pint down, turned and punched Craig straight in the face. Stunned, Craig stepped backwards as people tried to intervene. I know exactly why Richard has done this, he had been thinking back to what has been happening to me and has worked himself up to the point that he has finally snapped. Right now, I couldn't give a fuck, I'm only interested in getting next to my brother.

Okay, so Richard and I are side by side and enough is enough. Anyone who has a problem with that is going to have to deal with both of us, but Richard and I are going to walk out of this bar and on our own accord. There wasn't as much of a commotion as I thought there would be and I think people realised that there was bad blood between me and Craig, but it was Craig who was at fault and it was Craig who had started all of this by bullying me. Craig had quickly disappeared to the gents and was either checking his face out or snorting a line of cocaine to help him cope. Richard and I calmly walked out of the pub and started to walk in the direction of home; we'd only walked a slight distance from the Banyers when I heard shouting.

'You're gonna fucking get it,' Craig shouted as I looked back towards the pub. I could see Craig and another guy in the shadows walking at speed towards us; it was dark as they approached and I could just about work out which one Craig was.

'Good, I'm going to put an end to this,' I thought as I prepared myself to fight. I was very nonchalant about it, I wanted this to happen and I wasn't concerned at all. Richard was a little more agitated and seemed worried.

'Come on bro, let's go. Let's fuck this off,' he said to me.

'No, you stand your fucking ground,' I replied as both of them got closer. They weren't quite on us yet, but Craig's friend was moving towards us faster than Craig was. 'Fuck sake, that's not who I want, but I'm gonna have to deal with him first,' I thought.

At the time I never wanted to hurt someone as much as I wanted to hurt Craig; his friend was just in the way and was an inconvenience to me.

Richard was behind me as Craig's friend got closer, so I went at him, knocking him to the ground and dragging him along the floor; I could tell this guy's heart wasn't in it. Not like me, I was ready to go. I quickly looked over my shoulder and saw Craig go towards my brother—they had both gone to the floor and Craig was on top of Rich.

'No, mate, this is not going down like this,' I thought as I quickly dealt with his friend and threw him to the side.

I didn't want to hurt his mate and it felt like he was just there to even the score and keep an eye on things; he didn't want to be there. I was in control when I threw him away and sharply turned my attention towards Craig.

It took me about three steps to get to Rich as I grabbed Craig by the scruff of the neck and pulled him backwards. As I pulled him backwards, he released Rich and I went at him; it was now me and Craig—the guy who had been so horrible to me, the guy who had no care for how his behaviour in the past had affected me. After what Craig had done to me, I was not going to go easy on him.

I hit Craig so hard that he was now on the ground and on his back, moving just like an insect trying to recover and get back on its feet. I crouched down and I used my knees to pin him to the floor and everywhere he moved I moved. I was synchronised to Craig's movements and everywhere he went my knees followed and moved with him which kept him under control. Raining punches down into his face, wherever his face moved, my fists would also follow. I'm moving so smoothly just throwing punch after punch like a machine in a factory that has only one specific job and can just keep going without letting up.

The blood that came out of his mouth and nose was like a volcano erupting. He's on his back and he was gurgling while trying to stop swallowing his own blood as it covered his face drowning him. I was in full on attack mode and there was nothing he could do to stop me. 'I'll stop when he stops,' I thought, whatever that means, but I was comfortable and in the swing of things.

Craig went out of his way to attack me, bully me and violate me. I hadn't done anything wrong and I have to make him stop, punish him so badly that he would feel so frightened that it would become a struggle to ever leave his own house again.

What actually fucked me off more during the fight and I actually thought this at the time, 'Fucking hell, I'm scuffing my new Y3 trainers on the pavement.'

Then, all of a sudden, I heard shouting from down the street, 'Christian stop, please stop,' the voice shouted. I was still hitting Craig as I looked up.

It was my close friends, Adam and Matt, and they were both running towards me through the darkness dressed as Batman and Robin. It reminded me of a scene from 'Only Fools and Horses.'

Adam and Matt grabbed an arm each by sliding their arms underneath mine and dragged me away.

'How do you like that sweetheart?' I shouted at Craig as I was being dragged backwards with my heels scraping along the ground.

By the time I'd finished with him, I'd sent him back into that pub looking and making noises like a zombie. I heard screaming and a commotion coming from inside the pub and later found out it was my friend Tasha and a few other girls;

they screamed when Craig walked back in and they saw the state of him—he was in a bad way and needed some serious help.

I didn't have a scratch on me and by now everyone had made their way back into the pub as Richard and I stood there in the street, it was dead quiet.

'Fucking hell bro, what was that? You proper done him; you all right?' Rich said while standing there in complete shock.

'Yeah, I know, I'm all right. Hand hurts a little, but apart from that I'm okay,' I replied.

We stood for a moment without speaking and then we walked home. It wasn't until I got home and took my jeans off that I noticed both my knees were bruised, 'That must have happened when I had him pinned to the ground,' I thought.

I was in the bath when Abby got home from work and was just soaking my knees. The bathroom was at the top of the stairs and I heard the keys rattle in the front door.

'You all right, babe?' she shouted up the stairs.

'I'm good Abs, yeah, you?' I replied.

'I got a call from Beth telling me what happened down the pub. I heard what you did, he's in a bad way. I knew something like this was going to happen tonight,' she said.

'Yeah, I know, babe. I meant it, though, that's what happens if you're going to bully people: you'll pick on someone you shouldn't. I just wish people would realise that their actions can affect other people's lives, just be good to one another, love each other, and just be a fucking human,' I replied.

He was known around town as a hard man and a lot of people couldn't understand how he'd received such a beat down; I could have killed him that night. He was off work and out of action for weeks, if not a couple of months, and the next time I saw him I gave him a warm smile to show him that it was okay to approach me and he did just that. He came over and shook my hand.

As for Craig, I'm quite sure before he places his hands on anyone again that he'll remember what I did to him that night. There's a difference between beating someone and breaking them. I broke him and I remember one of my friends Cody asking me a couple a weeks later.

'What happened to you that night, mate? Did you get red mist or something?'

Chapter 14
It Takes Two to Tango

I needed to get away from Royston; I was feeling like this town was full of fucking idiots and we were sifting our way through all of them. Every day was a battle and we were literally fighting our way to the top, so I decided to go on holiday for a couple of weeks. I booked a holiday in Cuba with some of the lads and their girlfriends and I took my girlfriend, Abby. Richard stayed back and manned 'Fusion.' I wanted to relax and I would think of some new ideas when I got back. It would be nice to get away for a bit and recharge my batteries as I'd been struggling to switch off.

I have mixed memories of Cuba: a combination of relaxing, over-thinking and drinking. It was hard for me just to let go and, with my anxiety, most of the time I just wanted to get back behind my desk or potter about at home. I never took time to sit back and appreciate the moment. At this stage, my anxiety wasn't severe, but it would creep up on me and make me worry about all sorts. I felt like something was wrong even though I didn't know what that was and a feeling like I was losing control and that everything was upside down.

There were eight of us in total who went to Cuba, me and Abby went a week earlier then my friends so we could spend some time together, even though I spoke to Richard every day on the phone and we would always check in with each other. I remember Abby complaining about me being on the phone to Rich all the time. Rich and I have both experienced this with girls; they would become so jealous of our relationship and how much time we spent together.

Anyway, I organised what I thought would be a romantic day together, just me and Abby and no phones. I'd arranged for us to follow a tour guide on a Jet Ski and stop at a small island which had a bar and we could have some lunch together and drink champagne. I turned up in a pair of Gucci loafers and a Prada shirt looking and feeling sophisticated and Abby with her long blonde hair and slim figure looked gorgeous in a blue Burberry Bikini as the lagoon breeze lifted her hair ever so gently off of her shoulders.

We were totally unprepared for what was in store for us that day. I imagined us bobbing around on a Jet Ski, in crystal clear blue water, against an amazing background, waving at flamingos as we drove by. The reality was it felt like someone was continuously throwing buckets of dirty salt water in my face and I wasn't able to wipe my eyes because my hands were gripping the handle bar and accelerator so tightly. I was fearful of letting go and only going faster and faster as Abby was holding onto me for dear life. Her arms wrapped round my waist, squeezing the life out of me while screaming and crying the entire journey. I could barely see the tour guide in front of us as we smashed through the waves traversing through the dark green, muddy looking swamp that I was convinced was infested with crocodiles. It was absolutely terrifying!

Abby was so traumatised when we finally reached the location for drinks and something to eat that she just sat there. Abby was dazed and confused and looked a different colour; she was really pale and looked like she was going to be sick at any moment. The only time she spoke to me was to murmur quietly.

'I want to walk; I want to walk back. I can't get back on that thing,' she whispered.

This was impossible, we were stuck on a remote island and we had no choice but to get back on that Jet Ski. The return journey was just as traumatic and it took thirty minutes to get there and, on a Jet Ski, that feels like forever; there and back was sixty minutes of hell.

When our friends arrived for the second week of the holiday, that gave me and Abby a bit of a boost and we ended up having a great time together. I decided that I could see a real future with Abby; we'd grown closer and putting aside the Jet Ski incident, and not forgetting that I got so drunk on Sambuca when we stopped over in Havana for two days that I hallucinated, everything was going well.

Arriving back in the UK, my feet had barely touched the ground, but I went straight to see Richard. I hugged him as soon as he opened the front door and he said he had a surprise for me. One of our friends had invited us to Monza Race Track in Italy to watch his brother drive Formula 3 and we were flying on a private jet.

I literally landed back from Cuba and the following day flew back out to Italy. The jet itself was impressive but what I loved the most was when we arrived at the race track, the race car was covered in our company logo. It was touching; I smiled as I thought back to me and Richard basically living out of a garden shed and how far we'd come since then. When I finally made it home it wasn't long before I was back in town and in the local club called Fat Jax, with a few of the lads. This place certainly was rough around the edges, but the only place in Royston to go at the weekend when all the pubs had closed. As everybody poured out of the various pubs in town, people would head straight to Fat Jax and you would end up rubbing shoulders with people I wouldn't normally ever hang out with, people I didn't particularly like or they didn't like me for whatever reason. All squeezed into this one room with a capacity of around 250 people you would think it was a swanky VIP club in London as the queue snaked around the corner. It was the place to go if you weren't quite drunk enough and wanted to carry on, but it was a hotbed for trouble. I've seen no end of fights inside and outside of this place as everyone piles out of the club at the end of the night. I've seen the police turn up there in force on a number of occasions and once took a face full of pepper spray. On that night, I was outside the club talking to a couple of girls when this young officer got carried away; he was trying to disperse the crowd that was gathering in the street and started spraying pepper spray at everything in sight. I was so close that it hit me directly in the face and ricocheted off me onto these girls and back onto the officer and two of his colleagues. I'm not kidding, this stuff will stop you right in your tracks and you will go down. It sucks the breath right out of you while scorching your eyes at the same time, rendering you completely helpless. I remember there was one of the girls, me and the two officers all going to the ground at once, all of us blinded and this girl was holding onto me while we were crawling around on the pavement. Someone was even murdered outside the club once as a car deliberately ran them over.

On this particular night, I was in the club with one of my best mates, Cody; we were chatting away and both of us went

129

into the toilet together. There was a bit of a queue so Cody went first heading towards the empty urinal and I'd noticed the lad going for a piss next to Cody who was standing on his right-hand side. His body language was off and he was shouting and slurring while zipping himself back up. This lad had one mate behind him and another one who was washing his hands by the sink. As I'm watching a conversation unfold between Cody and this lad, something was said about a Ferrari which, at the time my mate, Cody owned. I think it was along the lines of 'You're the guy with that car,' and as Cody looked to his right this lad hit him straight in the face with an uppercut. This caused this lads mates to jump to attention and gather round Cody like a bunch of hyenas. The situation escalated very quickly and, before I knew it, the bouncers were wading in and grabbing hold of all of us; no questions asked, they chucked us all out on the street. By this time, Cody's brother Matt and a few of the other lads were there too. We were on one side and these lads were on the other—there were only a few metres between us. I shielded Cody as he stood behind me; Cody's face was a bit of a state and his lip looked like it was split in half—he'd suffered a lot of damage.

'Crystal, help me mate, I can't do anything,' his shaken voice said to me.

'It's all right, Cody, I've got this,' I replied as I stepped forward.

This lad who had hit Cody in the toilet came forward at me in a boxer's stance. He was bouncing all over the place and, as we clashed, he swung aimlessly as I grabbed him by the throat and started pushing him backwards at speed knowing he wouldn't be able to stay on his feet for long. By the time we both went to the floor, I was on top of him and I was in control.

'You've fucking had it now,' I thought.

I remember it well and I know exactly what he screamed out.

'Someone, get this fucking cunt off of me,' he screamed in a high-pitched voice. He sounded desperate for help and he was in trouble; he knew it and I knew it.

I had this guy on the ground and he was there because that's where I wanted him. Now that I had him pinned, I was in the process of deciding how to deal with him, rain down fists into his face or smash his head up and down off the pavement but, all of a sudden, I'm in retreat mode. I can feel the warmth of blood running down my face and, to be honest, I'm dumbstruck.

'What the fuck was that?' I thought—I was so dazed.

As I got to my feet, I backed up a moment and realised I'm on my own with these two lads circling me and an audience is gathering. Wiping the blood out of my eye, I know I've been hit in the face and it has done a lot of damage.

I moved backwards just enough to bring them both into view and my two assailants are now walking cautiously towards me while I'm slowly recovering my senses.

'I think I recognise these two; they are brothers,' I thought.

I'm outnumbered and bleeding everywhere as my eyes flick from one person to the other and I can tell they are deciding how to attack me and which one of them is brave enough to go first. I'm aware that this is not a situation I can win now and all I can do is try and hold my own. I'm not ready to run, I never run, and I'll give it all I've got.

Fights are over much faster than you would think, usually in seconds, but I know this has been going on for a while now and I know one of them is trying to get behind me so I backed up into a side street to narrow down their ability to do this. I am trying my hardest to fight them both as they keep coming at me. As they launched their next attack, the lad who I originally had on the ground was first to go as we traded blows, so I pulled him up against me and backed up against a shop window; he was now biting my arm while I watched the other one who was deciding when to make his move.

'Leave him alone! Look what you've done to him, you'll kill him,' a girl in the crowd shouted.

I need all the help I can get, right now, I'm running out of energy, my friends have fucked off and I'm hurt. I knew his brother was about to come at me so I threw the lad who was biting me to the ground and backed up again. When I threw him, he rolled across the ground and got back on his feet. I'm now facing both of them again, but I've managed to get some distance between us. I had to call it a day; I couldn't go on, but I wouldn't let them see I'm weak.

'I won't quit and if you keep coming at me, I'll just carry on,' I said defiantly at both of them.

They both moved forward and then looked at one another as though they were considering what to do next.

'I'm gonna walk away,' I said.

I summoned whatever strength I had left to stand strong and demonstrate to them that I had more in the tank and I could go all night, but the truth was I'm beat and starting to feel sick.

I slowly backed away and they didn't follow me but, as I backed away, I never took my eyes off either of them until I got further up the high street and out of sight.

I was now on my own as I made it to the top of the high street. I stopped for a moment and tried to see myself in the nearest shop window. As the street light flickered on and off, I could see my reflection in the glass, but all I could see was a lot of blood.

I'm panicking, I feel really rough, I feel sick and I have an instant migraine. I don't know what to do, but I wasn't far from my office and had my key card in my pocket.

'I'll be safe there. Come on Christian, it's not far, you can make it,' I thought.

Making my way slowly to the office, I swiped my key card and fell through the door.

'Drink, I need a drink,' I thought as I made my way to the kitchen.

The kitchen at our office was shared by a couple of other businesses that operate there including us. I knew nothing in there was ours, but I was so desperate as I opened the fridge door and stuck my hand in rooting around for anything that could save me. There was an unopened bottle of Lucozade which I grabbed and ripped the top off, guzzling down as much as I could.

For a moment, I felt better and then all of a sudden, my mouth turned to water.

'I'm gonna be sick,' I thought as I opened the downstairs toilet door and fell to my knees, puking up in the toilet.

Getting to my feet, I looked in the mirror; my face was a mess, but only half of it— I looked disfigured, it reminded me of the musical The Phantom of the Opera. The left side of my face was unrecognisable, so swollen and bruised I was covered in blood and had a really deep gash above my left eye; the cut ran along my left eyebrow and it was about an inch and half long. I was feeling so rough that I couldn't deal with anything else and just needed to get home. I started to suffer with an extreme migraine and all I wanted to do was lie down. I sat at the bottom of the stairs to our office until I was able to walk home and I fell into bed.

Richard hadn't heard about what had gone on that night and was trying to get hold of me the following morning; he was so worried, he drove round to my house and was knocking on the front door until I answered.

As I opened the door, my brother's face dropped and he welled up.

'No bro… no, no. What's happened to you? Who's done this?' he asked.

I explained to Richard what happened to me and he was really upset.

'Was anyone there to help you?' he asked.

'No, I don't know what happened, but I was left alone,' I replied.

Now Richard was getting to grips with the situation; he called Cody and went fucking bananas.

'Cody, do you wanna tell me what the fuck happened to my brother last night? Do you wanna explain to me why he's in such a state?'

'I don't know, mate, I can't remember much about last night or what happened,' Cody said sheepishly.

After making a few calls, Richard had got to the bottom of things and it turns out that Cody had jumped into a taxi and fucked off to hospital the very moment that I had intervened for him and the other lads who were there were just too scared to get involved.

The second I stepped forward for Cody, he turned and jumped into a taxi. All I needed was for someone to look out for me; I was expecting someone to at least cover my back, but that wasn't the case and I walked into battle on my own to protect my friend.

A couple of days later, I also found out that when this lad screamed out for help, it was his brother who had ran in and kicked me in the face with such ferocity it was like someone taking a penalty kick—that's what damaged me so badly.

Richard was so mad he told me, 'That's fucking it; I'm not having you end up in that state again. You having to fight two people at once, for the lads, while they got in a cab and fucked off leaving you to deal with it.'

'Yeah bro, I understand. It's just in my nature to protect people, though,' I said looking down at the floor.

'Christian, I couldn't give a fucking shit mate. From now on, the only people we protect are each other. I heard that you done well going up against both of them and you had the first lad no probs until you got kicked in the face, but so what. They could have killed you. Fuck this, we'll be all right, just me and you; we've got each other, haven't we? That's all we need and we can focus on the company,' he said as he put his arm around me and gave me a hug.

I knew Richard was right. I needed the cut above my eye glued together and, within a couple of weeks, once the swelling and bruising had gone down, I was back in action. We moved into a bigger office and threw ourselves into our business; there was more out there for us than this.

'What a joke, I'm running a successful business and rolling around in the streets at the weekend; I'm so much better than that,' I thought.

Chapter 15
A Little Something, Something

We moved into our new office, it was still at The Old Police Station, but we had moved across to the Old Court House. Our new office was on the upper level and positioned at the back of the property, right above the yard where the inmates used to exercise. It was three times bigger than our previous office. It was lovely, lots of character and so quiet. We had built up quite a lot of money in the business account and I was looking for something bigger to trade in while Richard focused on our core business. We also decided to try and expand the business and employed our first member of staff. The office was big enough to comfortably fit four or five people in it. Richard and I went to meet someone that Richard used to deal with from the Lightning days. We went to have a beer with him—an informal interview if you like. Rich assured me this guy was on his game and could make money and was good at what he did. I trusted Richard's judgement and thought, 'Why not? What's the worst that can happen? We'll give him a trial run and if he doesn't perform, we can just sack him.' Richard was more his mentor than I was, as I liked to get on with my own thing. I was looking for something bigger, something to impress and take this business further. For a two-man team, we were killing it in the electronics industry and could give our competitors a good run for their money, but I knew we could push it more.

There was something in the back of my mind nagging me to give Angela a call—this was the girl from Wales. I had her number on my phone and thought she would be a good starting point. We had got on so well, so I decided to give her a call. I called her mobile and it went straight through to her answering machine so I left a message. A couple of days later, Angela called me back; she had a strong Welsh accent and I would recognise that voice anywhere. We must have chatted for an hour or so, chatting away like two old friends that had lost touch with each other and had just been reunited. I was chatting with her about certain products and she said she mainly traded in Intel CPUs. I was familiar with this product, but needed to do a little homework on it. Even at this stage, I sensed I could do something here. A CPU is a central processing unit; you would recognise this chip, which is manufactured by Intel in all laptops and notebooks these days. One thing I knew for sure, these products were not cheap and were purchased in boxes containing 315 to 360 pieces.

'How's Ang? You and her spoke for ages,' Rich said.

'Yeah, Bro, she's good. She's so funny, it was great to catch up with her; I'm just checking a few things out with her at the moment,' I replied.

'Yeah, you get on really well with her,' he said.

For the moment, I didn't want to let Richard know what I was doing—it was early days. I wasn't keeping things from him, but I had a good feeling about it and I wanted to prove I could do this on my own. I also got in touch with a couple of customers I had based in Hong Kong, Europe and America to ask if they ever purchased these products and that I could help them with their requirements.

At the same time, I started to keep one eye on our new

member of staff; he'd started off well, but it wasn't long before I started to notice his flaws. He had made some good money in the first couple of months, which was fine, but I'd nipped out for lunch with him a couple of times in one week and both times he popped into the bookies before he grabbed a sandwich. I could count on one hand the amount of times in my life I'd been in the bookies as I walked in with him. I sat down on a stool and felt like the third wheel on a date while he started playing a slot machine which had a roulette wheel on it. These machines are now known as the crack cocaine of gambling addiction and I can see why. I watched him blast through £1,000.00 in half an hour and he did exactly the same the following day. I was shocked as he put on a brave face and acted like it wasn't a big deal. I was thinking, 'You've just spent two thirds of your monthly wage in less than an hour.' I mentioned it to Rich but, at the end of the day, it was his money and he could do what he likes with it. As long as it didn't affect the business, what harm could it do? I say that, but it did concern me.

Over the next couple of weeks, I worked hard as I sent emails and faxes, everywhere I could think of, looking for potential suppliers and customers to buy and sell CPUs. I came into the office one morning when I received a call from my customer who was looking for a specific CPU; it was quite a large quantity. I gave Angie a shout and she didn't have this particular CPU available, so at first it was a dead end, but I did have another supplier that I had found and gave them a call.

Richard could see me rushing around the office. The phones were going crazy for a few moments as I was dealing with things; there were a number of calls on hold as Richard and I methodically dealt with them. I had to be really on point not to get this wrong; the air was electric in those moments and then all of a sudden it was quiet. Sitting at my desk, I waited—I was waiting for the fax machine to ring and by now Richard had sensed something big was coming. I had been working on a deal and, as quickly and as sudden as it had started, the pandemonium suddenly stopped. I sat there at my desk for a moment to take a breath. I did it: I managed to secure my first order in the CPU industry. This was the moment I'd been waiting for, the moment that made me feel truly worthy, I was now Richard's equal in our business; in fact, from here moving forwards, I was the business. However, being his equal suited me just fine and Richard was about to recognise this when the fax machine rang.

'Christian, is that your order?' Rich asked curiously; he sounded nervous, but excited.

I looked over at him and he smiled at me; he looked really on edge. I delayed getting out of my chair deliberately. I wanted Rich to see this first and I watched him as he got up from his chair and wandered over to the fax machine. The fax machine using its roller grabbed a sheet of paper and started to drag it slowly inside itself and then started to print. After a couple of seconds, it ejected the paper like a hiccup as it spat out my order. Richard looked over his shoulder at me and his mouth dropped. The total of this order was in excess of £650,000.00. I had done a deal in one day that eclipsed any deal we'd ever done before; it was double what Fusion' had ever turned over in one year, but as they say, 'Turnover is vanity, profit is sanity.'

I loved that moment and remember it well, more for the devilment of it—it was just a great day. I was still pretty grounded and I didn't let it go to my head. They were just figures to me, I can do more.

'Let's push it and see how far I can go with this.' I thought.

The CPU industry isn't easy and is incredibly fast paced, even if you find stock for your customer, it could be sold by the time you've managed to secure an order and then phoned your supplier back. It takes a lot of money to buy these products and you have to be fast to secure the currency for the total order amount in the country that you are selling to with your foreign exchange agent. You could lose thousands of pounds, tens of thousands of pounds, in one deal if you get it wrong. When you're in the middle of a deal, it reminded me of the film *Rogue Trader*, frantically working the trading floor, trying to pull everything together to close the order. It was fast and at times very panicky, negotiating pricing, getting the customer order, securing the stock with your supplier, checking with your freight forwarder to inspect the product, buying and selling at the correct prices and locking in the currency at the correct rate to exchange dollars and euros into sterling. If the rate at which you tried to convert your currency dropped, this could greatly affect your margins. There was a lot to think about and as stressful as it was at the time, I thrived on it.

I've heard the word entrepreneur used a lot in my life and it's so easily slung around. Some people from the moment they pick a company name off the shelf consider themselves an entrepreneur and walk around like it's an instant badge to success; I have always hated the word. For me, I've always thought it's about having a little something, something and you either have it or you don't. I have always been able to make something from nothing. I'm a bit clumsy at times, but I will get there in the end; it doesn't matter how you get there, just get there.

There are different levels to having a little something, something. I thought that Richard was similar to me, but he aired more on the side of caution and this limited his ability to see potential in something. I am, in essence, quite a big risk-taker and don't get me wrong this can be a liability as I can make some bad decisions at times too.

It's a feeling I can't explain and if you have 'A little something, something' then you'll know what I mean.

As an exporter, Fusion would have to pay the VAT on each transaction. I started to do a lot more of these deals, but you could only trade with as much money as you had available in the bank. It would take a few days to deliver the product and get paid by your customer and I was literally spending every penny in the company account which was fine and, from my side of things, I was consistently making tens of thousands of pounds a month and with Richards core business, he was able to cover running costs and our salaries. It was the perfect combination.

This side of the business was like a well-oiled machine and then I'd look over at our employee Rob who had started off with potential, but was starting to drag us down a little. His desk was facing Richard and me so we couldn't see his computer screen, but we could see it from the reflection on the window behind him. He thought I hadn't noticed him playing solitaire all day, every day which I was prepared to let slide for now, but he was starting to take the piss bearing in mind we were paying him a salary of £36,000.00 a year. I used to laugh to myself because every time I got up to make a coffee, he would suddenly click off his screen and pretend he was looking at something else.

'Rich, does Rob think I'm a fucking idiot or what? He's playing solitaire all day long and is waiting till lunch so he can rush off down the bookies,' I said.

'What do you want to do, bro? Shall we talk to him?' Richard asked me.

'No don't worry for now; I've got my things going on at the minute. He's made about the same in profit as we've paid him so far—let's monitor his performance at the end of each month, but at this rate he'll be gone in two,' I replied.

I had my third rhinoplasty operation coming up at The Harley Medical Group and would be out of action for at least a couple of weeks and thought he could keep Rich company, although if it was me, I'd have rather been on my own.

I was walking into the office most mornings and had started to talk to Angie nearly every day. We started trading together and we just seemed to click; she loved that we were twins and she'd phone Rich sometimes in the morning and ask, 'Is he in yet?' We had done a few orders together and she was my go-to person when I was looking for stock; we'd chat about the market or generally just have a gossip—we could talk for hours. I was pretty much left to my own devices. I'd created two divisions within Fusion. Rich dealt with his customers and all of the paperwork which was quite a big job in itself and I would deal with my side of things. Without Richard, Fusion wouldn't have a spine to support me and, without me, we wouldn't be earning the money we were now making. We were becoming the biggest two-man team in the electronics industry. Even better than that, I hadn't boxed up a parcel for a long time that was left to Rob.

Fusion was taking up all of my time, I lived and breathed it. I was still living with Abby, but she was starting to become resentful towards me and had started to suffocate me a little. At times, it almost felt like an ultimatum; it was her or the business. Abby wanted the nice things and then would criticise me for working too much and not spending enough time with her. I had my suspicions she was becoming jealous of the relationship I had with Angie too and whenever her name was mentioned, she would say, 'Who is this girl you keep talking to? I'm not sure about this.'

Richard and I were spending more time together than ever, we couldn't help it. I was trading day and night pulling deals together in my sleep and I would call Rich at all hours to explain what I needed doing. I was enjoying life and really loved the new job that I had created for myself.

It was October 2004 and I was off getting organised to go to hospital for my rhinoplasty operation. I was really hopeful that they would finally be able to fix it aesthetically. Having your nose done on the NHS was okay, but they were more interested that it would function properly then getting it perfectly straight again and that's why I chose to pay for it privately. My nose has haunted me ever since Richard broke it with ongoing operations and procedures. I'm sure most people wouldn't even notice it, but for me it was gutting every time I looked in the mirror and could see the curve in my nose. It had been affecting my confidence for quite some time.

While I was out of action, my side of the business stopped completely until I was well enough to come back. Richard wasn't able to do his side of things and mine all at once; it would have been too daunting to even try it.

In the hospital, it was all so familiar. I'd been here and done this a number of times. I knew the procedure inside and out; I could have probably performed the operation myself. I'd always liked being put under general anaesthetic, trying to fight the drug once it has been administered and counting down from ten and, by the time I got to number eight, I was already under. In the blink of an eye, your awake again and feeling a bit beat up and woozy. Waking up wasn't as much fun as going under; they use nasal packing to stabilize and control the bleeding and that feels like you've had a scrunched-up football sock stuffed up each nostril. Your finally covered up with a splint which is placed on the top of your nose for support, black eyes, sweaty and oh my God it's all so itchy.

Chapter 16
Trust your Gut

Abby had come to pick me up after my operation. It was a quiet journey on the way home as I was really fragile and feeling nauseous; my head was banging and it felt like I was underwater. I climbed into bed to get some rest and Richard popped over to see the wounded solider.

'How are you doing, Bro? You look pretty bruised up,' he said; he looked sad to see me like that, as he leant over to kiss me on the head.

I was in and out of sleep so Richard left and was going to pop back to see how I was before the weekend. There wasn't much I could do as I was recovering; I lay in bed for the next few days, watching TV and just looking out of the window until it got dark and then I'd fall back to sleep again.

Richard came over to see me on the Friday and Abby was in the background saying how bored she was.

'Why don't I take her out down the town for a few drinks, Bro?' Richard said to me.

'Yeah, to be fair, mate, there's fuck all I can do while I'm stuck here; just promise me you'll look after her and bring her back home in one piece,' I said.

'Yeah, of course I will,' Rich replied.

Abby jumped at the chance to get out of the house, she'd been looking after me and I thought it would be nice for her to have a night out. I trusted my brother implicitly; he was an extension of me. He'd protect her and make sure that he dropped her back home safe and sound.

They didn't come home that night. I remember waking up around three in the morning and Abby still wasn't back. I had started to worry about both of them. 'It should be okay,' I thought as I lay there waiting for the keys to rattle in the front door. I'd thought back to all of the drama that I'd suffered fighting in town and just hoped everything was okay, but all I could do was lie there feeling helpless.

It was now four in the morning so I tried calling Rich, but there was no answer so I tried calling Abby, but it went straight through to her answering machine. By now, I'm really worried and thinking the worst must have happened.

I lay there wide awake just staring aimlessly at the ceiling, feeling vulnerable and not really able to do anything. I eventually drifted off to sleep when I heard the front door go at around eight in the morning. It was Abby and Rich, they were laughing and joking as they made their way up the stairs and breezed into my bedroom without a care in the world.

'Hey, Bro, how you doing?' Richard asked me.

'Fucking hell, are you serious, mate? Where the fuck have you been? I've been so worried about both of you,' I replied in a firm voice; they both knew I was annoyed.

'It's all good, Bro; we went down the pub and Abby ended up staying at mine,' Rich replied.

I sat there a bit dumbfounded and Abby didn't have much to say for herself as she loitered about in the background.

'You fucking what? I've been lying here clueless wondering what's going on and not been able to reach either of you,' I said.

'Yeah, sorry, Bro; we stopped at mine to carry on drinking and we both fell asleep. No big deal, we're back now and all is cool,' he said.

There was some more small talk and then Richard left, it felt really awkward. The atmosphere didn't feel right to me at all.

'This was not fucking okay,' I thought.

I knew this, Richard should have brought Abby back home as I instructed. I lived two minutes round the corner from Rich. Christ, I live at 115 Redwing Rise and he lives at number 46 Redwing Rise.

I disguised how I was feeling by using my operation as an excuse and saying that I had a headache and just wanted to be left alone. I didn't speak to Abby much while I lay there mulling this over; she definitely knew I wasn't happy and went downstairs and that's where she hid all day.

I didn't know what to make of it, but something didn't feel right. Without having to spell it out, something seemed and felt really wrong here. I didn't like anything about it, but for now I had to get stronger and heal properly. After a few weeks, I was back to normal, but the relationship with Abby was never the same after this and I didn't have the time to join the dots or deep down I didn't want to. As far as I was concerned, I was moving on without her, but not without my brother. Rich had told me all was fine so I took him at face value, but I think Abby should have made the right decision and that was to come home; they were both to blame, but Abby's behaviour at the very least showed me that she didn't care about me, so fuck her and it wasn't long before we split up—she packed all of her things, which fitted into two black plastic bin bags and left.

The lads call Richard 'Sleaze on Toast', which we all

found hilarious, but this situation wasn't funny. I know that Richard has preyed on a few girls that I used to date in the past and being an identical twin, this made it easy for him to swoop in, but even for him this would be an all-time low. To sleep with someone I was actually dating and living with, was bad enough and even worse doing it to me while I'm lying in bed trying to repair and heal myself after the damage that he had done to my nose all those years back. It could be totally innocent and Abby had just got carried away and genuinely had gone for more drinks. I honestly didn't know what to make of it, so I tried to put in to the back of my mind.

When Abby left the house, she became really spiteful; I guess living back with her mum wasn't the life that she had become accustomed to and this made her really resentful. I'd say she hated me and I ended up having a blazing row with her down the phone.

'I can get another one of you any day of the week,' I told her.

'So what, I fucked your brother!' she screamed back at me down the phone and hung up.

I was obviously stunned by her outburst, but was also aware that she could be really venomous. She could say anything; it was a cheap shot so I calmly went to my back door to have a cigarette outside.

Abby had obviously thought twice about what she had just shrieked at me down the phone and instantly confided in her best mate, Beth. My close friend Adam was dating Beth at the time and he told me what Abby had told her. Abby said, 'You have no idea what Christian is capable of; I can't believe what I just shouted at him down the phone,' she said.

Beth told Adam what had gone on so Adam phoned

Richard and said, 'I think you better get round to Christian's straight away.'

It must have only been five minutes since Abby's little outburst that Richard was knocking on my front door. Opening the front door, I stood there; Richard looked wary and really concerned.

'Adam just called me bro and told me what's gone on. That girl is a fucking liar, I promise you nothing happened; I'd never do that to you,' he frantically protested.

'Rich the whole thing is fucking questionable,' I said as Richard went on the defensive.

'Come on then, what are you accusing me of? You better not be thinking I've done anything. Why don't you tell me exactly what it is you're implying?' he replied.

'Hang on a fucking minute, I'm the innocent one in all of this and you clearly know what Abby has said to me so you do the fucking maths. I don't want to get into right now. Do yourself a favour and just go; go on, off you fuck,' I replied aggressively.

Richard going on the defensive was a clever strategy as it made me feel uncomfortable being asked to spell it out for him, this actually heightened my suspicions and weakened his innocence as I felt he was trying to do anything in his power to deflect the attention away from himself, then again he could be innocent; it was a tough situation for me and I had to weigh up what was important.

Here's the thing, I didn't care enough about Abby to give a shit what she did; she was in my past and not in my future so I actually couldn't care less. My brother's behaviour, as I said, was questionable to say the least and to be frank I didn't want to think anything untoward had gone on between Abby and my brother that night, but I certainly had my suspicions something wasn't quite right and told myself, 'To go with my gut.' Well, my gut was screaming at me, 'Open your eyes, Christian.' The problem for me was Richard meant so much to me that I chose to ignore any doubts that I had and move on; I'm far from stupid, but if I was wrong and started throwing accusations at Richard, it could destroy our relationship forever. I had to have faith that Richard loved me as much as I loved him and that we would never ever hurt each other, or cross a line that would make our relationship impossible to repair. Richard told me nothing happened, so I took his word for it. I put the whole sorry affair behind me and thought, 'Fuck it, if anything has gone on then shame on them.'

Moving on, my new nose was much better—not perfect, but it looked better than it did and I'd have to wait at least another year for it to heal properly. I was back at Fusion and ready to get things going again so the first person I called was Angie and she was so pleased to hear from me. Angie had a way of taking my mind off things. During the phone call, she invited me and Rich to a Christmas party; it was a Traders' Ball which was being held at a really posh hotel in London. I knew this would be a fantastic opportunity for us and a chance to meet Angie face to face.

The Traders' Ball was on a Friday night so Richard and I decided to leave a day early to spend some time together and relax, this Traders' Ball was a big deal for Richard and I, and we needed to be at our best. This could open up even more doors for us. We gave Rob simple instructions to look after Fusion while we were away, packed our tuxedos and left early Thursday morning.

What Rob did not realise at the time is that we also spoke

to a woman called Carol who worked in one of the other offices; we would never leave 'Fusion' alone with anyone without having a backup so we asked Carol to keep an eye on Rob—not to literally spy on him, but to keep an eye on him coming and going. Carol was really fond of Richard and I, and she had watched us evolve from the first day that we got our first office at The Old Police Station.

Rich telephoned the office just after nine o' clock on Thursday morning. That's when the office officially opened and Rob answered.

'Fusion, good morning,' Rob said.

'Hey, Rob, just checking you got in okay. Everything all right mate?' Rich asked him.

'Morning, Rich; yep everything's fine. I've got some quotes to sort out and a bit of boxing up to do, but don't worry, go and have a great time,' Rob confidently replied.

'Okay, Rob, nice one. Give me or Christian a shout if you need anything at all mate,' Rich said.

Richard and I were very protective of Fusion, like new parents leaving their baby for the first time with the babysitter. We were sitting at the hotel bar in the afternoon when Richard said, 'I'm just gonna give Rob a shout and see if he's okay.' Richard picked up his mobile phone and dialled the office.

'That's odd, it just went straight through to the answering machine,' he said worryingly.

'Really? Try it again,' I told him.

'Yeah, it's just going through to the answering machine,' Richard repeated.

'Okay, don't panic, have you tried Rob's mobile? If that doesn't work, give Carol a call,' I instructed Rich.

I'm sitting there sipping my drink and I can see Richard

was becoming agitated. Rob's mobile wasn't connecting and the office line was still going straight through to the answering machine.

'Right, I'm calling Carol,' Rich said as he selected her name from his contacts and put the phone to his ear.

'Carol, hiya, it's Rich. Listen, have you seen Rob about in the office?'

'Hey, Rich, yeah he just walked past the window. He went out around half nine this morning and he's just come back,' Carol said.

'Okay, Carol, thanks for that. I'll catch you later,' Richard replied.

Richard was getting madder by the second; he waited a couple of minutes and then called the office number again while putting his phone on speaker. I sat there having my drink and listened, but I already had a sneaking suspicion what was going on.

'Good afternoon, Fusion Electronics,' Rob answered.

'Rob, it's Rich; hello, mate, how are things going?' he asked.

'Hey, Rich, it's been quiet today. I've dealt with a few calls, but don't worry yourself, I've got it covered. Have a drink on me.,' Rob replied, sounding quite jovial.

'Oh, is that fucking right? So do you want to tell me how the fuck you've dealt with a few calls when you've not been there,' Richard said angrily.

Rob started to stutter and then tried to back track, 'I had to run, run, run down the town; I'm so sorry, I had to pay some of my bills and get to the bank. I literally ran down the town and came straight back,' he replied.

'Rob, I know that you've been out of the office for at least

152

five hours. We trusted you and left you to look after our business and you think it's okay to just fuck off down the town for a few hours? I'll speak with you when we get back and, in the meantime, go and get yourself a cup of tea and pull it together. I don't want to hear that you've left the office again,' Rich said.

'I won't leave my chair, even if I need the toilet. I won't let you down, I promise,' Rob replied.

The thing is, we had trusted him to look after our business and he had let us down. It's not okay to say 'I won't let you down,' after you got caught for letting us down.

We were paying him a great salary and he had a great job working for us and was basically his own boss. As long as he performed and was making money, we let him do his own thing, but he'd fucked it up the moment we were out of sight. I knew exactly what this clown had been doing; he'd taken that first call in the morning and thought he could get back before being noticed while he fucked off down the bookies to gamble—I would have bet my life on it.

'Can you fucking believe that he did that?' Rich asked me.

'It's a joke mate and he's a joke; he has it pretty good with us too and now he's just fucked it up. Fusion will be okay till we get back; honestly, Bro, don't let it stress you. We're here to have a good time and we've got a job to do.'

Chapter 17
Jet Setter, Go Getter, Nothing Better

Fusions last financial year had a turn over well in excess of 3 million pounds. Richard and I had only just turned 27 and it was the night of the Traders' Ball. We were getting ready and having a few drinks in our room. I knew that Angie was in the area as we'd spoken earlier on the phone. There was going to be a lot of people there tonight and we were sitting on a table set up for eight people, which Angie had paid for. Richard and I were putting on our tuxedos and faced one another to ask each other if we looked okay before we walked out the door; it was like staring at myself in the mirror, we both looked exactly the same, very dapper and very sharp in our jet black tuxes and black bow ties with a Rolex watch on our wrists.

'Rich, you look good, mate. I'm not a fan of wearing bow ties, though,' I said.

'Yeah, so do you, bro, I agree. First chance I get, I'm taking mine off,' he replied.

We walked from our room and headed towards the venue, this felt good and we looked good; I was excited. One of the perks of being a twin is that you're instantly noticeable. I was a little anxious, but I always am—particularly when I first approach a large group of people—but Richard and I bounce off one another and, once I'm warmed up, I can command a room, especially after a few drinks then I like to think I can out dance anyone in the room. I like dancing, not sure if I'm actually any good, but I don't care, I'll give it a go.

I'd called Angie and said we were on our way in and she said she'd be having a drink by the ice sculpture and told me to come and find her.

'Ice sculpture, nice,' I thought.

Making our way into the hotel and through these large double doors, there were waiters everywhere walking around with platters of fancy canapés and glasses of champagne.

As we walked into the venue, there was a sea of people: men in tuxedos and woman in dresses, some of them looked so elegant, and then you'd get the odd one out that must have missed the memo, wearing a short mini skirt and knee-high boots. There were Christmas lights and decorations wrapped around everything in sight, including the statues that were dotted about in the hotel reception.

'Get your game face on, Rich,' I told him.

'You too,' he replied.

We grabbed a couple of glasses of champagne and I'd spotted the ice sculpture; you couldn't miss it. It was big and in the shape of the company's logo that was hosting the Traders' Ball, a company called Capstar.

As I looked over, I could see a blonde woman, about 5ft 6 wearing a shimmering long black dress, it was beautiful; she was really good looking and was talking with some guys right next to the ice sculpture. As I've said before, you just can't miss her voice, it's so recognisable, and I knew it was her.

'Rich, that's Ang over there. Shall we finish these drinks and head over?' I said.

'Yep, ready when you are,' he replied.

We both downed our drinks and started to walk over to

her. Richard was just behind me and we had only got a couple of metres until she spotted us.

'It's my twins,' she shrieked; she was so excited to see both of us.

'Oh, my God! Which ones which? You two are going to get me in trouble tonight,' she laughed.

'Actually, I think it might be you getting us into trouble.' I replied as I gave her a hug and kissed her on the cheek.

'Okay, so you're definitely Christian. I'll have to put my lipstick on you so I can tell the difference,' she said while laughing.

'Hello, Angie, come on then gimme a hug too,' Rich said.

Angie was right up our street, so wild and she was really funny. She introduced us to a couple of people in the room and to the people who were also sitting at our table.

'These are my boys,' she would say in a joking way, but with 'a hands off they're mine' kind of way because there were other suppliers there too; she was marking her territory.

It wasn't long before the announcer came out and announced to all the guests that we could enter the main dining room. The main dining room was beautiful; there were huge chandeliers hanging from the ceiling and another ice sculpture in the room which was a vodka luge; you could pour vodka into the top of it and catch it at the bottom by a glass or even using your mouth. There was also a DJ and a dance floor in the centre of the room.

This was like no party that Richard and I had ever been to before; bottles of Crystal champagne at the table and great food. The whole night was amazing, hassle free and exactly what we'd been working towards. It certainly beat rolling around the streets of Royston on a Friday night and this lifestyle was only the tip of the iceberg for us.

We got drunk, laughed and danced the night away and had the hangovers in the morning to prove it; I knew that we had both presented ourselves really well.

After the party, we were back in the office on Monday to deal with Rob. We got into the office early before Rob started and when he walked through the door; he looked so sheepish.

'Hey, Rob, grab yourself a coffee, mate; we've got to sit down and have a chat,' I said.

We'd come back from having an amazing time and now had to deal with this shit.

'So tell me, Rob, what happened last week?' Rich asked him.

I interjected, 'No, Rob, what's going on with you in general? Your mind is elsewhere half the time so let's get to the bottom of things.'

I glanced over to our profit board that hung on the wall in our office and Rob hadn't made a single penny the entire month, not one single order. He kept promising us that he had some big orders in the pipeline, but nothing had materialised.

'I couldn't close a barn door this month; I have been trying,' Rob replied.

I couldn't help but feel sad for him, but up to this point, Rob had basically made what we had been paying him so we were even. Maybe we were down a little bit and this isn't good enough when you're running a company.

'To be fair, Rob, I know you're holding out on me,' I said firmly.

I was pushing him to be open and honest; it's not my business to know what he does in his personal life, but when it affects our company, I do have a right to know; suddenly,

Rob's eyes started to well up and then he just blurted it out.

'I'm about to lose my home and the wife doesn't know,' he said trying to hold back the tears.

I knew it, I knew deep down there was something bigger going on and it was down to his gambling.

We employed Rob based on the person that he used to be and that is the person that Richard used to know: a well-established business man in the electronics industry. He may have been back in the day but, right now, he was a gambling addict and once he got talking, we established he was £100,000.00 pounds in debt which his wife had no idea about and he hadn't been paying the mortgage for months or any of his bills; he had been hiding this double life from his wife for quite some time.

I really felt for his wife as well, we had met her once or twice and she was such a sweet girl. Rob was spending every penny he could get his hands on to try and get that big win, the win that could put everything right. I only know one person in my life that has ever done this. Rob was chasing the impossible; the big win is rarely achieved and takes someone really special to pull it off.

It now made sense after I'd seen him blowing all of his wages at lunch time; he would spend massive amounts of money in the bookies before he'd even got paid and it was certainly a lot more than we were paying him. We needed to protect the business and we couldn't allow a gambling addict to be part of our team; fucking hell, could you imagine if he got hold our company bank account?

It was true that when we left the office to go to the Traders' Ball, he had sneaked off down the bookies. We couldn't trust him and had no choice but to let him go. I don't know what happened to Rob after he left that day, I can't imagine going home and having to confess all of that to your wife.

It was just me and Rich again, just the way I liked it. Rob leaving had no impact whatsoever on us and, the following day, it was like he'd never been there in the first place.

The formula for Fusion was simple: Richard ran our core business as he always had done which would cover our salaries and all running costs, plus he would do all of the paperwork. I would focus on putting my deals together and both of us were working in tandem.

I was working all hours and my phone never stopped. Angie and I got on so well and, in this business, you need to work with people you can trust. The money involved was massive and this paved the way for crooks to try and operate in our industry. Just one deal with the wrong supplier, whose sole intention was to sell counterfeit goods, or a dummy company who would clone other companies in order to rip you off was huge and one wrong deal could destroy your business overnight.

Richard and I started to travel a lot more; I needed to build up our customer base as Angie could supply us more stock than we had customer requirements.

We went to so many trade shows building up our customers and contacts and were well known in the industry; you would only have to say, 'Do you know the twins?' and people knew exactly who we were. It felt like I was travelling or on a plane more than I was at home or in the office. Rich and I loved these adventures and streamlined the business so we could operate on the go.

We travelled to most of the countries in Europe all of the time; limousines picked us up from the airport, we stayed at the best hotels and booked the best suites they had available: The Ritz in Madrid, The Burj Al Arab in Dubai.

The Burj Al Arab made headlines as the world's first seven-star hotel and is the world's most luxurious hotel; the shape of the hotel is designed to resemble the sail of a ship and is positioned in the sea. We drove in a Rolls Royce, on its own private road that leads up to the hotel, and were greeted by a flurry of people all eager to carry your bags or pass you a hot flannel to freshen up. I just cannot begin to explain how luxurious it is; our room was bigger than my house and we had our own personal butler who was on hand 24/7.

I travelled to Dubai when it wasn't as well-known as it is now; it felt like a secret paradise nicknamed 'The Sands.'

One of our other visits to Dubai was to see Robbie Williams bang out a show at the Nad Al Sheba Racecourse.

Richard and I, dare I say it, deserved this lifestyle. We hadn't forgotten where we'd come from—how could we? Those memories will always stay with us forever, but we had worked so hard to achieve what we had and our lives at this point really were amazing.

I was back in the UK at our local Porsche dealership just walking around looking at the cars when I noticed a property that was being built; it was just down a side road and, at this stage, it wasn't quite finished yet. It looked big, it was a really unique looking property and could be ideal if we could snap this up at the right price and buy it as an investment and operate our business from it.

'Rich, come and take a look at this. There's a property being built over here that looks wicked,' I said.

Rich wandered over and we squeezed between the fencing to go on-site and have a proper look at it; I knew immediately we would have it and I could tell Richard was impressed with it.

'What do you want to do? This could really work if we can get it,' Rich said.

'Give the accountant a call in the morning and I'll come here first thing to see if anyone is on-site that I can speak to,' I replied.

I came back the following morning and the builder was on-site—his name was Alex.

'Is this property being built for someone, mate, or is it going up for sale?' I asked him.

'We're actually thinking, in the next couple of weeks, about getting in touch with a couple of estate agents,' he replied.

'Okay, mate, how much are you looking for?' I asked him.

'We could probably let it go for around £320,000.00,' Alex said.

'Hmmm, okay. I'll tell you what, I'll give you £310,000.00. I have the cash so you can save the money on estate agents fees,' I could tell Alex was quite taken aback when I made the offer.

'Okay that could work. Sorry, mate, what's your name again?' Alex asked me.

'It's Christian.'

'Okay, Christian, let me put a call into the office and speak to the boss, but I don't see why not.'

I wanted to put some pressure on him to get this sorted as I knew this was a really great price; at that price, we could already sell it on and make a profit.

'If you want, Alex, I'll go and have a coffee over the road and pop back in twenty if that works?'

'Yer, okay, speak in a bit,' Alex replied.

I called Rich straight away and told him how the conversation went, 'I'll get this property, Rich, you watch.'

I only left it about fifteen minutes before I went back and the deal was done.

'Hey, Christian. Yeah, that's fine, we're happy with that, so let me get your contact details,' Alex said.

It was that simple, Richard had already spoken to the accountant and we opened a second company which was going to be used as a holding company—it was called Excess Holdings Limited. The company was created to buy and own the shares of other companies that we opened, which it then controls, including Fusion Electronics Limited. In essence, it was like an umbrella that protected everything underneath it.

We purchased and completed on this property, Excess House, 37 New Road, Harston on the 6th of October 2005. It was a detached farmhouse-style property with a huge kitchen and utility room, and three large bedrooms and two large receptions areas. The landing upstairs had a stylish balcony that looked over into the downstairs area. The grounds circled the property with a large wooden gate which opened allowing cars to drive in and out. This was our new office for Fusion and it was time to leave The Old Police Station.

We were bigger and better than ever. This financial year, we had turned over well in excess of 6 million pounds. Just across from our new office was a Porsche dealership and next to the Porsche dealership was an Aston Martin dealership; we would often walk over there after work and look at the cars.

'What do you reckon, Rich? Shall we buy a couple of Aston Martins?' I said half-jokingly, but half serious.

'Could you imagine that? Twins with matching cars—I'd

fucking love that,' Rich said.

So that's what we did and for our 28th birthday, we walked in to Aston Martin and ordered two V8 Vantages. This car wasn't even out yet and they were taking orders for them; we sat all day customising them exactly how we wanted and put down a deposit of £5,000.00 each. They came in at about £95,000.00 each and the only difference between mine and Richard's cars was the colour: his was gun metal grey with red callipers and mine was electric blue with yellow callipers. The colour I had was specially made to order and no one else in the country had it.

Richard and I must have flown over 27 times this year on business so needed a time out; it wasn't all work and no play. In the evenings, whichever country we were in, we wined and dined at the best restaurants and went to the best clubs, but Rich and I decided to get away for Christmas just the two of us. We wanted to make it extra special as some of our Christmases hadn't been the best so we closed down the office on or around the 20th of December and spent a few days in Los Angeles, then flew on to Las Vegas and we finally arrived in New York to see in the New Year.

Mum and Dad crossed my mind occasionally. I wondered how they were and if they thought about us. They had missed out on so much and had no idea of the things we were doing or achieving.

Chapter 18
Brace Yourself for Impact

It was business as usual and Richard and I were considering buying a holiday home over in Dubai—another country was Spain. I absolutely loved Marbella and it was becoming a second home I travelled there so much; I dreamed of owning a place there one day.

We were looking at flights when Angie told me she was going over to the sands around the same time, so we arranged to meet up. We always had a great time; she liked having a twin on either side of her as we walked into bars and clubs. We looked out for her and were really protective; she knew she was in good hands. Angie was quite taken with me and I had a soft spot for her.

We were in this club in Dubai and I remember Richard pulling me aside one night; we'd both had a few drinks and were loving life.

'Bro, seriously, I've got to let you know how impressed I am; you're absolutely killing it. I'm really proud of you, we wouldn't be where we are now without you,' he said.

I was quite taken aback and it felt really nice to finally be acknowledged.

'Thanks, Rich, that means so much to me, but we do it together,' I replied as we hugged it out and did our little handshake before going back to partying.

Richard didn't praise me that often, so when he did, it was something I really noticed. It made me feel tearful, but in a good way. I felt accepted and worthy. It's been so many years and I still remember him saying that to me like it was yesterday.

We were only a few months into the New Year and Fusion was already reaching new heights; I was giving it everything I had. The bigger the deal, the more complex it became and I was juggling everything, but I was so used to it that they were just figures to me. If I could sell one box then I could sell twenty, you just had to be really focused, which I was.

Fusions' main business was now as an exporter and, as I mentioned, we delivered products all over the world. An exporter is reliant on receiving its VAT repayments from HMRC each month to be able to continue to trade; we pay our suppliers' VAT and are entitled to reclaim the VAT because our goods were exported overseas at a zero rate. Our VAT repayments were growing in size every month and we had never encountered any kind of problems before. For the last two months, I was now making over £100,000.00 a month in profit and within five months our turnover was well in excess of 18 million pounds. There were a number of other companies who traded like us and, in contrast, they made our figures look small but they were very large companies with a large number of employees and we were just a two-man team. From the very beginning, Fusion had gone from making thousands to tens of thousands and was now making hundreds of thousands of pounds each month. Richard and I were making in excess of 50K a month each, which we chose to put back into the business.

We were 28 years old and within a period of roughly six

years, between us, we owned three brand new houses—all kitted out brand new—and we had two brand new Aston Martins on order which were due for delivery at the end of May 2006. We had in excess of 1.3 million pounds in cash and assets in total and were unstoppable or at least that's what I thought. Fusion was at its peak in terms of performance and neither of us could ever have foreseen that it was all about to come crashing down around us.

We had a surprise visit in May 2006 from our contact at HMRC. We had always complied with any requests from HMRC but this time it felt a little different, the doorbell rang and it was our local officer who was accompanied by her senior officer. We had dealt with her for a number of years and she was always happy with the way in which we were trading and how we conducted our business. Her actual words were 'You're perfect and there is nothing further that you need to be doing.' We always received our VAT repayments not just on time but early and there were never any issues.

This surprise visit had raised my suspicions; it didn't matter to Richard and I when our contact decided to turn up, but it was the tone in her voice that I'd noticed and she was accompanied by another officer who ranked slightly higher than her and this was unusual.

There was some general chit-chat and then, out of the blue, she asked how much money we had left in the bank. 'This was a strange question,' I thought, but before I could decide whether or not to answer that, Richard just blurted out, 'At present, we have around £20,000.00 left.'

I was shocked when Richard said this as there are limits to what we are required to disclose and it was a really strange and personal question. To this day, I'm still miffed about

Richard divulging this information so freely. We had practically used everything that we had in the bank funding our deals for April and May 2006 and, as it stood, HMRC now had all of our funds which we were due back in repayments. I knew something was really wrong when she asked that question; there was some more small talk and then both the officers got up and left. It felt like they got what they came for and when the door closed behind them, I immediately said to Richard.

'That was really unusual, Rich, and I didn't like the sound of that one bit—something's up.'

'Yeah, that was weird,' he replied.

It crossed my mind based on what Richard had just told HMRC that they now knew that they had most of our money; actually, they had nearly all of it. I gave Angie a call who assured me all of her records and taxes were up-to-date and accounted for correctly, but she was hearing the same stories from her other customers. They were also receiving surprise visits from HMRC.

It transpires that HMRC were losing a catastrophic amount of money from other companies at the beginning of a supply chain in our industry. There were companies who were disappearing with the VAT and it was going unpaid somewhere else down the supply line. Angie was our supplier and I knew there were no problems there and that everything was accounted for correctly so we should be okay. These companies, who were setting up and disappearing, could be anyone and usually started at the very beginning of a supply chain; there could be any number of companies between us and the very beginning of a supply chain. This is what happened: HMRC in these two months for April and May 2006 had thrown a wide net over every exporter in the industry. I heard it was as many as 2,500 businesses. They wrongfully kept all of the exporters reclaims which was saving the treasury in excess of 2.5 billion pounds, but the figure was probably much higher; the bottom line is that it was easier for HMRC to deny our VAT repayments then it was to actually pursue the criminals that had disappeared with it at the beginning of the supply chain.

Richard and I were well and truly fucked and it stopped us dead in our tracks. The amount of money HMRC held from us was around £286,712.00 for April 2006 and £327,726.23 for May 2006 this was nearly all the money that we had in our company. This was our money and the total amount that was withheld from us by HMRC was in excess of £614,438.23 in total.

Angie was unaffected as our supplier and did not suffer at all financially; the only companies affected were the exporters and that included Fusion. The treatment we suffered at the hands of HMRC was deplorable. We were told by our contact at HMRC that enquiries were ongoing and until they had finished their investigations, they would not release our funds. We were given a central phone number to call and palmed off onto a call centre where nobody knew what was going on.

The reality was that every time we telephoned the call centre, someone with absolutely no experience in these matters simply read out whatever the last entry was in front of them from a computer screen.

It was sickening and the only reply you received was, 'The file has not been updated and is still being looked into.'

This is something that we'd hoped would rectify itself quite quickly and thought HMRC would soon release our funds. No law had been passed, allowing HMRC to do this and as an exporter, we were entitled to our VAT repayments. We had traded in accordance with any guidelines that were set out by HMRC and there was no evidence from HMRC of any wrong-doing.

This was a nightmare and I basically lost my job overnight; actually, our entire business had been crippled overnight. We still had Richard's core business that ticked us over, but what had happened totally took the wind out of our sails.

'Rich, when are those cars due?' I asked him.

'They are due any day now, mate,' he replied.

'Fucking hell, things are going from bad to worse. We've got ten grand between us in deposits on two cars and we haven't got the money to pay for them,' I said.

Richard and I were doing our best to support one another, but both had our own battles going on trying to deal with this. There was a feeling of disbelief that this couldn't be happening—it was like a bad dream.

Over the next couple of days Richard and I sat talking day and night about how to resolve this or what could we do about it. The truth was, we were at the mercy of HMRC who had put the shutters up and had taken our money and couldn't care less.

'This is bad, this is really bad. Thank fuck we bought the property in Harston outright,' I thought.

There was a large chunk of money in the house at Harston. It was a joke because HMRC could not have just taken our money if it was in our bank account, but due to the fact we had paid VAT to our supplier and HMRC owed us on the reclaim, they just kept it.

In its simplest form, it would be like someone owing you

money and because you are unable to recover your money from them, you simply take it from someone else in order offset the loss that you have incurred.

There was nothing we could do at this point; Richard and I had been staying late at the office most days.

'Bro, I've put the kettle on. Let's have a cuppa and go for a walk and try and think of a way forward,' I said.

'Yeah, okay, Bro,' he replied, sounding beat and exasperated.

We would often wander across the road to the Porsche and Aston Martin dealerships at night just to chat and look at the cars. We were standing outside the Aston Martin dealership; it was dark so it was hard to see through the window, but at certain angles where the street lights bounced off the glass, you could see some of the cars in the shadows. I had to look twice, crouching up and down, trying to get the right light to see better and there it was: an electric blue with yellow callipers Aston Martin V8 Vantage. My car was sitting on display with a notice saying ready for collection.

'Rich, is that my fucking car? That is! That's my fucking car!' I said; I was in shock and couldn't believe that it was right in front of my eyes.

In the background, I could see another one that looked like Richard's car.

'I think it is, yeah, Bro, that's gotta be your one; I can see the yellow callipers,' Rich replied.

Man was I fucked off, that was one of the most horrendous moments for both of us; we had worked so hard and to have a car like that staring back at you, which is yours, but you can't have it was truly devastating. Everything was going wrong all at once.

The conversation with Aston Martin the following day was uncomfortable and really embarrassing as we had to cancel the cars. The deposits were non-refundable, but because they knew us and we were local lads, the boss who we were friendly with at Aston Martin returned our deposits; however, only on the condition that we could have the deposits back once both of our cars had been sold.

We had been financially strangled by HMRC and to make matters worse, we eventually had to sell the property at Harston. This was to release enough funds for us to carry on because Fusion had started to grind to a halt; our hearts weren't in it anymore after such a big setback. We had lost the fire and the energy that we once had to carry on and it literally happened overnight.

Richard and I needed to retreat and start considering our options and perhaps consider legal advice. We were turning up for work and just waiting for the postman, in the hope he was bringing us some good news—a letter telling us that this nightmare was finally over. This went on initially for a few weeks and before we knew it months had gone past. The only information we ever received was that due to ongoing investigations, HMRC would be holding onto our money until the investigation was over. We were very much kept in the dark and HMRC strung us along for a couple of years until eventually, and all at the same time, a number of exporters—if not nearly all of them, including us—received a letter. This letter stated that HMRC were going to deny our VAT repayments. They were keeping our money.

A brown envelope landed on our doorstep on or around the 8th of February 2008.

The letter was dated the 7th of February 2008 and the

commissioners said that they, 'Are satisfied that the transactions set out in the attached appendix form part of an overall scheme to defraud the revenue, there are features of those transactions, and conduct on the part of Fusion Electronics Limited which demonstrate that they knew or should have known that this was the case.' We particularly note that the commissioners did not allege that Fusion was a party to such fraud.

They were careful not to actually accuse us of fraud, but the implication was that we should have known better. This is bullshit and laughable considering our suppliers were all still trading and had accounted for their taxes correctly; the only company who forfeited their money was us—the exporter, Fusion Electronics Limited.

'How the fuck am I supposed to know what's happening twenty people on down a supply chain?' I thought.

The accusation is ridiculous and HMRC were taking the easy route; why go hunting for the people that have not paid the VAT when they can simply just take it from me?

Was it even true that the money had not been accounted for and, even if that were true, what would Richard and I know about it? We had been trading a reputable business and accounting for all of our taxes correctly for years.

HMRC had taken around £615,000.00 and we had no other choice but to appeal the decision and commence with legal proceedings against HMRC to try and recover our money. This was the start of a court case against an unbeatable machine, HMRC. It would be like hitting a walnut with a sledgehammer and we were the walnut. It was a civil matter and the bench mark isn't set as high as that of a criminal case so this already gave HMRC the upper-hand; they didn't have to prove that we had acted in any way which could be considered fraudulent, just demonstrate that we should have known better. The whole situation was so contrived and corrupt, but Richard and I would—as we always have done— give it everything we've got.

We sold the property at Harston on the 28th of February 2008 for £410,000.00 and made £100,000.00 in profit. This enabled us to regroup and work out our next move.

Half of our wealth was snatched away overnight and the solicitor's costs to fund a case like this were mind boggling. The court case was gaining momentum slowly, but there was no quick fix and this would take years before we got in front of a judge. We were in this for the long haul and the work and preparation involved was immense. It felt like our lives were in suspended animation and it was difficult to move forwards. We tried our best to carry on but it was always in the back of our minds.

This was not the time to think, 'Oh well, stiff upper lip; onwards and upwards. This was damage-limitation time, retreat—we are fucked.'

Chapter 19
The Walnut vs The Sledgehammer

The situation was soul destroying and since 2006, the next few years had become a bit of a blur. Angie tried her best to help and support us and would do anything for me if I needed it but our relationship started to fizzle out as Richard and I became consumed with court papers and countless hours preparing bundles in readiness for our pending court case. This court case was all consuming; a job that you don't get paid for and the only reward were the sleepless nights.

We should only be liable for losses with our direct supplier and that's providing if something untoward has gone on and it hadn't, but there was a notice issued by HMRC called Notice 726 referred to as 'Joint and Several Liability'. The Notice 726 was introduced by HMRC so if any revenue was lost or fraud was established within a supply chain then all of the companies within that supply chain would be liable for the losses incurred; this meant any losses would be divided equally between the companies in a supply chain. Even though I knew we had done nothing wrong, this wasn't the point. We were being financially strangled and should have been able to rely on Notice 726 and been able to recoup some of our money back, but this was not the case and we took the full hit. We were having to fund the appeal against HMRC ourselves with what money we had left. I felt so much resentment. Richard and I both did towards all the companies in our industry that were happily still trading and were unaffected by this. Angie, who was our direct supplier, was still trading and never had any negative impact from HMRC. It was hard to carry on at times and there were days I felt really low and completely fucked over; getting out of bed was becoming harder and harder all of the time.

Richard and I carried on the best we could, but it was difficult and we ended up spending a lot of time together and less time with anyone else. That was until the start of 2009 when Richard and I were at a club together in Milton Keynes and he met a girl at the bar called Jennifer Potter. They instantly hit it off and Richard and Jen started dating; it wasn't that long until Jennifer moved into Richard's house, but first, she had to break up with her current boyfriend that she was living with. Jen reminded me of Cameron Diaz—she seemed really sweet. Richard and Jen were spending a lot of time together and I could tell Rich was really smitten with her; he was spending more time with Jen and less time with me. I sometimes had the feeling that Jen struggled with how close Richard and I were. I expected it—just another girl jealous of the bond that Richard and I have. Richard was more submissive when it came to girls and his loyalty sometimes wavered. As for me, I would never ever put a girl before my brother and I put him above all else—sometimes even myself.

I started spending more time out and about going to clubs and bars and the only good thing that happened to me during this court case that was hanging over us was meeting my girlfriend, Elizabeth Houlihan.

It was Halloween 2009 and I was on a coach going to a club in Newmarket. There were only two girls on this bus and

I'd noticed Elizabeth straight away, not that the other girl wasn't attractive, but it was Elizabeth who had got my attention. It turned out that the other girl was her cousin. I'd never seen her before around town; she was tall with long brown hair and really tanned—she was really pretty.

When everyone bundled off the coach, we went into the club and I deliberately got in front of her in the queue to the cloakroom. The girl behind the counter went to take my jacket and I turned to Elizabeth and said, 'Would you like to put your jacket with mine?' 'Sure, why not?' she replied as she smiled at me.

As the girl working in the cloakroom put both of our jackets on the same coat hanger, I was handed a pink ticket which I would need to collect our jackets later on.

'Now you've got to come and find me at the end of the night if you want your coat back, but don't worry I won't nick it,' I turned and said to her cheekily.

'Oh, and what's your name?' I asked her.

"Elizabeth and yours?" she replied wearing a big smile.

'Christian, it's nice to meet you and I'll see you at the bar.' As I walked away, I kind of strutted away with this cool limp thinking, 'That went pretty well; don't trip over, though, she might be watching.'

It wasn't long before we bumped heads in the club and started chatting and I'd noticed a tattoo on her wrist.

'What does that say?' I asked her.

Shyly, she tried to hide it from me at first. 'It's my daughter's name, her name is Shannon.'

Her reaction pulled at my heart strings a little. I must be honest. I'd always said I would never date a girl who had a child with someone else, not for any reason other than that was

176

my choice and it just wasn't for me—I'm not very familiar with children so struggle to understand them, but her reaction was really sweet and she had a shy vulnerability about her and she just wanted to have a good time with someone and not be put on the shelf because she was a single mum. In that moment, she changed my outlook, 'Maybe there is something here,' I thought and I was wrong to put someone on the shelf without getting to know them first; everyone has a history and I wanted to know hers.

We had a great night, laughing and dancing together and it was the first time in a long time that I forgot about my worries. That night, I didn't have a care in the world.

At the end of the night, we collected our jackets and we sat with each other on the coach as we made our way back to Royston. The coach pulled up outside her house and I kissed her goodbye and watched her walk down her drive and through her front door.

The coach pulled away and I was probably a bit keen and I text her straight away asking if she would like to go on a date sometime.

'Are you serious? You're ginger,' she jokingly text me back.

'Don't speak to your future guy like that, and the colour is actually Mediterranean brunette if you must know,' I replied.

We were flirty and I knew that there could be something really special between us and it wasn't long before we started dating.

We hadn't been dating that long when I had my fourth rhinoplasty operation; I still needed to improve the look of my nose. Lizzy was great and she drove me to the hospital and was there in my room when I opened my eyes; I really liked her and we were spending more and more time together.

I was running out of money fast, funding the court case. I'd paid off my mortgage which sounds great in theory, but not when all the money you have is tied up in a property; I sold my home at 115 Redwing Rise on the 5th of January 2010 to release some funds and I rented a flat for the short term.

We were informed that there was a backlog in the First Tier Tribunal so we had no idea when our court case would finally be heard. Richard and I knew that we had a strong case because of our electronics background and experience in the industry, we just knew our stuff. Word had spread that we were one of the companies to look out for and if any case could win and set a precedence for the other companies in a similar situation, then we were the ones to watch.

We had heard rumours of a judge who was particularly anti-trader, he was called Judge David Demack; he was a tribunal judge based in Manchester. Apparently, he was the last judge that any exporter would want dealing with their case. Sitting in court, you can also have two members; they play the same role as the judge and listen to each case and can outvote a judge's decision, by majority, if they think that the judge's decision is wrong—it's a fairer and pragmatic approach.

If you are appointed one member this, in my view, is slightly biased because the judge will listen to this member's opinion, but the judge's decision is final and he can overrule one member's decision.

To give us the best shot at this, we requested two members and expected a London judge as our case was going to be heard in London and then, out of the blue, I received a phone call from our solicitor and suddenly we were given dates for our hearing; this was really unexpected and guess what: it was a tribunal judge that had been drafted in from Manchester, called Judge David Demack. Apparently, as luck would have it, he had a gap in his diary and was available to deal with our case in London, and to top it off, we were only appointed one member. Richard and I were really opposed to this, but had no option but to continue.

From the moment our money was withheld and our repayments denied, we were finally given our court dates and it had taken us almost four years to get in front of a judge. We were sitting in public in London on the 20th of September 2010, 27th to 30th of September 2010, 4th to 6th of October 2010 and the 11th to 14th of October 2010.

We were as ready as we could be for the court case and whatever the outcome, the ending was in sight. It was our first day in court and we were already off to a really bad start. We were ambushed by HMRC with another bundle of A4 folders all containing further evidence; they wheeled them into the courtroom and there were around ten in total stuffed to the brim with new documents that we'd never seen before and we were unable to respond to this in such a short space of time— it was impossible. I mean, we were standing in court and ready to proceed. There was no way we could go through this, and why should we have to? There are strict guidelines given by the courts and a strict timetable to adhere to leading up to the actual court case; you're supposed to have your affairs in order to give each side a fair trial. We put it to the judge that this new evidence should be thrown out as the evidence was presented not just out of time but on the first day of our trial hearing and we were heavily prejudiced by this.

Richard and I were fuming as the judge asked us to consider the new evidence and basically adjourned the court for about 45 minutes so we could take a look at these files. This was fucking outrageous so we trundled off to the nearest coffee shop; it was pathetic, as Richard and I, our barrister and solicitor were all walking down the street carrying all these fucking files. Richard and I didn't even bother looking at any of it as we sat in the coffee shop.

I said to our solicitor and barrister about appealing against this new evidence as we were being blindsided by HMRC. This was a very big problem and all we could do is hope that the judge would throw it out. If the judge allowed this mountain of new evidence, we couldn't appeal his decision in time because our case would have been over long before it ever got into an appeal court.

Our lawyer said to us, 'We had a strong case and it was now or never,' I asked our lawyer to give us a minute to talk.

'Rich, what do you want to do? Everything about this is wrong: we are being set up,' I said to him.

'Yeah, I know Bro. This is our case and we shouldn't allow anyone to tell us what to do,' he replied.

I turned to our legal team and said, 'This is a fucking joke; we don't accept any further evidence. Tell the judge we will be heavily prejudiced if this new evidence is allowed in and we are not able to properly look through any of it and cannot possibly respond to any of it. HMRC have deliberately set up a surprise attack,' I said angrily.

Heading back, we took our positions in the courtroom; HMRC on the left side of the room and us on the right as we all waited for the judge and the member to enter through their special door at the back of the courtroom. The door handle clicked as they entered; we all stood up to bow and show respect to the judge and the member, and sat back down once they were seated.

Our barrister pleaded our position robustly. I sat there watching the judge and his body language; he was very hard to read and his facial expressions barely changed—his voice was very monotone.

HMRC were given the opportunity to plead their position and claimed that they could continue if the evidence was disallowed, but it would be with a very heavy heart. These files containing late evidence could be the difference of us winning or losing the entire case.

Once both sides had finished and sat back down, the judge gave a quick look over at us and then a quick look over at HMRC and said.

'In the interests of justice, I'll allow it,' the judge said, firmly looking straight down the middle of the room.

You could feel HMRC breathe a sigh of relief, while our side recoiled in horror at the decision.

Since this whole nightmare had started, we were always on the back foot and it always felt like it was out of our control. The impending doom, like a booby trap in an Indiana Jones movie, the feeling of being trapped in a room and the walls slowly closing in from both sides, each crank of the cog wheel slowly pushing the walls closer and closer till they would eventually crush us.

I still regret it to this day not just getting up there and then with Rich and both of us leaving the courtroom. I prefer the thought of putting the case into disarray and rolling the dice to see what would have happened if we'd done that.

HMRC carried out as I would expect a full investigation into all of our transactions; they actually cherry picked one of the deals and followed it through from start to finish. This deal was perfect and backfired on HMRC because there was no tax loss. The goods had been used by our customer—that is the customer we had sold the goods to—physically used them to build their products with. There was no question at all that this transaction was legitimate and this particular evidence should have raised doubts in HMRC's case.

Things went downhill gradually, Richard and I were fighting with everything we had and trying our hardest; we weren't there to lose, but sometimes even your best isn't good enough and you just know when you're beat, but that wouldn't stop us trying. We spent a lot of time being blasted by HMRC before Richard and I were asked to take the stand.

Our time on the stand and under oath was an onslaught; allegation after allegation, with no concrete evidence of any wrong-doing. The insinuation is that we should have known better. Our demise was from our own success. Yes, on the face of it, it was possible there had been wrong-doing by other companies in our supply chain, but this would have been impossible for us to know at the time of trading. The case was riddled with inaccuracies, but it all looks very different when you're standing in a courtroom with all of the information and diagrams in front of you. They made the story fit.

Chapter 20
He Who Casts the First Stone

Once you get in the stand, you believe that you will be allowed to speak and that you can start to put things right, but this isn't the case. The barrister appointed by HMRC was really fierce and he commanded the room. The thing is HMRC can chuck as much money as they like at each case and get the best legal team money can buy—our legal team paled in comparison. A David and Goliath situation except we were facing Goliath armed with a toothpick.

HMRC's barristers' line of questioning gave us very little opportunity to have a voice, with many questions only leaving you to respond with a yes or no answer. This made Richard come across as really evasive and combative. Richard got into the habit of avoiding a direct question which made him look dishonest, but he was doing his best. Richard spent two days on the stand and then it was my turn. As far as Richard was concerned, he hadn't given much away and believed that this approach left HMRC with very little to go on. We are identical twins but our characters are quite different; Rich can come across as very unapproachable and aggressive.

I'm a lot more open and softer in my approach than Richard so I just answered as honestly as I could; it was my second day in the stand and I was struggling. The whole situation was finally getting on top of me and I wished I'd gone first. I was tired and felt like I had gone through it with Richard on his two days and then had to do it myself so mentally I was finding it difficult.

Your voice is stifled on the witness stand as we were led on a journey by HMRC and if I'm honest, the way it was portrayed, it could make anyone look guilty. HMRC simply had to prove something wasn't quite right. Well, that was fucking obvious; there was a hole in HMRC's wallet and they wanted someone else to pay for the tab. Forget the actual criminals who had actually run off with the money, they were probably sunning themselves on a luxury yacht in Monaco while we were suffering in the courtroom. It was just before lunchtime on my second day in the stand and I remember HMRC's barrister asking me a question.

'Sorry, could you repeat the question for me? I didn't understand what you said,' I asked him politely.

The barrister repeated the question. I was focusing on his lips trying to understand what he was saying.

'I don't understand what you mean,' I said.

I could feel myself becoming frustrated because I could not understand what he was saying.

'Okay, let me try another way,' the barrister said before he asked me the same question but in a different way.

I listened intently while straining my eyes to watch his lips move. All I could see was movement and noise. He could have been speaking a foreign language for all I knew; I could not understand him. I looked at the judge for support who said, 'I think we'll break for lunch.'

I honestly could not understand a word the barrister had just said to me—try as I might, nothing was making any sense. This had never happened to me before, I had stalled and my mind had closed down, nothing was going in. My brain felt like a melted welly; my mind was gone and I was becoming really anxious.

We broke for lunch and, as I was still under oath, you're not allowed to discuss the case or communicate with anyone. I walked to a nearby Sainsbury's to grab a sandwich, but even the thought of eating made me feel sick. I was trying to pull myself together when my mobile started ringing, it was Rich.

'Get your shit together; you're fucking this all up and if we lose this, it's all your fault,' Richard screamed at me down the phone and then he hung up on me.

I didn't get a chance to reply or say a word and just sat there in Sainsbury's with a blank look on my face; this made me feel awful. I was trying my hardest and didn't deliberately set out to fuck anything up; why would I? This case was so important to me. What I really needed at the time was just a soft little nudge, something like, 'Come on, Christian, you got this—it's okay, you can do this.'

Richard berating me the way he did was an unnecessary stress and was totally uncalled for. It deflated me even further. I walked back into the courtroom and for the rest of the afternoon I was never quite back on track, but I did my best; I never fully recovered, but answered the best I could and I said to the judge on a couple of occasions, 'I promise I am trying to be truthful here and answer any questions the best I can, but I'm just struggling a bit at the minute.'

The judge ever so slightly nodded at me and interjected on a few occasions with HMRC's barrister to say, 'I think we get the point, let's move on.'

The judge could see I was being open and honest. I had nothing to hide and my testimony would not wreck our case entirely—this would not be the difference between winning and losing.

The court case was finally over and I was released from being under oath and we were free to leave—it was over. There was nothing more we could do; we left the courtroom. I'd always envisaged leaving the courtroom feeling uplifted and confident. I was feeling really low and rather than Rich and I hugging it out, he was the first to let me know what a failure he thought I was.

'What the fuck happened to you?' he said.

'I know bro. I don't know; my mind was gone,' I said defeated.

'Thing is Christian, you know this shit like the back of your hand, and what he was asking you was so easy,' Richard replied.

'I don't know, I couldn't understand what he was saying,' I was knackered and just wanted a quiet moment.

Richard and I went for drinks and I asked Richard to explain it to me slowly and when he did it was easy for me to answer. The pressure of court had got to me; what could I do?

I'd noticed even before going to court that I'd been struggling and feeling low; the thought that Richard now had an out and could blame me if we lost our case didn't make me feel any better. In the next few days, Richard and I didn't talk much and I just couldn't be fucked with his attitude. He had convinced himself that his efforts in court were outstanding and the only reason we could lose was because of me.

We were having an argument some months later and he screamed at me down the phone, 'It'll be your fault if we lose; you should have let me take your place—I would have fucking aced it.'

I absolutely hate the fucking term, 'Aced it.' I always have done, ever since Richard said that to me. It's so obnoxious and it still haunts me to this day.

As I mentioned previously, there were as many as 2,500 other exporters in the same position as us. Some had the money to fight on and some didn't, but all of them were losing and falling by the wayside. It was the 5th of August 2011 when our decision came out from the tribunal. We lost! Our appeal had been dismissed!

We were not just accused of having the 'Means of Knowledge'—which meant we ought to have known better that fraud was being committed somewhere in the supply chain—we were actually accused by the judge of having 'Actual Knowledge'. This means we knew fraud was being committed and were complicit in assisting with the fraud.

This was a clever and tactical strategy by the judge. Being accused of 'Actual Knowledge', which was becoming common place in these types of hearings, at the tribunal prevented us appealing the judge's decision, or have another judge look at the case to ensure the correct decision had been made using the right case law.

It was the end of the road; we had taken a massive hit financially and my mental health had started to suffer, it would take a lot for both of us to come back from this.

I was really upset and just found it hard to function when I heard the news; I sat in the corner of my bedroom in the dark and was really tearful.

I heard the front door go and knew it was Liz. I didn't want Liz to see me in this state, but I couldn't hide it either as she called out for me walking along the corridor to find me sat in my bedroom in the dark. She came straight to me.

'It's okay darling, we got each other; we'll be all right,' Lizzy said as she hugged me. My lip trembled; I couldn't speak I just didn't have the words.

I never read the decision itself, all 51 pages of it. Our accountant had though and called me.

'I'm sorry, mate, I've just read your court decision. Jesus, Rich took a kicking from the judge—'deceitful and not a credible witness' to name a few things. You didn't come off so bad,' he told me.

Turns out what happened to me on the stand was not detrimental to our case at all. We lost so what does it matter, but the judge did acknowledge—even though he found against us—he thought I was honest and, even though I had struggled to answer some of the questions, it was not seen as an attempt to deceive the courts. It made me feel slightly more at ease that Richard was mauled and the judge launched a scathing attack on him. It gave me a little comfort that it was not my fault, especially after how he had treated me saying, 'If we lose, it will be your fault.' Richard never apologised for it, then again, he rarely ever apologised for anything; why would he when there is always someone else to blame? You shouldn't criticise others when you are personally not perfect.

Fusion was technically over and so were our jobs; the company that we had started from scratch and dedicated so much of ourselves to was gone. It was running on fumes as we still had our core business, but it just wasn't the same again.

Fusion had finally run out of steam and Richard and I resigned as directors on the 14th of December 2012—this was quite devastating for both of us.

Trying to move on, I did find a good opportunity to buy a new house. A couple of my really close friends had purchased the entire site at The Old Police Station where our offices for Fusion used to be. Our first office and the lower floor were turned into two flats; the middle building was renovated into a one bedroomed house and The Old Magistrates Court was renovated into a 5-bedroom house—this place was huge.

I purchased the one-bedroom house on the 13th of January 2013 and it was quite strange owning a new home at The Old Police Station, which I called 'The Hayloft.' It was as big as my old three-bedroomed house at Redwing Rise and still the same on the outside with so much character, but brand new on the inside. I wouldn't have it any other way. I had gone full circle and ended up back at The Old Police Station, standing on the doorstep of an evening having a cigarette made me nostalgic, thinking back to us running a business here and now I lived here; it felt weird, but I loved my new place.

The fire had gone out and I was down as I floated along; days turned into months—a lot of months. I had enough money to get by for a while and was taking some time out. I can't just summon the magic when I feel like it, it would take as long as it takes for me to come up with some new ideas. I needed time to think, give myself a moment and wait for those ideas to start popping back into my head, not just for me, but for my brother too.

I was in the pub one evening when I was offered some cocaine; the first time I'd ever tried cocaine was on a lads' trip to Vegas when I was around 34. I'd never touched it before this, it just wasn't my thing, and because of how protective I was about my nose, I wouldn't risk damaging it. In Vegas, a friend said to me, 'You can stick it on your gums,' so I did and let's just say my jaw arrived at the party before I did—this wasn't a good look for me. When I tried it at the pub, I threw caution to the wind and thought, 'Fuck it, why not?' and I started sniffing it. I would occasionally do it, but I could take it or leave it; however, I did like it, especially the feeling it gave me. Once I wore my coke cloak, I was bigger, badder and a better version of me—I was already a handful to deal with as it was.

I had noticed changes within me and I was becoming afraid of large groups of people and was starting to feel awkward on social occasions; I would rarely walk into the pub without having a drink first to help lower my inhibitions and slip into my alter ego—the guy who could command a room and wanted to be the centre of attention. However, what you saw on the outside wasn't how I was feeling on the inside. The success I'd had was gone and the court case with HMRC had taken its toll on me. I just wanted to wake up, for even just one day, smiling. I couldn't remember the last time I'd genuinely felt happy. Things were going great with Elizabeth, and Rich and Jennifer were also still going strong, but most days felt cloudy in my head and I was a little lost.

I'd been self-employed at such a young age that I wasn't about to give up and get a job, now or ever; I don't work for other people.

I can't remember exactly, but sometime in 2013 Richard and Jennifer were over in Dubai on holiday when I received a panicky phone call from Rich.

'Bro, I can't be long. I know it's really spur of the moment, but Jens just getting ready and I've rushed down to a De Beers Jewellers shop in our hotel to buy a ring; I wanted you to be the first to know, but I'm going to propose,' he said.

I was really surprised and taken aback; it had come totally out of the blue.

'Wow, Rich, I'm really happy for you,' I said—I was in shock.

'We've got afternoon tea at the Burj Al Arab and I'm going to ask her there. I've gotta go mate; love you, Bro,' and he hung up the phone.

I stood there stunned. 'They were good together, so why not?' I thought.

I must admit I was feeling slightly jealous, like I was losing my brother a little bit to someone else. It's a twin thing and it's hard to explain.

When they got back, they were both so excited and Jennifer couldn't wait to show me the rock on her finger.

'We're getting married in Lake Garda in Italy,' she squealed with delight.

'Nice, babe, when are you thinking of doing that?' I replied.

'Well we're talking about going over to Italy in May next year to meet a wedding planner and thinking of getting married in May 2015,' she said; she was practically bouncing up and down.

I gave them both a hug and squeezed my brother extra tight, 'We better start making some money then, Bro,' I said jokingly.

'Yeah, tell me about it,' he replied.

There are times when things just pop into my head and I'd started thinking how difficult it was to borrow money from the banks; the banks were and still are not very flexible when it comes to lending money. I always had friends asking to borrow money from me or friends in business who were struggling with their cash flow.

'How could I lend money to people at higher interest

rates, but on a short-term basis without getting stung,' I thought to myself.

I started thinking that I would need some kind of security, but not your average items; I was thinking of items that were of high value. A second charge against someone's house is obvious, but that is long term and the rates involved are a lot lower. Placing a charge on someone's property is practically risk free, but it costs a lot to implement. I'm a risk-taker and I meant fast money, quick money, and was thinking about the risk to reward.

Then one night, the answer was literally staring at me straight in the face. I was watching TV and a programme on Channel 4 came on called *Posh Pawn*. It was about a successful business man called James Constantinou and he runs a high-end luxury pawn brokers in Weybridge called Prestige Pawn Brokers Limited. Weybridge is a very affluent area. This was not your average pawn brokers in the high street who would lend you a tenner for any old shit. That didn't interest me at all; this was a business loaning money against high-end luxury items, like jewellery, expensive cars and watches. Anything that you could loan against of high value in general would work. In the pawn broking sector, you could command as much as 7% per month on any one transaction— it's really good money, fast and efficient. This programme had got my attention; it wasn't a problem to me that Prestige had already cornered the market in loaning against high-end luxury items. It didn't scare me off or mean that I was too late to give it a go. I'd set my sights on doing it or possibly working with James Constantinou in one way or another. If I wanted to, I knew I could make it happen. I gave Rich a call after watching the programme.

'Hey, Rich, how's it going?' I asked him.

'Hey Bro, yeah not bad, what's up?'

'Listen, I was just watching this programme about pawn broking and it's given me a few ideas,' I then proceeded to explain to him how it works.

'Nah, that doesn't sound like something for me,' he replied.

'Okay, well I'm gonna give it a go; watch the programme, though, it's pretty good,' I told him.

Richard had basically rubbished my idea, but that didn't worry me at all; I started to do some homework on it that night. Then Richard gave me a call in the morning.

'Hey, Bro, listen, you might be onto something; I watched the programme and I can really see some potential there. What do you want to do?' he asked me.

'Leave it with me, I was already going to give Prestige a shout as I noticed on their website that there is an opportunity to own your own franchise.'

I didn't get chance to speak to James Constantinou on this occasion, but was put through to a guy called Mark who was in charge of the franchise opportunities within Prestige.

We would require approximately £220,000.00 to own a franchise. Rich and I could stump up £75,000.00 each and were a little short.

'We're fucked, Bro, I really want to do this, but we can't stretch enough money,' Rich said to me; it was quite a turnaround considering he had been so dismissive.

'Yeah, leave it with me. I've got a few thoughts on a couple of people who may be interested,' I replied.

Richard and I had the same circle of friends, but Richard didn't have the resources and strong friendships that I had so I

193

wasn't too worried. I made a couple of calls and in the same day I secured the other £75,000.00 needed. There was one condition my friend Carl stipulated—even though he was friends with both of us, me and Carl were much closer. He didn't want to work with Richard as he felt Richard couldn't be trusted and was too ruthless, but he would do it for me and act as a silent partner, but only if I was involved and would look out for him. I assured him I would protect his money and it would be okay. Richard was obviously over the moon that I secured the funding and now we could proceed.

I had the idea and I got us the money, with a little nudge here and there, we were ready to go and meet Prestige Pawn Brokers Limited and I arranged a meeting at their offices on the 11th of March 2014 in Weybridge.

Chapter 21
I Did it for Love Not Money

The meeting with Prestige went really well and when we walked away, as far as we were concerned, it was going to happen. We started thinking about the right location and looking for premises to run the shop, either in Harpenden or Cambridge.

Richard and I were excited to finally try again; unfortunately, due to the success of the programme on Channel 4, the franchise opportunity was placed on hold. Prestige was good enough to let us know that it wouldn't be fair on us to start a franchise as they couldn't give us the time needed to get the store up and running. Basically, the programme on Channel 4 had catapulted the company to become so successful that they ended up opening a chain of stores instead. Richard and I were understandably disappointed.

'I'm gutted, Bro, we'll have to think of something else to do,' Rich said with a big sigh.

'Maybe not, Rich, I still see potential here somewhere,' I replied.

It's business and some deals that look concrete can suddenly collapse and some deals you don't expect to work out do, but I thought if I can get involved in his business then maybe I could build up a relationship with James and who knows what could come from it. It took me some time, but I bullied my way into meeting with James Constantinou, the owner of Prestige Pawn Brokers Limited. I had money and thought, 'Okay, I'm gonna try and invest in his business and take a smaller percentage in return.'

I took Richard with me on the 8th of July 2014 to meet with James; he seemed a pretty decent guy and I walked out of the meeting and agreed to start off with an investment in his business for £50,000.00 which I sent as soon as I walked out of the door.

It was strange to me watching the programme, I liked sitting there thinking my money was being loaned against high-end luxury items like Ferraris, Lamborghinis, watches and diamonds.

Richard went off on his own and decided to renovate a house and do all of the work by himself. He purchased a property on the spur of the moment and I was concerned that he'd paid far too much money for the property. Richard had bought it as a renovation project and he outbid someone who was actually buying the property to live in it, so in my view, he was paying above market value but Rich was convinced it was a gold mine. It was totally up to him and he wouldn't be told any different; I had my reservations and my gut told me this was a bad idea and it didn't interest me at all—I'm a deal maker, not someone that wants to peel wallpaper or get on my hands and knees to paint a skirting board. That's just not for me, I'd rather hire a team to do it and make less money. I'd started filling some of my spare time in the evenings going out alone and occasionally went to a casino in Luton. I was still dabbling in cocaine and was also gambling occasionally online.

Richard had a wedding to pay for and had sunk all of his

money into this renovation property, but he was adamant that he was going to make a fortune once he sold the property at Olney. He was reliant on selling this house to pay for his wedding which was up in the region of £40,000.00 already, and the way Rich and Jen were spending, it could be much more than that by the time they had finished. He purchased 59 Wellingborough Road, Olney on the 1st of August 2014 for £249,995.00 and once he got the keys, he started renovating the property. I was thinking about Richard renovating this property and this had given me an idea so I asked Rich and Jennifer to meet me at a pub in Biggleswade called Stratton House; Rich and Jennifer were now living in Biggleswade. I pulled up and met them in the pub garden and walked over to the usual hugs and greetings.

'How's it going guys? Listen, I've had an idea that involves all of us and want to see what you think?' I said.

'Okay, what you thinking, Bro?' asked Rich while Jen sat there sipping on her drink.

'So, Jen earns a great salary and she can easily get mortgages, but she doesn't have the cash and we can't get the mortgages. We have the cash, though, so let's say we put in around £75,000.00 each—that's me and you, Rich—but obviously you don't have the money until you sell Olney, but I propose we try and buy some land and try to get planning to build a house on it. We can either build it out or sell it on with the planning permission. Alternatively, we could buy a property that has some land around it, knock it down and get planning for two properties—that kind of thing—just work it out as we go and see what works,' I explained to them.

They both listened intently as I went through the finer details; it was quite simple.

'Okay, what's the split or what you thinking?' Richard asked me.

I knew I had the contacts or friends, who could help us out, that they didn't, but I'm a team player and kept it straight forward.

'Okay, Rich, get a company sorted we'll call it XS Homes Limited. Jen gets 20% and you and I get 40% shares of the business; all Jen has to do is get the mortgages—we'll do the rest.'

'I like that idea,' Jen giggled.

'Rich, get onto the accountant and get the company set up,' I said.

'Yep, no problems, I'm on it,' Rich replied.

On the 1st of September 2014, XS Homes Limited was incorporated and we just parked it up until the time was right to do something, but I was keeping my ear close to the ground to see if anything cropped up.

In the meantime, Rich was spending every waking hour renovating Olney. It was towards the end of October 2014 when he called me.

'Hey, Rich, how's it going? What's up?' I asked him.

'I could do with your help to be honest, Bro. I'm running out of money to finish Olney.'

'How much do you need? I've already loaned you 15K,' I asked him.

'I was wondering if I could borrow the money you leant to Prestige; if you can do it, I need about another £40,000.00,' Richard asked me.

'Hmmm, okay, let me have a think about that Bro and I'll shout you back. I've only just given it to Prestige, so it'll be up to James, but if I can help you I will. I'm your big brother, aren't I? So I'll do what I can.'

'Your money will be safer with me than him, please Bro,' he replied.

This wasn't actually true; my money was safe with James and we had filled out a lot of paperwork and contracts to ensure my money was secure—moving my money was actually an annoying thing for me to do. I had an in with James and was sacrificing my opportunities to help Rich out. Rich phoned me the following day.

'Hey, Bro, have you thought any more about lending me that money? I'm getting worried. Once I finish Olney, I can pay you back and it'll sell no problems. I'd like to think you'll have your money back in March, but I promise it will definitely be back with you before our wedding,' Rich said to me; he sounded worried in his voice.

Rich was laying it on me really thick and the wedding was on the 23rd of May 2015. It did cross my mind that Olney was practically finished so 55K in total seemed like a lot and he'd already been working on the property for three months. I threw caution to the wind and didn't question it; he was my brother and he needed my help.

I emailed James at Prestige and basically said, 'I'm so sorry James and I know you've only had my investment for about three months, but my brother really needs my help; basically, he's renovating a house and he's run out of money.'

James was really cool about it and understood my dilemma; he sent my money back on the 14th of November 2014 and I loaned Rich another £40,000.00 and sent the money straight over to him. I loaned Rich £55,000.00 in total to help him—that's what big brothers do.

It wasn't long until Richard had finished renovating the

property and we had a drink to celebrate that he'd finished it. It was December 2014 and he'd already put Olney up for sale with a local estate agent. I didn't ask too many questions, but remember thinking to myself, 'You got that finished pretty quickly seeing as I'd only just sent you the money; you couldn't possibly have got through all that money in such a small amount of time for the work that needed doing to finish it.'

I was maybe a little too relaxed about it, but Rich was so happy and proud of himself. He was positive he'd done his homework and that it would be sold in no time; he was already spending the profit in his head and he put it on the market for £375,000.00—this was £125,000.00 more than he'd paid for it. The figures just didn't stack up to me, but he assured me my money would be back in no time.

As we were having a couple of drinks, Richard dropped a couple of secrets about the wedding; he just couldn't help himself. He told me that they had just booked and paid for a six-piece string quartet and a boat to ferry all of the guests to the wedding reception, this boat could ferry well over 150 people and was going to carry all of the guests and cruise along Lake Garda.

'I won't tell you all of the surprises we've arranged for the wedding, as I don't want to spoil it, but I've got something else to tell you,' he said.

'Go on Bro, what is it?' I replied.

'I've changed my surname; I'm going to take Jens surname. I've already changed it by deed poll,' Rich said to me with a big smile on his face.

I almost spat my drink out. 'You've done what?' I asked him, thinking I'd misheard him or hoped I had.

'I've changed my surname to Potter,' he repeated.

This came as a complete shock to me that he had actually gone ahead and done that. He had been rambling on a lot lately about doing this, but I just ignored him at the time and didn't really get it. However, it was true Richard Govan was now Richard Potter.

I was puzzled and thought, 'That's interesting; what the fuck's that all about? It's just fucking weird.'

His reasoning behind it was some nonsense about having nothing to do with Mum and Dad and he wanted to disassociate from them completely.

'Why all of a sudden? We haven't seen or spoken to Mum and Dad in years,' I thought.

Anyway, I thought it was bollocks and he hadn't taken into consideration how I might feel about it; I thought it was me and him forever—that hurt me.

It was just really fucking peculiar to me, or was it? I remember thinking, 'Maybe Rich has an ulterior motive or is hiding from something or someone.'

Richard changing his surname was distancing himself or dissociating himself from me and it had certainly raised my suspicions, 'Why would he do that?'

I started to question the relationship that Richard and I had these days; I was only needed if there was money to make or if he needed to borrow any money. It felt like Rich and Jen were setting off into the sunset without me.

It was the start of 2015 and I'm 38 years old, I had so much time on my hands and my house in Royston; 'The Hayloft' was my sanctuary, my hideout and I loved it. It was cool a proper bachelor pad except I wasn't a bachelor; I was still dating Lizzy so I spent time between houses—hers and mine. Things were going okay between us, but I sometimes questioned if I wanted to be single, but there was something so sweet about Lizzy; the thought of us splitting up and thinking of her face always pulled me back in. I wasn't being good to her and I knew it, but I wanted to do what I wanted to do. She's a good soul and I would have missed the little faces and smiles she pulled, but it was a constant tug of war. I wanted to get home, do coke and get smashed off my face or the alternative: sit feeling trapped at Lizzy's while sitting on the sofa and in bed by ten. I felt like I couldn't be me at times which was so frustrating and the nights I chose to be good, it was boring me. I wanted to go and do cocaine, drink and gamble. I was starting to wrestle with myself all of the time.

I was turning into a night owl and I liked what I was doing. Late at night, I'd started going out a lot more in the week. As I mentioned, I drove to the nearest casino which was in Luton for something to do, but I was starting to do it more frequently; it was a release for me and I was doing cocaine before I left and then while I was at the casino. I would sit at the poker tables with my headphones on and just melt away. I loved watching the cards come out and just relaxing, going outside occasionally to have a smoke. I had tried my hand at the roulette tables, but was always scared off with handing over chips and watching the croupier drag them away again and slide them down the black hole in the table when you lost and this wasn't fast enough for me. I remember thinking, 'What's the point of putting down £5 to win £180 which you'll only spend again? If you're going to do it, do it properly,' I thought.

I was sure that Lizzy wasn't onto me as I made my excuses and would leave hers. Most days, leaving around nine in the evening and saying, 'I just fancy sleeping at mine tonight, babe.' The truth was I wanted to spend less time with her and more time at home because at mine I was left to my own devices. I was out on the town a lot more and was doing more cocaine than I had ever done before. What started off as occasionally doing it perhaps once a month had started to increase to weekly, but I was in control or I felt like I was. I was at home and the front door was locked; I could do my own thing and nobody would be any the wiser. As I was standing there in the kitchen, I lined up around three or four lines of cocaine on the kitchen worktop and cracked open a bottle of wine. I opened my front door and stood there on the doorstep smoking a cigarette, I felt good and everything was okay. 'I'm going to go out,' I thought as I grabbed my hoodie, downed my glass of wine and locked my front door. I walked round the corner to the local pub; this was the same pub that I smashed my car into, all those years ago. I walked through the pub door like a celebrity; I was hyperactive and the life and soul of the party. This went on for a while and there would always be people back at my house once the pubs had shut. Even with my OCD, coke lowered my guard and, in that moment, I didn't care. It wasn't uncommon for me to have as many as 10–12 people at mine some weekends.

This lifestyle came quite normal to me and I could bounce back pretty quickly; I could come and go and no one would have a clue. Days and weeks were flying past so quickly; I lost count of the amount of times that I hadn't slept for a day or two—maybe even three.

Now I'm not saying I was making all the right choices, but I don't have to answer to anyone and these were my decisions to make. I had started to spend more time alone; I preferred my own company. On so many occasions I'd wake up to missed calls and texts from Rich trying to reach me and eventually I'd have to call him back. I remember this one particular occasion when I called him in the morning.

'Hey, Rich, sorry missed your call, mate. Phone was on silent,' I said making up an excuse.

'I know you're up to something; I know my brother. What you been up to?' he said, suspicious of me.

I deflected, 'More importantly, Rich, how's Olney coming along?'

'Not as good as I'd hoped. I've got a lot of interest though; don't worry, it will sell,' he said.

He was so optimistic that it clouded and blinkered his decisions; he was wearing rose tinted glasses and still wanted to believe that Olney was his cash cow. This, in my view, was a terrible purchase, but I wasn't concerned at this stage as I still had some money in the bank. I just couldn't see it though, whatever angle I looked at it from, but then again, I don't know everything and he might surprise me. I hoped I was wrong; I want the best for my brother and he had worked so hard on that property.

Rich then went on to tell me about his new Gucci loafers that he'd just bought for £400.00 and a blue Paul Smith suit that he'd bought as his wedding outfit—that cost £1,500.00. Additionally, he had paid for a 6-piece string quartet, the ferry and the money for the wedding planner and the film crew who were going to follow them around on their big day. They were also paying for every single drink for every single person attending their wedding day—and that so far, was 82 people.

I'd started to suspect that my money hadn't been used for the purpose that it was intended for.

Chapter 22
I Think I Prefer My Other Life

Olney was turning out to be the fucking nightmare that I thought it would be. If you're trying to charge £70,000.00 more than the suggested market price, no one is ever going to buy it and I think the reality of Richard's purchase was starting to sink in so Richard decided to lower the price, but he was still trying to charge too much money for it. In the meantime, I had my best friend call me—he owns a building company and is a housing developer. I'd asked him to call me if he came across anything I could be interested in and he'd seen a property in a village called Litlington. I gave Rich a call and we both went to take a look at it.

The Grove, Abington Road, Litlington was located in a small village in the surrounding area. The plot was quite large and had a really old looking property on it; the property was unliveable and derelict, but this site was large enough to potentially build two four-bedroom houses on it, which could possibly be around 2,000 square foot each. This was a no brainer: a good size plot, right place and great potential and I also had some inside knowledge at what price we could get it for.

The problem was is that Richard had all our money tied up in Olney and even if Jen could get a mortgage, it would be useless without money to finance the balance, not forgetting planning and all the other costs involved. Richard and Jen had their wedding coming up and had sunk whatever money they had into that, including mine, although they wouldn't admit it.

I knew this was a great opportunity; there was potentially a lot of money that could be made here and I wasn't prepared to miss out. I just had to think about how to juggle the funds to do it.

Rich and I went to a local pub to discuss it and Jen was on her way to meet us.

'Christian, what are we gonna do man? That's got so much potential,' Rich looked so frustrated and was already defeated.

'It'll be okay. I've got a few ideas and I think I have a way around it,' I said as Jen pulled up in the car and came to sit with us.

We got another round of drinks and sat down to bring Jen up to speed with things. As I sat there, I thought about Lizzy's dad and a friend of mine who could be interested and able to help us out.

Rich and Jen looked so disheartened and clueless how to proceed.

I told them, 'Hang on, I could approach Lizzy's dad and offer him a charge over the property, plus interest on his investment, and I've got an idea on the balance. I've just got to make a few calls.'

'Do you think you could, Bro?' Rich said.

'Just leave it with me a minute,' I replied.

'Do it Christian, get it for us,' Jen said.

I didn't like the way she said that, but I shrugged it off; doing business like this was way out of her depth and I think she was excited in the moment.

I spent the next few days in talks with Lizzy's dad who

said he'd support me and would require the first charge over the property if we were successful in getting it. A first charge is fool-proof and totally secures your money. I then spoke to my other friend about the balance and he agreed, but had a couple of conditions, so I had to call Rich.

'Rich, I'm trying to sort financing out on this property mate, but the other loan would require a charge on our own homes.'

'Not interested, mate. I can speak for Jen too and there is no way we are prepared to risk our own home or use it as security,' Rich said firmly.

'How the fuck do you expect to do any business if you won't even have faith to try, Rich?' I blasted at him.

'It's not happening, Bro. We'll have to give it a miss.'

'Fuck that, I'll make it happen,' and I put the phone down.

I spent the entire day negotiating. I had £310,000.00 secured with Lizzy's dad and I used my own house 'The Hayloft' as a personal guarantee to raise another £225,000.00. It took me about a week, but I secured a total of £535,000.00.

I sat there thinking, 'What a fucking joke, doing it on my own with no assistance from Rich and Jen at all—they're not even prepared to take a chance, and my own house is on the fucking line,' so, I called Rich.

'Rich, let me tell you something, don't go into business with me if you're not prepared to take a few risks. Having said that, I got us the money,' I told him.

'What? How the fuck have you done that?' he said; I could tell by his voice he was grinning.

'Well, I've had to use my own house as a personal guarantee, so I'm taking £25,000.00 as a finder's fee because you and Jen have done fuck all and we would lose this opportunity if it wasn't for me,' I said to him firmly.

I was fucked off and just so unimpressed with the pair of them; they were desperate to try and make a business work, but not prepared to take any risks at all. It was all on me as usual. I'm a team player and expected my team to help me out, but they did nothing.

'Wow, I'm impressed Bro; I can't believe that. It's funny 'cos Jen asked me the other day: do you think Christian can pull it off? And I told her you can never underestimate my brother,' Rich said to me.

The offer of £365,123.00 was accepted and, provided everything went okay with the paperwork and solicitors, XS Homes Limited had acquired its first property.

Everything was locked in as much as it could be at this stage so I had a lot of time on my hands again, so I went back to my other life: the life that I was not in control of, but was starting to prefer.

The life that involved me going out a lot, doing more cocaine, drinking and gambling. I'd got to a point where I remember thinking, 'I won't go out unless I have cocaine on me.' That was until I just stopped going out at all; one minute, I'm the life and soul of the party and before I knew it, I'd started to lock myself away at 'The Hayloft.' Cocaine keeps you awake and if you're alone, you either rattle around the house or stare up at the ceiling begging yourself to fall asleep, so I created my own escape, my own little world that I could totally submerge myself in—a vice. One of my friends was drawn into the world of webcam girls, but my vice was gambling while being seduced by coke.

I stopped heading over to the casino in Luton and started gambling online; I started playing live roulette. It was still in live play, like an actual casino, but I liked the variety of tables and speed at which they worked so I opened various accounts online. I only ever played the live tables in real time and never touched the computerised games; this was much more fun than going to the casino in Luton. I was in the comfort of my own home; I could do cocaine at the same time as play, and drink and smoke all on my own doorstep. I would always ensure my mobile had 100% battery as I only ever played using my mobile phone; using my phone gave me the freedom to walk about the house easier, never taking my eyes off the screen. I would block all incoming calls because any calls that came through would chuck me off a table—that pissed me off so much. I'd be right in the middle of a game and someone would call me. I couldn't tell you how much money I've lost before I started blocking people, but it was thousands of pounds. This is why Richard picked up on me being distant; Richard had always been able to reach me on speed dial, and in a heartbeat. I'd become vacant; although, most of the time I played, it was so late in the evening most people were asleep in bed—that was until I went through the night and straight through an entire day sometimes. It was a normal night just like any other and I started my ritual as always in my kitchen where I set up my base, I poured myself a glass of wine, took a couple of sips and racked up a couple of lines on the kitchen worktop. After sniffing the cocaine, I then had a cigarette. I was standing on the doorstep in the darkness, feeling the breeze, and felt the coke take effect. I was ready, I logged into my account and, putting my phone into horizontal mode, I started to play. I would spend hours analysing the tables flipping in and out of different roulette games, until I found one that I liked the look of. I got so used to playing and knew exactly where all of the numbers were that I could place bets on one table quickly enough to view what was happening on other tables before the ball had even landed on a number. I was viewing so many tables all at once and watching the statistics; that's one of the things I was enjoying the most about it, but I had no off switch.

When I finally stopped—and the main reason I did was because I'd run out of cocaine or I'd won or lost enough money—I'd slip back into normal mode and get some sleep if I could. I would have a shower to rinse away the night before or, on many occasions, rinse away the last two days. Opening my front door, I was ready for action and had an excuse for anyone asking where I'd been or why I was unreachable. I became very skilled at lying through my teeth; not to harm people, but lies to hide my secret life. 'It shouldn't have to be a secret; it's my life and I'll do what I like,' I thought, but I knew I was a little out of control and the judgement from other people on how I should be living was driving me underground, or I knew what I was doing to myself wasn't quite right.

I projected to everyone on the outside the Christian that everyone knew and loved and I was there in presence, but not always in person. I was becoming a bit slower, but was still on point when needed—but only if needed—and I was becoming fatigued while trying to keep my severely, ever-increasing anxiety at bay. That was impossible because no one suffering from anxiety calls the shots. Anxiety comes knocking and leaves you when it wants to.

I used to look in the mirror; I didn't dislike what I saw, but was starting to wonder who I was and what the fuck I was doing.

The wedding was looming and Richard had obviously asked me to be his best man, and I was honoured until I found out that Rich had also asked my cousin to be his best man too; this was weird, it had only ever been me and Rich and now he's asking strangers in the family to be one of his best men.

'What the fuck is that all about? My cousin has not been there for you; why do you need to have two best men?' I thought.

I wasn't a fan of my cousin; he's the type of guy that thinks no one works as hard as he does and the world owes him a living. He is so envious of others, me included, and such a shit stirrer. He's the sort of guy that would catch his cock in his zip and would be too fearful to rip it out so, instead, would cover it with a long T-shirt and go out dressed like that. He dreams of running his own businesses and would go down the shops looking for the manual to do it but, unfortunately, life doesn't come with a manual; you need that little something, something. Remember, you either have it or you don't, and he most definitely didn't. I spoke to him about being my brother's best man and he said to me on the phone, 'I don't know why your brother has asked me to be his best man, to be honest—it's all a bit awkward.'

'What a fucking insult, my cousin didn't even want the job as best man; what was Rich thinking?' I thought.

I told my cousin to take a back seat; and I arranged my brother's stag do. This is something that I wanted to do alone; this was my job and I wanted it to be the most amazing stag do for my little brother. On the 30th of April 2015, we went to Budapest. We were picked up from the airport in a stretched Hummer with lap dancers on-board; it was just a bit of fun—just what lads do—and I'd arranged the best tables at the best restaurants, bars and clubs in Budapest.

By now, I was starting to run out of money; the roulette

tables weren't being so kind to me and my new lifestyle was expensive, so I called Rich.

'Rich, how's it going? You good?' I asked him.

'Hey Bro; where you been hiding? I haven't heard from you much lately,' he replied.

'Any news on Olney?' I asked him.

'Yeah, I was going to talk to you about that. I've had an offer, but the person wants to live in it first.'

'Huh? What the fuck are you talking about? No, Rich, don't even consider it. That's a big mistake and the stupidest idea I've ever heard of. Not only do you have no commitment that the person will buy it, but you're selling it as new; it won't be new once someone has lived in it and trashed it. And what about my money? This isn't what you promised; you're changing what we agreed. You said I'd have my money back before the wedding so you need to sort something out,' I told him.

'I've already agreed to it,' he said, sounding a bit sheepish.

'Are you fucking mad? This could be the worst decision you've ever made; you're going to let someone live in that house on a promise they'll live in it and, if they like it they'll buy it. What a fucking joke! Where does that leave me with my money? This isn't what we agreed,' I said angrily.

'I thought you had plenty to get by and I gave you £2,000.00 back in March,' Rich said curiously.

If you remember, Richard had told me I should have all my money back by March. It was now May, and only a couple of weeks before their wedding.

'Rich, that's not the fucking point. You're changing what we agreed. You told me what a great house the property in Olney is and you'll make a fortune, and now you're renting it out; Olney is a fucking joke,' I said to him.

'No, it's not. It'll work out,' he replied.

'Work out? Work out for whom? Work out for you and your timescales; it's not your money, it's mine, and you're juggling it all over the place. You claimed that you had no money to finish Olney and asked to borrow it from me to finish the renovation and all I've heard since then is how great your new Gucci fucking loafers are. Listen, I don't need to tell you shit about my money or what I do with it, but I'm running low, so you need to get something sorted,' I hung up on him, I was absolutely fuming.

Rich, Jen and Lizzy all knew I had a flutter, but were not aware that I was doing it as much as I was and, yes, my current lifestyle was getting the better of me financially, but right now Richard had £53,000.00 of my money and was using it like it was actually his and that he owned it.

'He doesn't give a fuck,' I thought.

He has the property at Olney which he's now decided to rent out at a pittance per month. He has all of my money and miraculously doesn't need to sell Olney now until it suits him because his lavish wedding is all paid for.

Chapter 23
Am I at the Right Wedding?

Richard and I have always strived to be the best so it didn't shock me how impressive his wedding actually was, and it is still the most lavish and extravagant wedding that I have ever been to. He was on a mission to outdo any of our friend's previous weddings and demonstrate his wealth and success.

The truth is that I was the one propping up his bank balance so he was currently living a champagne lifestyle on a lemonade budget.

The relationship was so strained between me and my brother that Richard, even to this day, still doesn't realise how close me and Lizzy came to not going to his wedding. I had no money as we packed our cases and I was getting so worked up about everything. We were due to meet them at lunchtime and spend a lovely day at a beautiful hotel that we'd booked the night before we flew out to Italy.

Lizzy was trying her best to salvage everything, but my mood was bringing us both down. Rich was just oblivious to what was going on with me so I picked up the phone and called him.

'You on your way mate? We're already at the hotel,' he said excitedly down the phone at me.

'Rich, I'm struggling. I've got no money and I'm not prepared to spend the next few days trying to get by when I should be with you and enjoying the wedding; you're going to have to help me out,' I said.

'I don't know where all your money has gone Bro, or what the fuck you're doing with it, but I can't help you; it's starting to really piss me off. I'll have to see if I can borrow some off Jen's mum and dad. I'll call you back,' Richard said abruptly and he put the phone down on me.

I went and had a cigarette and, before I'd finished my cigarette, my phone rang.

'Hey, Rich,' I said.

'Listen, I've borrowed £1,000.00 off Jen's mum and dad, but that's your fucking lot. You're financially strangling everyone; you won't be getting any more—Jen and I are fed up with it. I'm gonna go and I'll catch you later; I'm meant to be enjoying my wedding and instead I'm dealing with you,' he replied and hung up on me again.

'Okay, so now you only owe me £52,000.00,' I thought.

He made me feel inferior and I hated that I had to grovel to him. It made me feel awful begging for my own money and the conversation was really awkward. Me and Lizzy took our time to get ready and didn't turn up at the hotel until midnight, so I didn't see my brother and Jen until the morning; there wasn't much time to chat while we rushed around getting ready to go to the airport. Rich and I had a huge group of friends and there were 82 people attending this wedding. I didn't get a chance to catch up with Rich properly and kept in the background to let him enjoy his time. He was greeting friends and family; well, Jen's side of the family, should I say? On my side, there was only me and Lizzy, and my cousin and his wife and kids.

We were staying at a hotel in a town called Riva Del

Garda, which is situated in Northern Italy. The town itself is so beautiful and surrounded by the Garda Mountains. It really is stunning and very romantic. I wanted to put any negative vibes behind me and just crack on and have a great time, plus I had a job to do—I was the best man.

Richard had booked this quaint little restaurant on our first night; it was small and only catered for a handful of guests because it was quite exclusive. There was a small group of us just before the masses arrived the following day. When the time was right, I was going to pull Richard aside and have a quick word.

At the restaurant, everyone was in good spirits and on great form. I got up and went outside for a cigarette and Richard followed me; the cobbled streets were barely visible, but looked warm from the glow of the dimmed street lamps. The lights carried on into the distance and through the dark alley ways that were leading in all directions; you could see street signs dotted up all over the place for different bars and restaurants.

'What do you think to the place so far, Bro?' Rich said excitedly.

It was just me and him and this seemed like the right time to say something.

'Yeah, mate, it is lovely round here. Listen, while I've got you to myself, I just wanted to say something. I feel things haven't been quite right lately, but I want to put all of that aside. I know there is an issue with the finances, but I'm your best man and I'm going to be your best man. I want the best for you; you're my brother and I love you.'

Things weren't sitting quite right with me, particularly the situation with my money, but for now, I was prepared to park everything up until I got home.

It was the first time in a while that I'd seen my brother's eyes glaze over; I think he was emotional with everything that was going on.

'Okay, Bro, don't be silly; come here,' he said as he put his arm around me; we hugged and he kissed me on the cheek.

The following day, Rich and Jen had arranged transport from the airport for all of our friends and guests; they had arranged two coaches that arrived at our hotel the day before the wedding. There were bags, suitcases and people dotted about all over the place.

The wedding day was upon us and the turnout was spectacular; everybody was dressed up to the nines. The day itself consisted of two separate venues. Walking to our first venue, through the cobblestone streets of Malcesine Village, we made our way to Malcesine Castle. As I stood there on the rooftop of the castle it was so magical, everywhere I looked was decorated with flowers. We had a 360-degree view over Lake Garda—it really was stunning—and it wasn't long before everyone was in position and the string quartet started to play. I was standing next to Rich as we watched Jen and her dad approach from the distance; they finally reached us and Jen took her position standing next to Richard so that they could declare their vows. After the ceremony had taken place, there was champagne, food and aperitifs served as waiters rushed around looking after guests, or you could mingle and explore the castle. Richard and Jen had hired a company to film their wedding day and a wedding photographer who followed them around all day long.

Richard and Jen also hired a beautifully dressed up Fiat 500 to whisk them away through the narrow cobblestone streets of Malcesine Village and they would meet all of the guests at the harbour where a ferry was waiting to take us to our second venue. There was champagne on the boat as we cruised along Lake Garda to the next venue.

It was the first time after the ceremony that Richard and I had a moment to talk properly. There was a platform that we were standing on at the back of the ferry.

'Congratulations, Rich,' I said as I gave him a hug and a kiss.

'What do you think to the wedding so far?' he asked me.

He knew very well how amazing it was and was just looking for my acknowledgement that he'd done well. There is a slight difference between Richard and me in that I look for his approval, but he looks for me to massage his ego.

'Honestly, Rich, it's amazing; I'm proud of you,' I said as we clinked our glasses of champagne.

'What do you think everyone else thinks?' he asked me.

'Richard, honestly, mate your wedding is impressive so don't worry about that,' I replied.

I'll never forget that moment as I stood by my brother on the back of the ferry. We clinked our glasses of champagne and I stared into the distance as we cruised by the Garda Mountains; it was so picturesque but, in the back of my mind, I had mixed feelings of happiness and at the same time was feeling a little deflated. I had no doubt that Richard would pay me back when he'd sold Olney—that wasn't the issue—but it was just the way that he'd gone about it.

I'm standing here clinking champagne glasses with my brother and this whole event is being funded with my money, from the champagne that everyone is drinking to those Gucci fucking loafers on his feet. I'd paid for all of it.

In essence, and as the old saying goes, he'd robbed Peter to pay Paul.

This happens in business all the time and there is nothing necessarily wrong with juggling funds this way, but it is risky as you are taking money from one source to give it to another. This is fine as long as you can, and intend to, pay the money back or pay Peter back going by the saying.

Anyway, Jen's brother-in-law's timing couldn't have been better as he came bouncing out to the back of the ferry with a joint in his hand.

It was the first time I'd really spoken to or seen him.

'Jesus, you two don't half look the same; here, try this. It's good shit,' he said as he passed Rich half a joint.

Smoking cannabis has never been my thing, I just don't get along with it, but we both had a drag and I flicked the roach into the sea as we moored up at our final destination, The Grand Hotel Riva.

Rich and Jen had hired the entire top floor, including the rooftop. The table setting and decor was exquisite and the food was amazing, all 9 courses of it.

In between courses, the best man speeches were imminent and I saw my cousin sneak out onto the rooftop and down his bottle of beer for some Dutch courage. This made me laugh, a deer in the headlights sprang to mind.

To give him his dues, he did a good job and without realising it, he had prepped me up nicely to take centre stage.

I had made notes which felt scripted, but I really kept questioning myself if I should actually use them; it made me feel robotic, so I slid the notes under my plate and stood up and walked around the table to the front so everyone could see me and I just went with what came to me in the moment.

'Thanks for that Cuz. Just like a fluffer on a porn set, let's get into the main event,' I said laughing.

I delivered a very punchy best man's speech with a lot of humour and it was heart-felt where I needed it to be; I'm a bit backward in coming forward sometimes, but if you listen carefully, you will see everything has a meaning and I will go full circle, but it will tie up nicely at the end. Just like this book, there is a method to the madness.

I wanted to make people laugh but, most importantly, I wanted them to know how important my brother was to me and I'd hoped that I could touch people in a way that they might even shed a tear, and I did just that as I started to wrap up my speech.

'So, will you please join me in raising a glass to the happy couple Richard and Jennifer Potter. I am the best man, but for today at least my brother is the better man,' I said.

Richard had got out of his chair and was making his way over to me and by the time I'd finished that final sentence, he snatched the microphone out my hands.

'Gimme that; let someone else have a go,' he shouted down the mic as he gave me a massive hug. We were both hugging each other and laughing.

The atmosphere in the room was electric and everyone was having a great time. After all of the food and a short timeout, it was time for the DJ. Rich and Jen took to the dance floor and started dancing together as the first wedding song started to play; the song came booming out of the speakers, that distinctive sound as the piano starts to play. It was John Legend's song, 'All of Me'. It wasn't long until everyone hit the dance floor; everybody partied and danced until the very end.

The fairy-tale wedding was over and I was back at mine at 'The Hayloft.' Everything was going to plan with XS Homes Limited and the property looked likely to exchange and complete on the 14th of July 2015. I had been back on the tables gambling and had won enough money to keep me going for a while; I could be down one moment and a couple of spins later, I could be thousands of pounds up.

A friend of mine had booked a nice hotel and tickets to go and see Fleetwood Mac on the 9th of June at Genting Arena in Birmingham, but he couldn't make it and he called me up to see if I was interested. Fleetwood Mac wasn't my cup of tea really, but I knew some of their songs and I wanted to spend some time just me and Lizzy as I'd been distant lately.

Foolishly, I didn't sleep that night and Lizzy was due to pick me up at mine to go to the concert. I still had some cocaine which was in the kitchen cupboard; it was in a sealed bag, sitting inside a mug. As I was getting ready, I told myself to behave but just like a mermaid luring a sailor to his doom with their enchanting music and beautiful singing voice the coke had got my attention. As soon as it crossed my mind, there was no going back: it was beckoning me over to the kitchen cupboard.

'What harm could a couple of lines do?' I thought.

Racking up a couple of lines as quick as I could in my usual spot on the kitchen worktop, I was aware Lizzy could pull up any second so I locked the front door.

Racing back into the kitchen and rolling up a note, I sniffed two lines—I felt good. I was ready for action as I grabbed my phone and cigarettes and, just as I got to the front door, I thought, 'Ah fuck it, I'm taking it with me.' So, I grabbed the bag of coke and put it down the side of my sock.

It was a pretty decent sized bag of gear. Moments later, Lizzy pulled up and I jumped into the car.

'Hiya babe, how's it going?' I said.

'I'm good, babe, you?' she replied.

'Yeah, I'm okay. You excited about today and have you kissed me lately?' I asked her.

She leant over and kissed me and we pulled off the drive and headed off on our adventure.

I had gone out of my way to keep certain things from Lizzy, but she was aware that I was gambling and perhaps dabbled a little bit here and there. She certainly didn't approve, but trusted I had it under control. I have always been an open book, upfront and honest, but when it came to coke and gambling, I hadn't advertised that it was something that I liked to do in my spare time; well, it was becoming nearly all of the time.

Deep down, I knew she wasn't stupid, but she loved me dearly and perhaps chose to overlook some of my questionable behaviour and especially because I don't like being told what to do, she would rather not make waves with me. My attitude was 'you do you and I'll do me' and as long as no one is getting hurt and we are having a good time then what's the problem? But maybe I'd missed the point because there certainly were days that I was definitely feeling hurt and most definitely there were days that I wasn't having a good time.

We were making our way to Birmingham and we had to stop for petrol.

'Result, I'll get another line in,' I thought as she filled up the car and I went in to pay, making a detour into the toilets at the petrol station.

Travelling down the motorway, we started to notice signs saying that the Fleetwood Mac concert was cancelled.

'Christian, take a look online to see if it's cancelled or what's going on?' she asked me.

'Yes, babe looking at this they've cancelled due to illness and it's being rescheduled.' I replied.

'Oh, shit what we going to do? We are nearly at the hotel,' she said.

'It's cool babe, don't panic. I'll take you for dinner and we'll go for drinks; It's not a big deal, I bet we'll have a better time out on the town,' I said.

We arrived at our hotel in Birmingham and the hotel was really cool; we checked in and literally threw our stuff down, chucked on some different clothes and went out. I took her to a lovely restaurant for something to eat, even though my appetite was shot to pieces and after, we hit the bars and clubs in the town centre. We were having such a good time and always loved dancing together; we were laughing and enjoying each other's company until the early hours when we headed back to the hotel.

Lizzy fell into bed so I seized my opportunity to do a couple more lines. I walked into the bathroom and didn't even shut the door as I put the toilet seat down and straddled the toilet backwards; I was facing the wall. I'd never done that before, but facing the wall meant I could use the cistern as a table, so I poured out most of the coke that I had left onto it and racked up a couple of lines. I remember thinking, 'That looks like a pretty big pile of coke.' I suddenly came over so tired and exhausted so I lent backwards while still sitting down to look at myself in the mirror. Staring at myself in the mirror, I also remember thinking, 'Fucking hell, I'm really tired.' As I faced the wall again, preparing myself to do the lines of gear, that's the last thing I remember and all of a sudden, I woke up being slapped around the head by Lizzy and all sorts of commotion and shouting was going on. Confused and dazed, it only took me a second to realise that I hadn't even managed to sniff those lines and I'd fallen asleep while sitting on the toilet. I was face first in a pile of gear and Lizzy was going ballistic as I jumped to attention.

'Fuck, how am I gonna salvage this?' I thought.

There was no stopping her, she was on a mission to get out of that room as quickly as possible and was gone in a flash.

I sat on the bed and the first thing that crossed my mind was, 'For fuck sake, Christian if you'd have just summoned the energy to sniff those fucking lines on the way down, you might not have face planted into all of it and fallen asleep; that would have saved you a lot of drama.'

Lizzy had left and I was fucked. I was so ashamed and disappointed with myself being found like that but, to be truthful, I was also thinking, 'Okay it's not ideal, but we both had a good time and it would have been easier if she had of been a bit gentler with me.' This sort of reaction is what forces people to hide things in the first place, but I accept it's not a good look.

I gathered my bits and made my way into the hotel reception to work out my next move and there she was. Lizzy had pulled up outside the front of the hotel and it felt like even her car was snarling at me. I walked over and she wound down the window.

'Get in the fucking car,' she shouted at me.

I opened the back door and lay across the back seat. There were no words on the journey home and it was a nightmare— honestly, a fucking nightmare.

This is when Lizzy first realised that I was doing a lot more coke then she first thought; not a once a month thing, but a more, on it than off it, scenario.

Chapter 24
A Brief Interlude

It was a rocky few days and Lizzy wouldn't even talk to me and when she did, they were only one-word answers. It took some time before things were on the mend after my indiscretion.

I was feeling fragile and decided to pull it together, I needed to catch up on my sleeping and eating and get back into the gym and generally just sort myself out. I received a call from Richard, to make matters worse, and I knew straight away from the tone of his voice that something was up.

'Bro, I've got you on speaker and Jen's here as well,' he said to me down the phone; his voice was very stern.

'Hey Rich, Jen what's up?' I asked them.

'I logged into your bank account and was checking what you've been up to; I wanted to see why you're spending so much money,' he replied.

Richard, since I can remember, had always known all of my passwords and usernames; in fact, Richard could have stepped into my shoes whenever he wanted. He looked like me, had access to everything and anything about me: my passport, my driving licence and my banking information, he could even do my signature. He could have even travelled using my passport if he wanted to. Identical twins are exactly the same down to their DNA; the only slight difference between Richard and I are our fingerprints.

He was my twin brother and I trusted him implicitly, there was never any reason for me to care or think anything about it.

'Hang on; you're calling me up on speaker to tell me, you and Jen have been sifting through my bank account?' I said angrily.

'I can see you've been gambling a lot,' he quickly replied.

'So fucking what! So you two think you can go through my bank accounts without my permission and spy on me and then have the audacity to call me up and you want me to explain to you what I've been spending my money on! Is that what you're saying? What's laughable about that is that you owe me money,' I replied.

'No, it's not that, we just worry about you—that's all,' Jen said interjecting.

Jen had adopted a softer tone to try and keep things calm, as Rich went in on me; calm is not one of Richard's specialities. He does not have the ability to speak rationally if he doesn't like what's happening in the moment as he shouted down the phone.

'Listen to me, Jen and I have been chatting and we're phoning to tell you if you don't sort it out, we've both decided we're going to disown you,' he screamed.

'No, you listen to me you fucking idiots, you two clowns think you can phone me up on speaker and team up on me because I don't fit into your perfect little world, which is all a facade,' I said.

'What's that supposed to mean?' Rich replied.

I was raging and far too angry to get upset or tearful at this stage, but they had really hurt my feelings. What had really bothered me is the thought of the two of them sitting at home colluding together before calling me and making a pact that if the call doesn't go the way they want, they could just throw me away. They were calling because I didn't fit their mould and they were doing it together as a show of strength against me—well, fuck that. Richard just thinks if he doesn't like something, he will just throw it away, get rid of it or disown it and move on.

'Bro, do you know how embarrassing it is for us with the way you are behaving? Why do you think I changed my surname? To get away from you; I've always hated being a twin,' he shouted at me.

'Embarrassing for whom? I couldn't give a fuck mate,' I replied.

Now I am seeing red, but I spoke very calmly for maximum effect rather than scream down the phone which is what I really wanted to do.

'Even at my worst, I'm still more capable then both of you put together so let me tell you what's going to happen. I will pull 'XS Homes' and do it on my own; I don't need either of you. I'm bringing the finances, I found the property and I'll fucking disown you,' I said.

Jen interjected again, 'Christian, Rich doesn't mean what he just said, I think he struggles to get his point across because he cares so much and things are getting out of hand.'

'If I hear the word disown one more time, I'll disown you two; you can't just throw people away when you feel like it. The only reason this deal exists is because of me so both of you go and fuck yourselves. Whatever I do in my own time with my money is none of your business. I call the shots and Rich is just a paper boy, I can do this without you, but choose not to because I thought we were a team.'

Richard then went to speak and interrupt me, 'No Bro, let me finish; most of the wealth you have is because of me but we made it together and you're fucking out of order treating me this way and, forgetting that, do you know how much it hurts my feelings?' I said.

'Yeah, okay, bro I get it, I understand,' he replied.

I put the phone down and started ranting to myself in the kitchen while I grabbed a cigarette. Honestly, what a fucking liberty, these two calling me up on speaker and talking to me like that. I sent them packing, but I was aware that as soon as I'd threatened to pull the deal they changed their tune; these two were coming at me and I felt there was no room for me in their team, which is what Jen wanted I'm sure—to try and drive a wedge between us. I was aware of it as I stood on my doorstep staring up into the sky as I muttered, 'Fucking clowns,' under my breath and took a drag of my cigarette.

From here onwards, things are about to get really serious. My identical twin brother is about to turn on me and become the biggest enemy I will ever face in my life and I will fight against an array of problems while battling to stay alive.

Chapter 25
Pantomime Gangster

It was around five o' clock in the morning on the 14th of July 2015, knackered and with blood-shot eyes, I poured the last of the cocaine that I had out onto the kitchen work top. There were two empty bags to my right while I made two lines out of what was left and sniffed a line up each nostril. I'd only just finished the last line when, suddenly, there was a large bang on my front door; it sounded like a fist against my door.

'What the fuck was that?' I thought.

It startled me so I went to the front door and looked through my peep hole; there were two guys standing there. I took a step back and then leaned forward and looked through the peep hole again. I didn't recognise either of these two men. On the main road, I could just about make out a couple of vehicles parked a little further up the road to my right and maybe another vehicle to the left.

They knocked the door again, but the next hit was a lot harder than the first time. 'Am I about to have a fight,' I thought as I methodically went through my mind like a rolodex trying to recall anyone I'd upset recently. I hadn't had a fight in a while and couldn't think of anyone that I'd pissed off enough to knock on my front door at this hour and it wasn't the police as they had plain clothes on; my mind was running a million miles an hour.

I rushed into the kitchen, grabbed the two empty bags of coke and ran upstairs to my en-suite and flushed them down the toilet; there was nothing else here to worry about. All the shutters were down around my ground floor so from the outside it would have been impossible to see in. I ran down the stairs, skipping steps, and positioned myself in the kitchen while this was going on—which, in reality, had only been a couple of minutes at most—and the coke had started to kick in and I was feeling excited, but not in a good way; my adrenaline had started to simmer too.

Again, they banged on the door; this time, even harder and using a lot more force. It felt like the whole house breathed in and then exhaled back out. Then I heard a man's a voice come from outside my kitchen window.

'The lights on in the kitchen there's definitely someone in,' the man said.

'Okay, so that's three men; two at the front door and one at the kitchen window,' I thought to myself.

I approached the peep hole again and saw the flicker of another man; he was loitering by the right-hand side of my house. 'Fuck, okay, right so that's four men surrounding my house.' There was no way anyone could be at the back, it was impossible for anyone to get round the back of my house because the property backed up against a twenty foot wall.

If I had wanted to, I could have climbed out of my bedroom window and stood on the top of this wall and escaped.

'I am, I'm about to have a fight with at least four men and I don't even know who the fuck they are,' I thought.

It felt like forever but, in reality, it had still only been a matter of minutes. I reached for the front door handle, my adrenaline had fully kicked in and I was in fight mode. As I grabbed the door handle, a voice bellowed at me through the door.

'If you don't open this door right now, we're going to break it in.'

I took a deep breath and opened the front door, I had only opened the door by about an inch before I was rushed. The door flew open and these men came through the door one after the other at me, badges in hand shouting.

'It's the police, don't move, and stay where you are.'

I was surrounded by four plain-clothed officers; they cuffed me and went through protocol while another four people followed in after them. In a matter of seconds, there were eight people inside my house in total and a number of cars on my drive. They started to wander round my house. One of them was a giant of a man; his head almost hit the ceiling as he walked into my kitchen. He was wearing a black suit, and I couldn't quite recognise the first few words he'd said to a woman that was with him—they spoke between themselves and I thought he was speaking German. As it transpires, he was and he had been sent by the German authorities to overlook the raid and ensure the operation was carried out successfully. This man stood there leaning against a wall next to the entrance of my kitchen; he was watching everyone rushing around. He looked so pleased with himself; he had a big smug smile on his face as he stood there and then just stared at me.

I'm now handcuffed and the officer that I first saw on the door step started talking to me. Bearing in mind I'm high, drowned in adrenaline and struggling to catch my breath. Sometimes your adrenaline can be your own worst enemy as it had saturated my body and I couldn't calm down; I was struggling to breathe. I couldn't take in a word he was saying.

'Hang on a second; let me catch my breath a minute. Slow down for me so I can understand what's happening,' I said.

It felt so busy, there was so much going on and they had started to dismantle and rummage through my house. I can't recall the exact order of things, it's a little hazy and I was under the influence of alcohol and cocaine at the time, but I remember flash backs like snippets on a movie reel.

'Christian Govan, today we are executing a European Arrest Warrant, an extradition request has been sent to us from Germany and we have a search warrant issued by the courts in London to search your house and car for anything that could be considered as evidence in a case against you for tax evasion in Germany. I take it that's your Porsche on the drive?' the officer said to me.

I zoned out and stood there cuffed letting them do whatever they were here to do. I was shown all sorts of paperwork and informed I'm about to be transported to the police station in Stevenage where I will be booked in and processed. I knew that whatever is going on right now, it was best not to say anything until I'd spoken to a solicitor; the police as polite as they were are not my friends and, anyway, I could barely string a sentence together—I was still in shock.

They performed the usual checks, and asked if I had any drugs or weapons on me or in the house.

'Thank fuck I'd flushed those empty bags of coke; I would have been charged with possession of a controlled substance to make matters worse,' I thought, but right now that would have been the least of my worries.

'Hold on, stop. I don't understand what's about to happen to me now,' I said.

'We are taking you to the police station in Stevenage to be processed; they are already waiting for us and then you will be going to court in London today and possibly flown out this evening and detained in Germany,' the officer replied.

I didn't know what the fuck they were talking about or what any of this was about. The first thing I needed to do was gather my senses as I couldn't deal with anything in my current state so I didn't ask anything further or say another word. These officers were part of an elite task force and not your ordinary police officers; one thing I did know was that this was serious.

Handcuffed, I was walked out of my house by two detectives and put into what looked like any ordinary vehicle and driven away. I was just going through the motions; I was in shock and just stunned as I looked back at my house. The front door was left wide open while they turned my house upside down and it was just a blur as we pulled away; the fuzzy images of people already rooting around in my car, the doors and boot were wide open as we turned the corner and headed to Stevenage.

On the way to Stevenage, I could hear them discussing between each other about the other teams who had gone out this morning. I picked up on what they were talking about, they had picked up seven out of the nine people they had gone out to arrest today.

They had co-ordinated and executed a number of search warrants and arrests. This was all part of something so much bigger.

As we reached Stevenage, these two officers were ahead of time and pulled into a McDonalds and parked up.

'Would you like anything to eat?' one of them asked me.

'I'm fine, thanks,' I replied.

I sat in the car while one of them went into McDonalds and the other one stood guard over me.

Twenty minutes before, I was at home doing a couple of lines of coke and now I was sitting in a carpark outside McDonalds in Stevenage, handcuffed and under arrest. I couldn't get my head round it all.

I was on autopilot as I was processed at the police station in Stevenage. I was allowed to make one call and I called my brother, but it was still so early in the morning, I didn't know if he'd pick up or simply ignore the phone because I assumed it would come up with a No Caller ID—thank God he picked up the call.

He sounded so sleepy, 'Rich it's me; don't talk just listen. I've just been arrested and I'm being taken to a court in London, shortly. Keep your phone on you at all times and answer any calls you receive as it could be me. I'll be in touch again as soon as I can,' then I hung up on him.

The officers that had taken me from my home were my chaperones as I was led back to the car in cuffs and driven to London. I just stared out of the car window as we travelled to court; this situation was so surreal. Driving through the grotty streets of London, I now felt a million miles away from home. I was entering the unknown; I didn't know what the court was called or where it was, even though I had probably been told a number of times, but nothing was sinking in.

We pulled up at the back of these large buildings and waited for this huge green door to roll aside and let us through; it was the back entrance to the court.

Walking in with the officers, I was processed again; the handcuffs were taken off and I was placed in a holding cell.

There are a number of cells that lie hidden underneath the court itself.

I sat there in disbelief and was starting to feel rough as fuck; when was this going to stop? I just wanted my bed. I'd been ripped out of my house and everything that was familiar to me was gone. I felt really uncomfortable in my own skin and my anxiety was kicking in big time.

I can't remember if I asked for a lawyer or was just given one and I couldn't tell you how long I'd sat in that holding cell for, but I do know that I wasn't put in front of a judge till late that afternoon.

A duty solicitor had been appointed to me. The hatch on my cell door opened and a warm and friendly voice spoke to me.

'Christian, my name is Lorenzo and I'm the duty solicitor who will be looking after you okay; I'll be with you shortly.'

I looked up at him and said, 'Lorenzo, how bad is this?'

'I'm not going to lie, Christian, it is 60 million euros bad,' he replied.

I knew from the moment I heard those words that I was in serious trouble. The gravity of the situation had started to sink in and as hard as I fought it, I started to cry. I knew I hadn't done anything wrong and shouldn't even be here, but that didn't bring me any comfort because right now I was sitting in a holding cell, underneath the court when I should have been at home in bed.

When I first got in front of Lorenzo and we spoke, I said to him, 'Hi, Lorenzo, how are you?'

'More to the point, Christian, how are you?' he replied.

'I don't understand what's happening and what I'm doing here,' I said; I was feeling so overwhelmed.

Lorenzo explained to me that the German authorities were accusing me of assisting in tax evasion and that the amount lost was in excess of 60 million euros.

I was at the mercy of a juggernaut, the powerhouse coming after me was Germany.

In an instant, I had two fights to deal with. The first was to fight the European Arrest Warrant (EAW) that was issued against me. This was incredibly difficult, almost impossible, and the second fight which was running alongside the EAW at the same time was the case against me in Germany for tax evasion. The final choice was that I could go to Germany to try and resolve this and face the charges. I would be held on remand and, if found guilty, possibly spend the next 8 to 10 years in a German prison. I was not guilty of anything so that was not an option and the thought of it terrified me; I don't care how big and strong anyone thinks they are, this situation will rock any man—I had to try and stop Germany taking me away.

Lorenzo explained to me what was about to happen next and that he would do his best to protect me as his client. I was instructed that under no circumstances when I get in front of the judge must I say the word, 'Yes'. I must say the word, 'No'. This was because there was a plane ready and waiting on the tarmac and the judge was going to ask me if I wanted to go and face the charges in Germany. If I said 'Yes', I would be immediately taken to the airport and flown to Germany and remanded in custody in a German prison until a later date when a trial or sentencing hearing will take place.

'My main priority, Christian, is to get you out of here and then take this step by step; there is no doubt you're in a lot of trouble and dependant on the judge's decision, you may be remanded in custody here in the UK or released on bail,' Lorenzo said.

'Lorenzo, can you please do something for me? Can you call my brother and explain to him what's going on and check he's okay?' I said.

'Yes, Christian, I will do that for you,' he replied.

I was returned back to my holding cell and waited to be called to go to court. It was all so surreal and I was trying to break it all down into smaller pieces in my head so I could start protecting myself. I was not all right and just summoning everything I had to try and cope, but I was running on empty.

'Okay, all I need to do right now is say no and then hopefully I can go home,' I thought—that's all I wanted—all I wanted to do was go home.

I can't remember if I was handcuffed again when they unlocked my cell door and led me to the courtroom, but we travelled along these long underground corridors. It felt like you were in the belly of the beast and you were gradually making your way up to the surface.

The custody officer that was taking me to court stopped at the end of a corridor and pressed a button on the wall calling for the lift. I was just standing there as the lift made its way down to us when a group of people started gathering behind me; they were waiting for the same lift. The lift doors opened and we all squeezed in. I didn't even realise it at the time, but these were the other six people that were arrested today along with me and I only realised this because these people walked into the same courtroom as me. I was standing there next to these six strangers, all of us in a line and silent now facing the judge.

What happened next is a blur, but I know that when the judge asked me the question, 'Are you prepared to leave today and answer the case against you in Germany?' I firmly, but politely, replied, 'NO.'

I struggle to recall the memory of even being inside that courtroom or exactly what was said. I've tried so hard, but it's just not there. I do know this though, when I was released on bail, I thought I was going home.

There were a number of bail conditions set out by the judge which I'll get to as I go along, but what I hadn't realised was the security had been set at £10,000.00. This amount had to be paid before they would release you back into the real world and, until it was paid, I would be remanded in prison.

There is a process and you can't just hand the judge your debit card and walk out of the court there and then and, anyway, I didn't have 10K. I know this now, but I didn't know this at the time and I was learning as these events were unfolding. It still hadn't sunk in and I still think I'm going home shortly.

I was taken back to the holding cell and I'm sure there was a conversation with Lorenzo and that he was now in close contact with my brother. I sat there in the holding cell until a vehicle was ready to take me to Wandsworth Prison.

I was crushed, I wasn't going home; I was going to prison. I was just a robot by this point and doing as I was told; I was there in body, but not in mind.

I was placed into a secure vehicle that transports prisoners between court and prison—what's known as a meat wagon. The vehicle has a number of separate compartments all with their own doors and a metal pole that you're cuffed to, just like a hanging piece of meat in a butcher's shop. That's what I was right now, a piece of meat; my hollow and bloodshot eyes stared aimlessly through the darkened glass of the window, sat in my little compartment which was just about big enough for one person as we traversed the streets of London. I could see shop owners of little newsagents' and stores closing their shutters and locking up for the day as we drove by; I was jealous of them, they were free and walking the streets. There's still daylight, but I didn't even know what time it was anymore; I was switched off.

Chapter 26
I Used to be Worth My Weight in Gold

We arrived at Wandsworth Prison. Wandsworth was a huge depressing looking building, a concrete fortress and the entrance was in the centre of these two perfectly aligned towers that sat on either side. The entrance reminded me of a drawbridge; it was dark green in colour as it slowly rolled to the right allowing enough space for the meat wagon to drive through. Once we were on the other side, it immediately started to close again behind us, slowly rolling and grinding.

'Fuck me, this is really happening. I'm being put in prison,' I thought.

The meat wagon eventually pulled up outside a building within the prison. Once I got through that main entrance, there were buildings everywhere and in every direction that I looked.

'Time to switch myself on; I don't know what the fuck I'm walking into, but I need to be alert and aware of everything because everything right now is a threat to me,' I thought.

One by one, we were taken out of the meat wagon and walked into this building; there was a waiting room and you are gradually processed. I would describe it as the front desk. You are then taken through another large metal door that is opened and locked behind you and then you have to go through security. Similar to what you would think of when you go through an airport, but just not as exciting; a line of people in single file slowly moving along a conveyor belt of officers who ask you to empty your pockets then another officer takes you into a side room where you are stripped. By the time you reach the end, you are handed a sealed bag which contains all of your belongings, including a plastic plate and plastic mug, some rolling tobacco and Rizla paper and a phone card which contained £1 credit on it. The officer dealing with me was kind enough to allow me to keep my box of cigarettes that I had in my pocket.

'I think you'll need these, but keep it quiet,' he said.

I was immediately aware of the clunking of heavy-metal doors and the jingling of keys before I entered the wing that I was assigned to. Walking through the prison, I looked up and could see security netting stretched from wall to wall. I didn't get past one door without the other inmates shouting or hammering at their doors as I was led to my cell. The other six strangers that had stood with me in court were all paired up and had asked to be cell mates; I thought that was strange and I didn't want to be anywhere near them. I was put in a cell with a Moroccan who was inside for burglary.

As I entered my cell, I thought living out of the shed at Therfield was bad enough, but that paled in comparison to this cell and it wasn't much bigger than the shed either. Thick obscured glass squares for a window, a smashed-up bunk bed, a broken cabinet and, at the bottom of the bunk bed, a metal toilet and sink in the corner of the room. There was a green plastic shower curtain for a little privacy. This curtain was only the length of the toilet and looked like it had been hacked to bits by Freddy Kruger; there were more rips than curtain.

The Moroccan burglar didn't speak much English which

was good for me as I had no intention of making small talk. I placed my bag on the bottom of the bed and sat down for a moment to think. I needed to reach my brother; it was around seven o' clock in the evening and I was allowed to make a phone call. Picking up the card that was given to me with £1 credit on it, I went to the nearest phone and called Richard.

I called Rich and it just rang until it went through to his answering machine, so I tried again after waiting a couple of minutes and the same thing happened. I was running out of credit and only had enough to make one more call, so I called Lizzy and thank fuck she picked up.

'Babe it's me; listen, I haven't got long and I can't explain everything right now, but I'm in Wandsworth Prison and I can't reach Rich. Right now, there is nothing more important then you getting hold of him and getting me the fuck out of here; also, tell him to call my solicitor, Lorenzo. I've got to go, I'm running out of credit, I love you,' I said.

'Yeah right until the next time,' she replied.

I didn't even know what that meant and then the phone cut off. All I wanted was to hear those words, I wanted Lizzy to tell me she loved me too. It would have helped me and given me a little comfort, but I walked back to my cell disheartened and I felt alone.

I could not believe that Richard hadn't picked up the phone and that it went through to his answering machine or the parting words between me and Lizzy. Back in my cell, I lay on my plastic mattress and tried to go to sleep. This was impossible because of the continuous pounding on the metal cell doors and the yelling and screaming coming from other inmates—it was unrelenting. The noise never once surrendered and, throughout the night, when one inmate stopped there was always another one ready to take his place. I hadn't even had the time to think about being banged up for something that I hadn't even done—I was raging and bubbling over on the inside, but was too exhausted. I looked up and stared aimlessly at the wooden slates above me of the bunk bed until the morning.

It was eleven o' clock in the morning and I was allowed out into the yard; you are locked up for twenty-three hours of the day and able to walk around the yard for one hour. This was quite overwhelming; I walked out into what looked like a large concrete space the size of a basketball court and it was surrounded by metal fencing. My 'spidey senses' were going haywire; there were so many inmates all over the place so I backed up against a wall. This way, I only had to worry about what was in front of me; there must have been at least 200 people and most of them were walking around the yard anti-clockwise. Round and round they went, some would drop out and others would join in; for one hour, continuously just walking round and round in a circle. I got the occasional look from people as they went past me. I felt extremely uncomfortable in this situation and vowed once I got back in that I wasn't going out there again. I can hold my own, but this was a lot to deal with. Returning back to my cell, I asked one of the prison officers if they could find out what was happening to me and then I spent the rest of the day locked in my cell. Once you're locked away from the outside world it really does feel like you've been forgotten about.

I stared out of the window in my cell, pushing my face up against the obscured glass blocks, I could see the yard and in the very distance, lads playing football. The world was still going on as normal without me. It wasn't until very late in the evening that I was told that my bail money had been paid, but they were still processing the paperwork and I wouldn't be released until sometime tomorrow. The money had been paid and Rich had come through for me, but I was going to have to spend another night in this shithole. It's hard to explain; I felt a sense of relief that I was going home, yet I felt nothing. Even though I was only in there for a short period of time, what I'd been through and going to prison literally sucked the life out of me; the emptiness and desperation—this place reeked of it and this life wasn't for me.

'I won't be caged up again, I'd rather be dead,' I thought.

I hadn't slept and it was exactly the same as the night before, it was now eleven o' clock in the morning, and I refused to go out into the yard and being released was dragging on. Just after lunchtime, a prison officer came to my cell and told me I was free to go.

I walked out of my cell and gave the Moroccan burglar my pouch of tobacco and Rizla paper. He looked so happy as he thanked me and shook my hand. It was like all his Christmases had come at once; he was touched that human kindness still existed because it was so lacking in this place. I was a civilian again and walked straight through the prison and down the stairs like I was just visiting; I could walk around freely and instantly felt a weight off my shoulders. I was processed and given a card which allowed me to travel on the train and they returned my belongings, which was a blue hoodie and a few coins. I was then led outside and walked along with a prison guard until I reached the big green drawbridge. I could see it clearer now than I could when I first got here and it had a normal sized door inside it. A door within a door, which they opened, and I walked out. The moment I went through the door it was like I had walked through an invisible barrier and the air instantly smelled different. I was now free, out on the street and standing there.

'What the fuck was that? What just happened to me?' I thought as I walked along the pavement.

I was like a normal person again and people were just passing me in the street going about their daily business completely oblivious to what I had just gone through. I stopped and looked back at Wandsworth Prison and it made me shudder; I felt dirty and violated by the experience—it had been incredibly traumatic and I hadn't slept for about 4 days. Even writing about it now has been really difficult for me, a feeling of immense sadness. I feel like I was actually there again.

Walking along the street, I found a payphone and called my brother.

'Rich, it's me,' I said.

'Ah thank fuck, are you okay? Bro where are you?' he asked me.

'I've literally just walked out of prison; I need to get out of here, Rich, and I don't really know where I am. I'm going to head for the nearest train station.'

'Okay, stop at Ashwell and I'll meet you at The Jester. Call me when you get there,' he said.

'Sure, I will do,' I replied.

I hung the phone up and headed towards the nearest train station and made my way to Ashwell. Once the train stopped at Ashwell, I was back in territory that I was familiar with and I called Rich.

A journey that should have taken him twenty minutes, only took him ten as he pulled up, parked the car and got out and ran towards me, giving me a big hug.

'Fucking hell, mate. I was so worried about you; are you okay? You look okay, not sure what I expected, but you don't look too bad,' he said.

It was so nice to see him and we had a lot to talk about. I had also been thinking while I was on the train journey back 'How did he manage to pay my bail money of £10,000.00 when he had been unable to pay me back any of the money that he owed me and why hadn't he picked up my phone calls whilst I was in prison?'

'Fucking hell, Rich, I don't know where to begin. It's been horrendous, absolutely shocking,' I said.

'Bro, one of the first things Lorenzo said to me when I spoke to him: he said Christian hasn't done this, in all my years I can tell; he doesn't know anything and I'll do everything I can to help him.'

'Why didn't you pick up the phone, Rich, when I called?' I asked him and he deflected.

'Trust me, Bro; I knew where you were at all times. Lorenzo's been amazing and I stayed in close contact with him; I couldn't tell you how many times we spoke, but it was a lot. Liz was worried she was really upset and frantically called me after she spoke to you in prison; she didn't realise how serious things were.'

I proceeded to tell Rich everything I knew, which wasn't very much at this stage as I hadn't gone through any of the paperwork. All I knew were three things: Germany, tax evasion and 60 million euros. I assumed the paperwork was waiting for me at my house after the raid. When I first spoke to Lorenzo, we had so much to deal with that we had to deal with things one step at a time. The first step was to get me out of prison and then we would approach everything else step by step.

Richard certainly didn't shed any light on the situation and remained tight lipped, but he did proceed to tell me that on the first day I was locked up that he had exchanged and completed on 'The Grove' at Litlington and we now owned it, well XS Homes Limited owned it.

'Fucking hell, Rich; I hadn't even thought about that. What have you done? So we exchanged and completed on the same day that I got arrested and put in prison?' I asked him.

'Yer, I had all the paperwork ready so I just told Lizzy's Mum where to send the money. I didn't tell her you'd been locked up though,' Rich said.

'Ah fuck me, mate, this isn't ideal,' I replied.

'I had to do that or we might have lost the sale,' Rich said.

'How the fuck am I going to explain that, Rich? Jesus, I'll have to deal with it another day,' I said.

I was so tired and desperately in need of sleep, so many questions and so few answers—this was a minefield. I asked Rich to take me home. Walking through my front door was strange and it was eerily quiet; the house looked the same, but felt different. With my OCD, I knew that every single item in my house had been touched or moved in some way; they had gone through the entire place. There was a bunch of paperwork on the side and a receipt of the personal possessions that had been taken away from my house, including my phone, some gambling receipts and a Belkin wireless stick which is used for a wireless mouse. I assume they thought this was a memory stick.

'The UK has raided my house looking for evidence to assist Germany with their case against me, that would make sense seeing as there were people from Germany here,' I thought.

I wasn't concerned about this at all, I knew there was nothing of any evidential value because I hadn't done anything wrong, so that side of things simply didn't worry me and I pushed the paperwork to the side for now. I did need a new phone though, so that's going to be my first job tomorrow.

It wasn't long before Lizzy's car pulled up on the drive and I opened the front door as soon as she pulled up; she wrapped her arms around me so tightly which felt really comforting. We both struggled to talk to each other without getting tearful so we just held one another—I couldn't speak.

'It'll be okay,' she whispered.

Lizzy didn't stay long; she was so quiet and I knew that she was struggling inside. I've always promised her that everything is fixable and always come to me because I'm the one to fix it, but even for me this looked impossible. I'd already been pushing my luck for a while and now I was really out of my depth. This was going to test our relationship and push us both to our breaking points.

I watched Lizzy pull off the drive while I had a cigarette then I went upstairs and fell into bed. It was the early hours and my mind was racing all night as I lay there—I could still hear the banging of the cell doors in my head and there was something that had been bugging me and had been at the back of my mind since I'd got out of prison.

'I needed to see that paperwork,' I thought.

I got out of bed and went downstairs to sift through some of the documents; the list of charges against me was longer than a receipt from Lizzy when she does the big shop. It was unfathomable and painful to look at. There were thirty odd charges in total, conspiracy to defraud, being a member of a criminal organisation, money laundering, tax evasion—the list was exhaustive. There was so much of it I didn't understand but there was a company name on there that I recognised, that's what I was looking for.

It was confusing because this company was not based in Germany and it was incredibly far reaching of Germany to swoop in and rip me out of my house, and based on the information that I was looking at, it demonstrated to me how powerful they were.

Chapter 27
What's Yours is Mine and What's Mine is Mine

One of my bail conditions was that I must have my mobile phone on me 24/7, but the police had taken my phone so this is the first thing that I got sorted out. My phone was my lifeline to the outside world. I surrendered my passport at the police station in Stevenage and had to sign in every single day between 8pm and 10pm at night and was under house arrest between 10pm and 3am in the morning, I had to wear an ankle tag. This made things tricky because it was an hour round trip to Stevenage so I couldn't exactly sign in just before 10pm and be back home in time for my curfew, so I always had to leave around 8pm to make sure I was back in good time; my nights were no longer my own as my ankle bracelet ensured I never left my house. While under house arrest, an invisible barrier covered my whole house and prevented me crossing the threshold of my front door. I was a prisoner in my own home, I was affected by what had happened to me and I think it started at my front door so I decided to sleep downstairs on an inflatable double bed. I'd been struggling to sleep and it gave me a little comfort to be nearer the front door, I felt like I had more control. Over the next few days, Richard was all over me; he kept phoning me up and pressuring me to sign over XS Homes Limited to him.

'Christian, you need to seriously think about signing the

company over to me; who knows what else Germany can do? And if you sign it all over to me, at least we know it's safe and I can look after it while you deal with them,' he told me.

Thinking back to my state of mind at the time, I was so vulnerable and unable to think straight, I didn't even discuss this with Lizzy.

'If Germany can do that to me, who knows what else they are capable of?' I thought.

I needed to protect everyone around me, so I reluctantly had to think about signing the business over to Richard. When I called Rich, he had already spoken to the accountant and was getting the paperwork raised. I was feeling really pressured and wanted everyone to back off, but also had a feeling that time was of the essence.

'Rich, I've been thinking about it and I know I need to protect everyone,' I said.

'You know it's the right decision and I'll look after everything. I'm your brother; I'll look out for you. I've also raised some paperwork between us that shows behind the scenes you're still involved. I know you're not gonna like the idea, but I was also thinking it would be a good idea to sell your house,' he said.

I was at home on a Wednesday afternoon when I got a call from Rich and he asked where I was, and in less than 5 minutes, there was a knock at my front door. I opened the door and Rich came bounding through.

'Hey bro, I got some paperwork for you to sign. I can't be long; Jesus, what the fuck is that inflatable bed doing there?' he asked me.

'That's where I sleep at the moment. What is it? What's the paperwork?' I asked him.

'It's your resignation for XS Homes Limited. We've got to do this; you know it's the right thing to do,' he said firmly to me.

I felt caught off guard and was resisting a little, I just needed more time.

'Bro, if you don't sign this and they take control of the business, then what?' he said to me.

'Yeah I get it Bro, but I feel like everything is being taken away from me,' I replied.

'Well, it's not really is it? 'Cos I will look after it for us and I'm just an extension of you,' he said.

'I feel like I have nothing, but I know it's the right thing to do; I want to protect everybody,' I replied. I was feeling really sad and unsure what to do.

Richard also had the paperwork with him that he had raised confirming that I still had a financial interest in XS Homes Limited. It was a contract and it was signed by Rich and Jen and he needed me to sign it too; it gave me a little comfort, but it wasn't ideal. I was beat and just signed all of the paperwork that Richard shoved in my face.

'Also, Bro, I know it's a touchy subject but we might as well sort it all out now. I paid your bail money so I'll deduct that off of what I owe you, so now it's £42,000.00 in total that I owe you and I was also thinking when your house sells, I can look after your money and keep it out of the way, but if the worst comes to the worst, I can use it and build you a little pot, for when you get out,' he said.

I couldn't believe what I was hearing, 'Get out? Get the fuck out of where? I won't be going to prison, Rich; I'd rather check out,' I said to him defiantly.

'Don't say that, Bro. Sorry I didn't mean to upset you, that upsets me. It's okay, we'll get you through this and I know you can fix it; I'm just looking out for you,' he said and with that, he gave me a quick hug and left again to race off to the accountants.

When Richard left my house, he had picked up all of the paperwork, including my copy of our agreement which confirmed that I was still involved with XS Homes Limited. I felt so lost and so lonely as he slammed my front door and sped off. Richard was keeping his distance from me I could tell; I could sense it.

It was astonishing to me the speed at which Richard got the paperwork raised, we had only just talked over the weekend and a couple of days later, he just turned up at mine armed with a pen. I was released from prison on the 16th of July 2015 and by the 22nd of July 2015, I had already signed the paperwork and had resigned from XS Homes Limited giving Richard all of my company shares; he had complete control. My resignation was executed on the same day that I signed the paperwork.

There wasn't much left for Rich to take; he hadn't paid me back my money from the renovation at Olney and now he owned a company with assets and cash worth £535,000.00. All that I had left was the money from my house, 'The Hayloft', and he was already trying to earmark that.

I felt beaten and wasn't functioning correctly to think about things logically; I was worried that Germany would try and take my house from me so I did put my house up for sale.

It had only been two weeks since my arrest and I came downstairs to make my breakfast; I went into the kitchen and stopped.

'What have I come down here for? I can't remember,' I

thought.

I didn't feel right, it was a feeling I was unfamiliar with as I stood there puzzled.

'Oh yeah, I was gonna have something to eat,' I said to myself.

It took me an eternity to sort my breakfast out and I was struggling to just make a bowl of Weetabix; I slammed my spoon on the kitchen worktop.

I was tearful as I just stared into the abyss and I felt hopeless and really sad, a darkness that was just attached to me it was blacker than my own shadow, a black that I'd never seen before and I couldn't shake it off. I've been down before, but not like this; this was different, it was the first time I became aware of feelings that I didn't want to be here anymore; I didn't want to live anymore. In the next coming days, I didn't want to get out of bed or face the world and when I did wake up, I woke up to my negative rolodex and would flip through it over and over in my mind. I had an 'I don't give a fuck anymore' attitude; 'what's the point?'

I fell down so much quicker than I ever thought I would; I couldn't take any more and I had no control of when my mind decided to give up on me. I hadn't realised it at the time, but this was the first time that severe depression had revealed itself to me. It wrapped itself around my mind, like Japanese knotweed, breaking me down and targeting my weak points. It had crept up on me stealthier than a hitman and now that it had arrived, thinking back, it was very noticeable. If I had just taken the time to listen to myself, it sounds odd, but just asked myself if I was doing okay then maybe I could have heeded the warning signs. You need to listen to your body; ask yourself how you are feeling. I didn't and now it's too late.

'I'm fucked, I'm well and truly broken.'

To top it off, I was losing everything while Richard was methodically taking or securing everything I owned.

'He's only trying to help me,' I tried to convince myself, but at the same time, I also had a feeling that made me feel unsure about everything.

I've always been super sensitive and wear my heart on my sleeve, but at the same time, I'm strong and can hold my own. I'm someone you just wouldn't want to fuck about with. I know my lifestyle before my arrest was not ideal and I hadn't helped myself, but I'd always thought I was so strong and could handle anything. However, since my arrest and only two weeks later, I was rapidly falling apart.

It was all a build-up of everything and everyone has a trigger or a point at which they will break. The trigger for me was my arrest and the crushing feeling from Germany that was weighing heavier and heavier on me as each day passed.

Me, Lizzy, Rich and Jen were the only ones that knew that I had been arrested and I wanted to keep it that way for a moment while I tried to make sense of this mess. I didn't know this at the time, but an employee who works for one of my closest friends, had been watching the drama unfold the day I got arrested, from her living room window; her house is over the road, and directly opposite mine.

My close friend, Chink, called me and asked, 'Is everything okay, mate? I've been meaning to call you, but thought you'd come to me if something was wrong.'

He was rocked to the core when I told him what had happened to me.

'I'm always here if you need me. Love you, mate; you do you and you know where I am if you need me and I won't say a word,' Chink said.

He had reached out to try and help me, but I turned it away and then there was my identical twin brother Richard. He had only been to my house once and that was with his bundle of paperwork and since then he'd left me and I just knew he was deliberately keeping his distance. There was only the odd phone call asking how I was; it was pathetic. I wanted him to grab me by the scruff of the neck and say, 'I've got you Bro. I'm gonna do everything in my power to stop these fuckers hurting you; they are not taking you anywhere, so bring it on.'

That's what I wanted, that's exactly what I would have done for him.

I felt alone and Lizzy had to look after her daughter Shannon which I totally understood. To be honest, I was a nightmare, a total handful for her; she had to protect her daughter, not from me as I love Shannon, but from everything around me that was going on—which was me, I suppose. It was just too much for her, but she was still trying her best by me; she would never give up on me, never surrender.

I was trying to fight, but I was at the mercy of Germany and under their control. This wasn't something that I could fix instantly, if at all, so I took back what I did have control of which wasn't much, but I could choose how I spent the rest of my time. I know they may not have been the right choices, but they were still mine to make.

'I can do whatever I want inside my own home so I'll do whatever the fuck I like.'

So, what now? Well, perhaps while I'm rattling around this place as a prisoner in my own home, maybe I don't want to sit on the sofa and watch *EastEnders*. Maybe I want to get pissed so I reached for a bottle of wine that was in the fridge and with that I pressed the self-destruct button.

'Do you think I'm gonna give a fuck how many bottles of wine I've had when I look out of the window from my prison cell in Germany?' I thought to myself.

It was only an hour later that I had run out of wine and it was gone 10pm and I couldn't leave the house to get more.

'Hmmm, that was not quite as explosive as I thought, that won't be happening again,' so I made sure that I got supplies of everything and lots of it: alcohol, cigarettes and cocaine.

I completely shut myself away from the outside world. I thought I had been doing a lot of alcohol and cocaine before, but things escalated quickly. In the next days, weeks and months, I functioned only when I had to; I was an unstoppable train wreck. The only reason I wasn't either drinking, gambling or doing cocaine was because I was asleep. Being asleep was the only time I ever got away from it all.

I was living and breathing for the cocaine and the gambling, with alcohol and cigarettes as a side-line. Analysing the roulette wheels and tables, not just for hours at a time but for days at a time, and if I wasn't doing that then there were so many nights that I just broke down and cried, either sitting on my stairs in a state of despair or lying on the inflatable bed downstairs beating my fist down into the pillow.

'I don't wanna fucking be here,' I screamed.

On a good day, I would submerge myself into music, dancing around the house; certain songs became a big part of my life inside the Fortress of Solitude.

Lizzy and I were invited to a christening and when I turned up, everyone knew instantly something was wrong. I could see people looking over at me and talking which made me feel uncomfortable; I'd lost a lot of weight and it was a struggle for me to even get dressed in the morning. I wasn't in the right frame of mind to have even gone and it wasn't long before it all finally came out. The news of my arrest spread through Royston like a plague of locust.

I was becoming more of a recluse as I floated along trapped in all directions, time was of the essence fighting against the European Arrest Warrant but in this process, things took time. I had appointed Lorenzo to help me fight the European Arrest Warrant and assist me with the case against me in Germany. Lorenzo also found me a solicitor in Germany who was prepared to take on my case, so for now there was nothing more I could do but sit and wait for any new developments.

Chapter 28
No Caller ID

I had a meeting coming up with Lorenzo and was asked to prepare a written statement, so I gave my brother a call while I was on the way to sign in at the police station in Stevenage.

'Hey, Rich how's it going?' I asked him.

'Hey, Bro, you sound happier today; what's up?' he replied.

'I've had to prepare a written statement and was hoping you could take a look at it for me,' I said.

'Sorry, Bro, I'm a bit busy tonight; can you pop round mine and I'll take a look at it then?' he replied.

'Yeah, but I can't get to you in time and get back to mine before curfew, that's why I'm asking can you come to mine,' I said.

'To be honest, Christian, I don't know how I can help you with it; you know what you're doing. You're good at that sort of stuff,' he replied.

'Listen, Rich, I'm gonna go. I'll catch you later,' I said and I hung up the phone.

I was so down about how unsupportive he was being towards me; I knew what it was and why he didn't want to be anywhere near me or my house. Out of everything, this was really starting to get to me. Richard didn't even attend the meeting I had with Lorenzo or take the time to understand what was going on with me; Lizzy was there for me, but Richard swerved going to the meeting at the last minute. Everything Richard did was about creating distance.

At the meeting, Lorenzo informed me that I had a court date set for a hearing in November regarding the European Arrest Warrant. I at least hoped Richard could take the time out of his busy schedule to come with me to this. With everything that was happening in my life and even with all the friends that I have, they didn't know what to do with me or they didn't know how to help me, so a lot of them stayed away. I didn't want to be around me so why would anyone else? But two of my closest friends, Kirk and Tasha, invited me round their house for dinner and, to be fair, they were trying hard to be supportive. I love both of them and I remember this night in particular because it was one of the rare occasions that I dared to leave the house; this was a real effort for me and I had to be back before ten o' clock so it was an early dinner, but I decided to put on my nicest outfit and just go and try and have a good time. I was struggling with my anxiety and I didn't want to leave the house when the time came. I had promised myself not to do any cocaine, but I just couldn't cope; I thought about cancelling, but felt bad as they had gone too so much effort for me. I leant against my front door and contemplated what I was going to do, but by now my anxiety was bubbling over and I was getting in a real state so I reached for the cocaine. I did a couple of lines and took a little with me when I left. I know I shouldn't have done it, but as I was walking to their house a calmness came over me as I slipped into character. They opened their front door with open arms and greeted me with hugs and kisses; this was just what I needed. We talked and laughed and it took my mind away from everything for a while, but I could feel the cocaine wearing off so I made my excuses and walked into their downstairs toilet and flushed the toilet to disguise the fact that I was doing cocaine. I felt bad and I was putting on a front, but I was doing my best. After dinner and saying goodbye to Kirk and Tasha, I was walking back to mine and eventually made it to my front door. I lit up a cigarette and stood there for a moment and spoke to myself, 'Okay, you're home now. You've done it and all is okay.'

I went through a check list in my head: Kirk likes you, Tasha likes you, we had a good time and I'm okay; all is okay. Doing this kind of ritual in my head put me more at ease. I smiled that I'd got through it and was glad that I went; it was the first time that I'd smiled in a long time.

Now I was back at home it turned into every other evening and it wasn't long before I was drunk and, in a drug-fuelled haze standing on my front door step having a cigarette making sure not to pass the threshold for fear of setting off my ankle bracelet. I had started to venture out of the house when it had gone past three o' clock in the morning as I could leave the house again without my tag going off, I would spend a lot of time walking round the nearby park until it got light just because I could. I didn't like to smoke in the house so I adopted this position where I could practically have most of my body outside. I was sitting on the floor with my right leg over the door step and my left leg to my side, making sure my ankle never crossed the invisible barrier that would set off my tag. The main road into town goes straight past my house and at times it was so peaceful just sitting there in the dark. I sat there and watched the cars go by while smoking a cigarette, staring into the headlights as they drove past and at times, they were so bright and dazzling that it would almost put me into a trance. I would transport myself to a tropical beach somewhere or pictured myself owning a new place in Marbella sitting on my balcony clinking champagne and looking forward to a fresh start; actually, I imagined myself being anywhere else but here. I'd noticed that there was this car that drove past my house on a number of occasions and at the time I hadn't thought much about it and it wasn't until I was driving back one evening from signing in at the police station in Stevenage that I pulled into a petrol station, when I heard.

'All right, Christian, how you doing babe?' a girl's voice hollered at me from across the petrol station forecourt.

I recognised this girl from school; she was a real live wire and was as mad as a box of frogs. She was quite attractive, slightly taller than me with long dark hair and she reminded me of the character Tasha St. Patrick from the Netflix drama, Power. I looked across at her car, it was that car, the same car that I'd seen driving past my house on so many different occasions.

'That's so random,' I thought. 'You stalking me,' I said to her jokingly.

'Yeah babes, you wish; how you been, all right?' she replied.

'Yeah so-so; long story,' I said and with that she walked into the petrol station for some cigarettes and came out and strutted back to her car.

'Take care, babes, I'll see you soon,' she said pausing to look me up and down as she got in her car and then drove off.

'What happened there? That was so flirty, that was weird.' I thought as I finished putting petrol in my car.

It wasn't until a couple of days later whilst I was having a cigarette on my front doorstep, that she pulled her car straight onto my drive.

'Thought I'd stop and say hello,' she said as she got out of her car.

'Hello, Nadine, how's it going?' I replied.

'You gonna invite me in then?' she said.

'Sure; how's your day been? I've seen you drive past me so many times,' I said to her as she walked straight into my house.

'Well, I only live up the road, don't I? And I've seen you out here nearly every day for a while now, thought I'd say hi and check in on you,' she said as she unbuttoned her jacket and threw it over the back of my sofa.

We stood in the kitchen and I poured her a drink and we just started chatting; she saw I had some coke on the side.

'Mind if I have some?' she asked me.

'Course you can, I'll rack us up a couple of lines,' I replied.

'Rumour has it you're involved in something pretty big,' she said to me.

'Small town… yeah, you could say that,' I replied.

'60 million or something,' she said as she tried to stop herself smiling.

I proceeded to tell her about what had happened and what was currently happening to me and she listened intently. There was some more small talk before she made her excuses and left. Nadine would come and go dropping by unannounced every now and again to have a drink with me and do some coke. I was aware she was becoming more and more interested in my case, but then again everyone knew about it; perhaps I should have been a little more guarded as I didn't really know her that well but, to be honest, I liked the company and couldn't see the harm in it.

This current lifestyle I was leading wasn't doing me any favours, especially with what I was up against. There came a point that I decided to go the doctor's with Lizzy and try and piece myself back together. I was struggling at the doctors' as I explained what was happening to me and the doctor was shocked and mystified as my story unfolded. It broke Lizzy's heart to see me in so much pain, some of it, admittedly, 'self-inflicted', but sometimes people fall and just need some help to get back up again. Therefore, when they fall, catch them, and when they ask for help, give it but don't judge. The truth is there is not a thing anyone can do to help a friend or loved one unless that person wants to help themselves and as much as it hurts to watch from the side-line and see people you love fall down, trust me, the only one that can fix you is you. There's nothing anyone can do but ride this rollercoaster with you until you stop it and I'm not preaching—don't forget: I'm still my own worst enemy.

The doctor wasn't shocked that I was in such a state after I told him my story so far and he prescribed me an anti-depressant called Sertraline. I was also referred to a nearby clinic in Letchworth called Spectrum for drink and drug abuse. I didn't even know if I was an addict, but I was looking for help, so if you want to call me an addict, call me an addict; it's not a dirty word and I don't need a label. What I need is a little bit of help and support.

My coke cloak started off as something I wore that made me bigger and badder, a better version of myself, but not anymore; I was now wearing it as a comfort blanket. Doing a line of coke so that I could zoom away in my head and get away from all of this, just doing something to feel different; the truth is, I liked doing cocaine. Coke was my friend, even when I was dealing with the brief moments of paranoia that kicked in which were becoming more and more frequent. The countless times I went backwards and forwards to my front door to look out of the peephole or peer through the blinds was absolutely ridiculous.

'No one is there, the coast is clear,' I thought. I'd only checked it a minute ago; it was nonstop and relentless and I never found what I was looking for because there was never anybody there.

That was until October when, out of the blue, I heard a knock at the door. I looked through the peephole and I could see it was Nadine so I opened the door.

'Hey, Nadine, how's it going? What you up to?' I asked her.

Nadine stormed straight past me and into my house; she was drunk and had parked her car at a funny angle on my drive. 'Why don't you just come in?' I said to her sarcastically.

'You all right, babe? Just thought I'd stop by, catch up on the gossip. Is there any news on your case? I was just thinking the other day what happened to all that money,' she slurred at me and she was really unsteady on her feet.

'What money?' I replied.

'Don't act stupid with me; you know exactly what I'm talking about, that 60 million, where is it?'

Her demeanour was a bit off and that's an understatement; she was being really feisty. It felt like she was determined for a row and was being so obnoxious; she was showing her true colours and was a handful for me to deal with.

'Seriously? You're asking me that? I'm selling my house

and losing everything I own and you think I've got 60 million euros hidden somewhere; don't be a fucking idiot,' I was quickly starting to lose my patience with her and it wasn't long before I asked her to leave.

'You're not throwing me out,' she screamed in my face.

'I'm not throwing you out. I'm asking you, politely, to leave my house and go and take a time out,' I said as the situation had got out of hand really quickly.

'I'll tell your girlfriend about us,' she snarled at me.

'Nadine, where the fuck is all of this coming from? Has something happened to you today or something?' I asked her.

'I will, babes, I'll tell your girlfriend about us,' she repeated.

'Tell her what? Tell her that you come around my house and do coke with me? I couldn't give a fuck; go for it, she's heard worse,' I replied.

'You don't tell me when to leave, I'll get out of dodge when I want to,' she replied.

'Nadine, you're really testing my patience; seriously, what the fuck has got into you? What are you all about?' I asked her.

The next ten minutes were the longest ten minutes of my life. I stood in my kitchen as she staggered around my house bumping into things, occasionally looking at me and smiling; quite frankly, it was really weird and so awkward.

'You gonna drive me home then or what? I'm drunk,' she asked me.

'You fucking drove here; no, I'm not driving you home,' I replied.

'Fuck you then,' she said as she fumbled about in her bag looking for her keys as she slowly walked out of my front door, looking back at me over her shoulder and grinning.

As she climbed into her car and started the engine, the music was blaring as she sped off the wrong way up the road.

'Oh wow, what the fuck was that?' I said to myself and I actually nervously laughed out loud. I was so relieved that she'd gone and I lifted the blinds a couple of times to look out my living room window just in case she came back.

'Fucking lunatic; I can't get my head round it, that's it: she's never setting foot in my house again—fuck that,' I said to myself.

The following morning, I woke up to my phone ringing in my ear because I'd fallen asleep with it next to me on my bed. I looked at my phone and the display had No Caller ID. I would never usually answer the phone if I didn't know who it was, but I picked up the call.

'Where's the money?' a girl's voice screamed at me down the phone.

I was still half asleep and getting my bearings. As my ears adjusted, I recognised the voice—it was Nadine.

'Why the fuck are you calling me up and blocking your ID?' I asked her.

'I want to know where the money is! Did you put something in my drink last night?' she replied.

'What? Did I put something in your drink? What do you mean? Did I put something in your drink? What the fuck for?' I said to her; I didn't like how this conversation was going.

'Well, I can't remember anything from last night and I've woke up with all bruises on me and thought something might have happened. I thought you might have put something in my drink,' she said.

I sprung out of bed and, to this day, I have never unleashed hell on a girl or shouted at a girl the way I did to her.

'Listen to me, you fucking cunt, let's not sugar coat this; are you implying that I did something to you last night?' I shouted at her in full volume.

'No, I'm not saying that, but if you give me some money we'll say no more about it, she replied.

'Give you some money? And how much is it you're after?' I said angrily.

'Let's start off with, say, sixty quid? And we'll go from there,' she replied.

'Sixty fucking quid? you joker; you think you can call me up and dance around me, implying I slipped something in your drink and then ask me for money? Let's call it for what it is: you're implying—and doing a really bad job at it—that if I don't pay you money, you're going to accuse me of raping you,' I said.

'No, no, I'm not saying that and I didn't use that word.' she replied.

'Yes, you fucking are!' I was fuming, absolutely raging. 'Let me tell you what's going to happen; I sign in at the police station every day of my fucking life and when I walk in there this evening, I'm going to explain to them that you're saying I raped you and you're asking me for money.'

'Why are you getting the police involved? There's no need for that and I never used the word rape,' she replied as she started to back track.

'You're trying to be clever by not using the word, but that's what you're implying. I'll make a statement to the police this evening and I'll tell them what's gone on and they will be in contact with you; I couldn't give a fuck,' I said to her.

'We don't need to be contacting the police; what are you

doing running off to the police for?' she replied.

'Listen to me, you fucking idiot, I'm the kind of guy that would protect a girl and you're implying that I have harmed you in some way; it's a fucking liberty. You came to my house and all I've ever done is be nice to you. What do you need 60 quid for? Have you run out of crack?' I said.

Nadine hung up the phone up on me and I never heard from her again, and have never seen her again. It was audacious of her calling me like that and trying to exploit money from me; it really pissed me off—I wasn't fazed as I knew I'd done nothing wrong.

'Okay, deep breath, Christian,' I thought

This was just so ridiculous that yet again another person was taking advantage of my good nature. I called Rich just to vent and tell him what had happened; I wanted some support and I felt like he needed to know.

'Bro, what the fuck are you doing? I could have told you something like that would happen; she's fucking mental, mate. I remember she used to go down the Banyers with clients when she was working as a hooker. I didn't know she was turning up at yours; you never said anything about it, but I'd have told you to stay well away,' Rich said to me sternly.

'I didn't know any of that Rich,' I said to him feeling rather foolish.

'Did you not think it was weird that she just turned up out of the blue? It's obvious you could be a target; you have to be more careful. If I were you, I would just forget about it; I wouldn't mention anything to Liz either. I know my brother and you're the last person that could be capable of anything like that—it's a joke,' he said.

'Trust me, Bro, Lizzy is struggling as it is; not sure she

can take much more,' I replied.

I decided not tell Lizzy what had happened; firstly, it wouldn't have been an easy subject to approach and, secondly, I was trying to protect her from any more drama. I could kick myself at times; I'm far too trusting in people and leave myself wide open.

I mulled over what had gone on and questioned whether I had been set up. This girl appeared in my life not long after everyone in Royston had heard about my situation and this included the amount of money involved. It was just after the christening and I'm not sure—even to this day—if that first meeting at the petrol station could have been a set up. I wondered if she had been watching me and chose that as the perfect moment to slowly infiltrate my life. One thing I do know—for a fact—is that she had attempted to extort money from me. I was just being a nice guy and looking for a distraction so I didn't feel so lonely at times. I would never commit such a heinous crime; it's unthinkable and writing about it creeps me out a little bit. It makes me feel uncomfortable, but it's my story and I have to write it.

Chapter 29
My Guardian Angel

I attended my first therapy session at Spectrum in Letchworth; I remember pulling up in the car and thinking 'How has it come to this?' I entered the building and sat patiently in the reception area staring blankly at the brochures and posters on the wall when my therapist came out and invited me into a private room. I wanted to sort myself out and start to cope with things better if I had any chance of getting through this; why else would I go to therapy? I sat down with my therapist and we started to talk; I'm usually very open and honest but the line of questioning had already started to niggle at me. I had my therapist sussed out and knew where all of her leading questions were going as I spent the next hour getting wound up, even though I didn't let it show. I couldn't wait to get out of there and was starting to feel choked up. We hadn't even scratched the surface or the formalities and I was just getting pissed off.

'What the fuck am I doing here letting people try and unravel me?' I thought.

I finished the session and sat in my car; pausing for a moment, I burst into tears. I was getting myself really worked up when Lizzy called to see how I got on. Clicking hands free, I answered the phone and sat there silent for a moment—I couldn't speak.

'You there, babe?' Lizzy asked me and, in that moment, it felt like the enormity of everything came crashing down on top of me; I don't know why, but I just snapped.

'I just want everyone to leave me alone; why won't everyone just leave me the fuck alone?' I shouted as I was hitting the steering wheel with my fist.

'Hang on, Christian, calm down. Why are you getting yourself so worked up?' Lizzy asked me with a really soft and gentle tone in her voice.

'I shouldn't even be in this mess; why won't everyone just leave me the fuck alone?' I shouted.

'Are you still there, still in Letchworth? I'll come to you,' she replied.

'No, I just want to be alone; I've had enough, I'm gonna go,' I said and I hung up on her.

I sat in the car feeling so hopeless and desperate; the suicidal feelings were back and the unwanted thoughts and images I'd been having lately kept flashing up in my mind— images of me hanging from the wooden beam attached to my ceiling in my bedroom or smashing my Porsche into a wall and I was the crash test dummy. I started the engine and drove to a pub called George the Fourth; it's in a town called Baldock and when I got there, I ordered a pint of Fosters.

I felt so many emotions while I contemplated my next move.

'Maybe I'll just sit here and get pissed until I've decided what I'm going to do next,' I thought while I looked into the bottom of my empty pint glass and got up to order another drink.

I was sitting outside the pub having a cigarette and started to feel aggressive.

'I will not conform; I haven't done anything wrong. Fuck all of you,' I thought.

That's when I noticed someone loitering about on my right-hand side; I'd not seen or met him before. He looked like a country boy. He was wearing a big chunky jumper and blue jeans; he was about my height and his brown hair was covered up by a baseball cap—he was wearing a green pair of wellington boots which were covered in mud. I could tell he wanted to approach me, but was hesitant.

'Not today, mate, of all the fucking days,' I thought to myself.

He went to walk towards me and then his feet took him off in another direction as he changed his mind and went back into the pub. Whatever it was he was thinking, he'd bottled the first attempt to approach me. I continued to sit outside drinking and smoking and out of the corner of my eye he was back. He hovered for a moment and then he approached me.

'Can I buy you a drink mate?' he said nervously.

I looked at my glass which was nearly empty again.

'Yeah, why not? Go on then,' I replied.

He scuttled off back into the pub and surfaced a couple of moments later with two pints and set one of them down on the table for me.

'Is it okay for me to sit down? I don't want to bother you,' he asked as he gingerly placed his hand on the chair next to me.

I wasn't in the mood for small talk and there was an awkward silence for a moment.

'How's your day going? I'm Joseph?' he said as he pulled the chair out from under the table and sat down next to me while, at the same time, putting out his other hand to shake mine.

I shook his hand and said, 'My name's, Christian, I've had better days mate; saying that, I can't actually remember the last time I had a good day. How about you?' I replied looking at him with a sombre expression.

'I'm celebrating my brothers' birthday today; I've got a twin brother,' Joseph said to me.

This comment caught my attention. I'd hardly said a word to this guy and I certainly hadn't revealed anything to him about myself or my current situation.

'Really? I have a twin brother too, so it's your birthday as well then.' I replied.

'Yeah, my birthday too,' he said as he flipped out his wallet and showed me a picture and, it was true, he did have an identical twin brother.

'Carry him everywhere I go, his name is Richard,' he said as he looked up.

'Really? Wow, my brother's name is Richard; is he coming down here to meet you?' I asked him.

'I lost him a few years ago,' he replied.

'Oh fuck, mate, I'm so sorry,' I said and I didn't know where to look; I must admit, I was a bit taken aback by his revelation.

'It's fine, you weren't to know; I always go for a drink on our birthday. I celebrate it just me and him; I always come to this pub,' he said.

I struggled not to well up, 'Fucking hell that's so sad, I couldn't imagine what I'd do if I lost my brother, especially being a twin; I always say twins are a gift. I hope you don't mind me asking, but how did you lose him?' I approached the subject as tactfully as I could, but this was a difficult conversation.

'It's okay, you can ask me,' he paused for a moment and then he said, 'He committed suicide; he was having a bad time of it and he hung himself from his gym equipment in his bedroom. It still bothers me to this day, when they found him and I got there, the police wouldn't let me in to try and save him.'

'Mate, that's heart-breaking; I don't know what I'd do if my twin brother died. I know exactly what you mean though and nothing would stop me trying to save my twin brother either. In one way or another, I save him all the time. Tell you what, let me grab us another drink and we can talk some more. What you drinking Joseph?' I asked him.

'The same again would be really nice,' he replied.

I went to the bar and, when I was out of sight, I paused for a moment; this had totally taken me by surprise and I was perplexed. 'This could be my brother sitting there,' I was staring into the face of someone who had lost his twin brother. If I committed suicide, this could be my twin brother celebrating our birthdays alone. Joseph trudged around like he was carrying his twin brother on his back, like he was still there in his shadow. It was a very humbling experience and I found all of my bad emotions melt away—for a day at least. I wanted Joseph to have a good day, considering what I'd just heard.

Joseph and I chatted for the rest of the day until it got too cold to sit outside anymore, so we went indoors. Joseph ordered a couple more drinks and we sat down at a table; about ten minutes later, one of the waitresses came over and put down a bowl of chilli and some nachos.

'I hope it was okay, mate, I ordered us some food as well;

I get the feeling you haven't eaten for a couple of days, be good to get some food inside you,' he said.

'Awww, mate, that's very sweet of you,' I replied and he was right I hadn't eaten much at all.

'Can I be honest about something?' Joseph said to me.

'Yeah, sure, go for it,' I said.

'I could tell you were in trouble that's why I approached you this morning,' he said.

The whole day had weirded me out and I didn't know if it was him helping me or me helping him, but us meeting like this was incredibly strange and I didn't know what to make of it.

As we ate chilli and nachos, Lizzy turned up at the pub with Shannon right behind her.

'Christian, fucking hell; I've been so worried about you. I've been looking for you everywhere,' she said, her face was a mixture of happy to see me and puzzled that I was sitting having food and drink with some stranger.

'I'm okay, babe; this is Joseph. I've just been sitting here chatting with him.'

'Hello Joseph, I'm Elizabeth, well Lizzy. I hope he's been behaving,' she said.

'Yeah, he's been fine. I got him some food too; he's a good old boy,' he replied.

'Ah, thank you. Yeah, he probably hasn't eaten in a couple of days, knowing him,' she said.

It was starting to feel a little awkward with all of us there at the same time so that was my cue to leave as I got up.

'Thanks, Joseph, you've helped me more than you know,' I said and I gave him a hug.

'Take care of yourself, Christian,' he said as I left the pub.

I left my car in the pub carpark and Lizzy drove me to the police station in Stevenage to sign in. On the journey, I was telling Lizzy snippets of what had happened, but she was more concerned with me and how I was feeling. I was talking selectively as Shan was in the back of the car.

'I'm okay babe, closest I've felt today; though, it was just a hard day,' I said.

'Yeah, I could tell something was wrong in your voice; you sounded so different, me and Shannon were in tears,' she said.

'Ah fuck, did Shannon hear that?' I asked her.

'Yes, I was driving in the car at the time and you were on speaker, Shan was with me,' she said.

'Is Shan okay? I don't want her to hear me in that state,' I said.

'Yeah she's okay. She's not stupid, she knows what's going on; she's worried about you,' Lizzy replied.

I looked over my right shoulder and looked Shan straight in the face; her big blue eyes were looking back at me.

'Don't worry about me, Shanny; I'll be all right, okay. You know if anyone can fix it, I will,' I told her.

Meeting Joseph had a profound effect on me; I knew I couldn't just flip a switch and turn off all of my emotions—they attacked me when they felt like it—but I would try harder, I would fight harder.

'Not all guardian angels wear wings,' I thought to myself.

I'd sold my house, 'The Hayloft', but that wouldn't be completed until early December 2015. I hadn't even thought about where I was moving onto, it was a bit of a toss-up which one out of Lizzy or Rich were going to have me. I was really volatile and the truthful answer is no one really wanted me.

Richard had his reasons and Lizzy had hers, but each of them assumed that I was staying with the other so it hadn't come up until I started moving all of my furniture out of my house which was being put into storage. I totally understood Lizzy's situation: she's a mum and had to protect Shannon. Due to my behaviour, I was unpredictable with the drink and drugs and she needed to shield Shannon from this. Richard's reasons will become clearer, but Richard had a meeting with Jen to decide if they would allow me to stay; they had drawn the short straw and with a little resistance I moved in with them on the 18th of November 2015. I had to arrange things early so that I made sure I complied with my bail conditions. Richard and Jen had taken pity on me; how grateful I was to be allowed to live in Richard's perfect home with his perfect wife, they had allowed me to encroach on their lavish and wonderful lifestyles. I just hoped I wasn't too much of an inconvenience and I didn't get in the way while Richard was running my business XS Homes Limited, the business that I'd signed over to him.

'We're going to let you stay in what will be the nursery; me and Jen are thinking of having children in the next six months so hopefully everything will be sorted by then,' Richard said to me as I placed my bag on the floor.

My life was in a bag and I already felt so uncomfortable; crazy as it sounds, I felt uncomfortable with my own identical twin brother. With everything that was going on in my life, my identical twin brother made me feel inferior and that he was doing me a favour letting me stay there. I sat on the edge of the bed; it was awful, feeling that neither of them wanted me there.

I'd only been there a day when Richard asked me to go for breakfast with him; he wanted to speak to me about something and said it was urgent.

'Bro, listen, I've been speaking to Jen's brother-in-law and he has some friends and some contacts in Thailand. I told him what's happening with you and he reckons it's time to go. I can give you my passport and you'll be able to travel on that and you can post it back to me; I'm just looking out for you if the worst comes to the worst,' he said looking at me with a very serious face on.

I scowled back at him over my cup of coffee, 'Rich don't be a fucking idiot, mate; do you know how ridiculous that sounds? I haven't done anything wrong and I'd rather stay here and fight,' I couldn't believe my ears at the suggestion Richard had just made; he was so desperate to get rid of me.

'Okay, Bro, just so you know it's an option,' he replied.

He was trying to get rid of me and was about as subtle as a brick through a window. The suggestion was ludicrous and he knew very fucking well that I hadn't done anything wrong and now he wants me running for the rest of my life. I sat there quietly and didn't say another word while I finished my coffee. I was disgusted and starting to see him in a completely different light; I was starting to open my eyes.

My first court appearance was late in November at Westminster Magistrates Court in London. I had a hearing concerning the European Arrest Warrant. Providing the EAW had been executed correctly, they could send me away immediately to answer the case against me in Germany. We were going to argue that the EAW was not correctly executed and that some of the vital information needed was missing. This was a job for Lorenzo and my barrister to argue on my behalf.

I arrived at court with Lizzy, Rich and Jen. I was so

279

pleased that they were there to support me, but it wasn't like Richard and Jen had much choice unless they were going to completely abandon me; they had to try and keep me on side, at least for now. As I went through security and up the stairs, I sat outside the courtroom and took a seat with Lizzy. Rich and Jen went and stood out of the way they weren't close to me, but they weren't far either. The six strangers that had been arrested and taken up in the lift with me and sent to prison were also there. They all sat in a group together while their lawyers were coming and going. The nerves and anxiety had me on high alert when, all of a sudden, I saw a group of men running up the stairs; they were plain clothed officers. The officers darted in all directions until one of them was standing over me while I was sitting down, everything felt like it went into slow motion.

'Christian Govan, we're arresting you on suspicion of tax evasion in Germany,' the officer said as he read me my rights.

'Are you going to take me away again?' I asked the officer. I was confused as I looked over to my brother and Jen; Jen burst into tears—she couldn't watch so she looked away.

'No, Christian, but we have to re-arrest you and serve you with a new European Arrest Warrant; this replaces your existing one, its formality,' the officer said to me.

This new European Arrest Warrant replaced my existing EAW and was served on me just before I was about to walk into court. Basically, Germany was aware that the first EAW that had been given to me was missing vital information. They had now fine-tuned the original EAW and corrected any mistakes or added to it so that they could now take me away pending the judge's decision in court. I thought this could be the last time I saw Lizzy, Rich and Jen; I just didn't know what was about to happen to me. All of us in court that day were served with new European Arrest Warrants and were called into court moments later. Nothing seemed real anymore, but this was very real and my life was slipping away right in front of my eyes.

In single file, we entered the courtroom and were asked to stand in what looked like a big glass box with a row of chairs inside it. The wall behind us had a door in it and if you were taken down, then that's where you would go. I looked across at Rich, Jen and Lizzy; they were sitting in the public gallery: Jen was still crying, Rich was as white as a ghost and Lizzy had her stern face on and was holding it together on the face of it. You could cut the atmosphere with a knife. Inside the glass cage, there was a strong smell of booze and a couple of the strangers were being rowdy and talking to one another. They, like me, had been hitting the drink hard, even to the point they were drunk in the courtroom. In that environment, I couldn't think of anything worse; I was still scarred from the last time.

In layman's terms, it was argued by each barrister for each defendant that being served with a new EAW so late in the day was improper and each defendant hadn't been given any time to consider the new documents or evidence attached, or how it would affect each individual's case. This was not fair or in the interests of justice, particularly when the stakes were so high.

Like I said, the case in Germany is a fight of its own; it forms part of the EAW paperwork, but would not be taken into consideration by a UK judge. This was a different fight for another day in a different country. With an EAW, if you're fit to go, there's no reason they won't take you unless it infringes on your human rights or there is a compelling reason for you not to go, but we are all entitled to a fair trial and being ambushed before we walked into court had not given anyone a chance to review the new paperwork. The frustrating thing for me was that we were not being heard on our own individual cases, we were all put into one big melting point; me and the strangers.

On hearing the pleas from each barrister, the judge adjourned the court hearing based on the late service of the new EAW's and a new court date would be given for the case to be heard again. I wasn't thrilled about the new European Arrest Warrant because the first one looked so ugly and scary to me as it was, but I was interested to know what was different and receiving a revised EAW today had given me a lifeline; I was still here and hanging on.

Before we left the courtroom, one of the barristers took issue with how heavy the bail conditions were and the unnecessary restrictions that had been placed on his client for such a long period of time. It was argued that a European Arrest Warrant is meant to be expedited efficiently and, basically, you're snatched and gone before you know it. However, we were all floating around after our initial arrest four months later. They had my passport so I wasn't a flight risk. The judge agreed that we were all suffering under these conditions and that they should be relaxed. The judge ordered for all of our tags to be removed and it was only a requirement for me to sign in at the police station in Stevenage once a week on a Wednesday between 6pm and 8pm.

The following day, the guy who had installed the system and tag to monitor me turned up at my brother's house; I cut through the rubber bracelet myself and felt instant freedom. I was mobile again and, since meeting Joseph in the pub that day, I had been putting things into perspective. I decided to go and see Mum and Dad; I hadn't seen either of them in over 12 years. I don't know why, really, but I just wanted to make peace with everything. It was late in the evening when I walked up their garden path as I came in through the back of the property. It was an assault course with old furniture strewn everywhere; the garden was still like a chewed-up racecourse. I could see little footprints in the mud where the dogs had been charging about.

I wasn't even in the house before I recognised that smell; it was pouring out of the house like smoke from a witch's cauldron. The dogs were aware I was there as the barking started and I entered through the front door; the front door was always open because it was so knackered—it couldn't be shut properly or even locked, a slight push with my finger and I was in. I stood there on the landing at the bottom of the stairs. I knew behind that living room door there was an army of dogs waiting to get their teeth into me.

'Mum, Dad, it's Christian,' I shouted and stood there with uncertainty of what was about to happen.

I heard movement and shouting from inside the living room.

'David, get the dogs back,' I heard Mum's voice shout from inside the living room.

As the door opened, Mum and Dad squeezed themselves through a small gap while trying to keep the dogs at bay; they were snarling and going crazy. I glimpsed through the gap in the door as they squeezed through. It was honestly a wall of dogs all clambering over one another, violently sticking their paws through the gap and trying to scratch at me; Mum and Dad were hitting them all back as they finally managed to seal the door behind them.

Mum and Dad were now standing in the landing with me.

'Hello, Mum; all right, Dad,' I said to them.

'Hello, Christian, what are you doing here?' Dad asked me.

'No, Christian, we're not interested; I won't have it,' Mum said, folding her arms, as she gave me that look of anger that I was so familiar with.

'Hang on, Marilyn, let him speak,' Dad said to my mum.

'No, David, you shut up; I won't,' she replied aggressively.

It wasn't the warmest reception, but I didn't expect them to welcome me with open arms either. I went onto explain I was in trouble and, by the end of the conversation, Dad was listening intently and Mum's arms were now down by her side; she was warming to me. I kept it short and sweet, I gave them my number and told them they can contact me anytime they like and then I left. It must have been quite a shock for them to see me after all this time.

When I got back to Richard's, I told him where I'd been and he wasn't that pleased about it.

'What the fuck did you go there for?' he said while looking at me really puzzled.

'I don't know. I don't know what's going to happen to me and I wanted to check in on them in case the worst comes to the worst and, anyway, I can do what the fuck I like,' I told him.

'Well don't expect me to get involved; I'm not interested,' he said defiantly, he wasn't happy.

'Funny, that's exactly what Mum said; you're a bit like her,' I replied sarcastically.

'Fuck off, mate, I'm nothing like either of them,' he said as he walked off unimpressed.

I'd moved into Richard's and I'd only stayed there a matter of days and I couldn't take it. The truth is, he made me feel so wretched being there and that I was a burden on him and Jen. It filled me with dread and made my anxiety go through the roof being there. Now I was able to move about again without a tag on, I asked Lizzy if I could stay with her, which I did.

Chapter 30
Me, Myself and Why

It was late in the afternoon on Friday the 27th of November 2015, I'd been with Liz for the last few days now, so I went back to Richard and Jen's. As I walked through the front door, Richard was there.

'Hey, Bro, haven't seen you about in the last few days; how's it going?' he asked me.

'Yeah, I just thought I'd keep out the way,' I replied.

'You don't need to do that, Bro, you live here; do you fancy going down to Stratton House for a few beers? Jen's not back till later, she's out tonight in London with some of her mates from work.'

'Sure, that's cool,' I said, thinking it would be nice for it just to be me and him; maybe we could have a laugh together like the old days and just spend some decent time with each other.

We walked from Richard's house down to Stratton House, which is a pub in Biggleswade, walking and talking along the way. It felt nice just to be able to walk around; you take it for granted until you're in the position that I was in with my bail conditions. Things were going okay, it was just me and him catching up; a sense of some normality since my arrest which had only been four and a half months ago, so much had happened to me since then and it was about nine in the evening when we finally walked home.

'Bro, I'll cook us up a lasagne when we get in and we can stick a movie on,' he said to me as we started to approach his estate.

'That sounds good; yeah cool, bro, I'd like that,' I replied.

'We can eat it in the living room, but don't you dare spill anything on my carpet,' he said and I knew from the tone in his voice that I had to be careful; his carpet was his pride and joy.

Richard's carpet was the thickest pile you could get and was so luxurious—champagne in colour. You could lie down on it and it felt like you were suspended off the floor, even leaving footprints when you walked on it; this was as good as carpet gets. We sat down on the sofa to eat and I was cautious to position my plate on my lap for fear of spilling anything on the floor; we had only just sat down when Jen came stumbling through the front door. She looked like she'd been dragged through a hedge backwards, while she struggled to stand on one foot and unzip her boots.

'Jen, what are you doing back babe? I thought you weren't back till later?' Rich asked her.

'Yeah some of the girls went home early so I thought I'd come home too,' she slurred back.

'How did you get home? You've been drinking. Jen, I'm talking to you.'

Richard started to question her and Jen was still stumbling around with her boots as she looked up and I could see in her face just how drunk she was, she was all bleary eyed; you just know when someone is pissed. I was starting to feel anxious as I saw my brother's face change, that same face that he wears when he's angry and he was rapidly getting angrier by the second.

'Jen, are you gonna tell me how the fuck you got home or what?' Richard said to her firmly; by now, he had got up and placed his plate in the kitchen and was standing next to her.

'I drove; it's only down the road from the train station,' she said looking down at the floor.

'Jen, I know where the fucking train station is; you shouldn't be driving, you're drunk.'

The atmosphere changed very quickly and I could tell Rich was about to kick off. I tried to interject and calm everything down, but it was quickly getting out of hand.

'Well she's home now. Granted, Rich, it's not ideal but—' I didn't get the chance to finish my sentence.

'Christian, shut the fuck up, I'm talking to my wife. Say that to me again, Jen, you drove home drunk and then what?' Richard said, and by now his volume was increasing after every word.

I was still sitting on the sofa and starting to get really anxious; my anxiety went through the roof and I felt my legs starting to jump up and down and I couldn't control them and, before I could do anything to stop it, the plate of lasagne flipped out of my lap. I watched in slow motion as the plate spun in mid-air and landed face down on Richard's carpet; my lasagne had face planted into Richard's pride and joy: the worlds thickest carpet.

As I looked up, I knew instantly this was bad, perhaps not as bad as it was about to actually go down, but I knew this wasn't going to end well—especially as Rich was already vexed with Jen.

Jen looked over at me and burst out laughing—this was purely a nervous laugh—she, like me, knew this was bad. I jumped up off of the sofa and picked up the plate to look at the damage.

'Fuck, the lasagne looked like a hot coal that had just sunk into the snow,' I thought to myself and was instantly overcome with dread.

The lasagne was embedded into the carpet and Richard was already fuelled up by Jens indiscretion. He was about to take all of his anger out on me; he has OCD like me and was already thinking this is not fixable—in his head, he was already pulling out the entire carpet and dragging it out of the house to dump it in the street or cutting a big square in the carpet with a Stanley knife to remove the abomination.

'I'm so sorry, Rich; honestly, it was an accident. I can fix this,' I said panicking.

'What the fuck are you going to do about it? That can't be fixed,' he said as he stood there rigid and he looked furious.

I was out of the front door in seconds and in the car to the local shop to buy up every spray and cleaner I could get my hands on. When I pulled up at the house, I came through the front door and Richard and Jen were both standing there in the living room and neither of them were speaking. Richard had his aggressive, snarling face on: the one he wears just before he's about to have a fight. I hurried over to where I had spilt the lasagne and set the bag of cleaning products down.

'Just leave it, don't fucking touch anything,' he growled at me.

I stood there as he looked at me dead in the face and erupted like a volcano; I'll never forget his exact words.

'This ain't gonna work out is it? You, cunt,' he bellowed at me, while taking a step forward, and squared up to me leaning right into my face.

'Oh my God, this is all my fault,' Jen shrieked.

'Rich, I suggest you get the fuck out of my face,' I said to him firmly as I squared up to him.

I was very nonchalant and I knew there was no going back and Richard now had the excuse he needed to get rid of me.

'Listen to me, you fucking cunt, I couldn't give a fuck about you and I want you out of my house right now,' he said pointing his finger at me.

Jen was still in the background sailing up and down unsure what to do; there was no way she could stop either of us if we went at it and I was now standing up to him. In Richard's eyes, I had served my purpose and I was a liability; I was no longer of any use to either of them, but I'm still a fighter and now I had nothing to lose. Richard would have come off a lot worse, he knew it and I knew it.

'Listen, Rich, if you want to square up to me, we can go outside. I'll at least show you some respect and not splash your face all over your own fucking house. I'll go for Jen's sake, but I just need a moment to get my things,' I told him and I waited for him to respond, he did nothing.

'Christian, I'm so sorry; this is all my fault. I'm so, so sorry,' Jen said crying hysterically.

'It's okay Jen, don't worry about it; I can take it,' I replied.

With that, I went outside and pulled my Porsche up outside Rich's front door and left the engine running, I went upstairs and picked up my bag; the bag that had my life in it. I grabbed my toiletries and placed my suit on the parcel shelf. I left my key on the kitchen work top and drove away. I was heading for my home, 'The Hayloft'. It wasn't due to complete until the 4th of December and I still had my inflatable bed there; there was so much going through my head as I drove to the

Fortress of Solitude.

I moved into Richard's house on the 18th of November 2015; I had only stayed there a few days in total and by the 27th of November 2015 Richard had thrown me out. Rich didn't give a shit about throwing me away and I was breaking my bail conditions because I was registered at his address; for all I knew, he had called the police. I could end up in prison for breaking them, but that's right where he wanted me: locked away, silenced and unable to reveal the truth.

'Do you know what? Fuck this,' I thought as I pulled the car over.

Pulling my car off the motorway and into the nearest lay-by, I turned off the engine and I began typing out a text message on my phone. I was about to reveal the secret that I had been guarding so heavily this whole time, I was not prepared to suffer in silence anymore, protecting my little brother while he watched me collapse. In the darkness and with only the illumination from my screen, I started hitting the keys; I set up a group text to all of the lads and selected a number of my closest friends and I also added Richard, I wrote:

Sometimes in life, you have to call a cunt out for just being a cunt, as you all know I have been arrested for tax evasion in Germany. I have been carrying this burden on my own and guarding my brother who thinks he can just throw me away. I only ever wanted him to support me and help me while I deal with this. I was blinded by the love that I have for my brother who doesn't give a shit about anyone but himself. I had nothing to do with what I am being accused of because it was Richard that operated that business and it was Richard who did all of the transactions. Now I'm not implying that there is anything wrong with the transactions or the company; the truth is, I just don't know, but I'm the one who is suffering while Richard leaves me to deal with it. I just want some support from people to help me get through this. P.S Over to you, Rich x

I sat there for a moment and then pressed send.

I started the engine and drove home and I could hear messages immediately pinging into my inbox; messages of shock and support.

'Be strong, Christian, you'll get through this.'

'You can beat this, Crystal, chin up mate.'

'I don't know what to say, I feel so sorry for you, love ya mate.'

'I had no idea, I'm shocked. Stay positive mate.'

'Stay strong, bruva.'

I didn't want Rich anywhere near my situation with Germany; he wasn't clever enough to help and would have just made things worse. All I wanted was unwavering, rock solid, support. I wanted Richard to have my back while I fight from the front—that wasn't too much to expect, but Rich couldn't even get that right. I called out the elephant in the room and hoped people would be more sympathetic towards my situation and stop kicking me when I'm already down, so I could be left to focus. I was sick of being Richard and Jen's dirty little secret; they hadn't been supporting me and were tearing me down piece by piece.

I knew that it would not change anything with my case and I would go it alone, but I didn't care that I called Rich out, it made me feel better. I would have loved to have seen his face when that text dropped in; I bet he nearly choked on his lasagne. I could not suffer any longer while being treated so badly by him.

I was foolish enough not to get a contract or raise any paperwork for the money that I had loaned Richard for the property at Olney; I was foolish enough to sign over XS Homes Limited with assets and cash worth £535,000.00 and I was foolish enough to have allowed Richard to use my name to operate a business because Germany now had me in their crosshairs.

The reason I didn't know about any of it is because I didn't do any of it. I had trusted Richard implicitly and he had thrown me under the bus for his own greed and financial gain. He had become accustomed to money through me and now he would do anything and everything to keep it. I had protected him all of my life because that's what big brothers do and it may be too late, but I had to start protecting myself.

It was my birthday on Monday the 30th of November 2015 and I'm 38 years old when I received a call from my solicitor, Lorenzo; it was really early in the morning.

'Hello, Christian, it's Lorenzo,' he sounded really alarmed and worried.

'Hi, Lorenzo, I was going to call you this morning, but you just beat me to it.'

'Listen, Christian, we've received an email from your brother over the weekend and it's quite nasty; I don't want to tell you what's in it. You're my client and my job is to look after you and your best interests; what concerns me is that I'm aware he threw you out on Friday so can you please give me an address. We mustn't delay, right now, you're breaking your bail conditions.'

'Can you tell me anything it says in the email he sent?' I asked Lorenzo.

'I'm not going to, Christian; honestly, you wouldn't want to see it. Let's just focus on you.'

'Okay, Lorenzo, I understand and I have got an address for you.'

I'd already spoken to Lizzy over the weekend and she might not have liked the idea, but I had nowhere else to go—especially at such short notice—so Lizzy said I could move in with her and I gave Lorenzo Lizzy's home address.

'Christian, on another note, we've been reviewing and comparing your new European Arrest Warrant against the first one and there really isn't much difference. I'm aware that all of the other people arrested were also issued with new European Arrests Warrants and theirs are significantly different.'

'What does that mean, Lorenzo?' I asked him.

'If I was to hazard a guess: when they raided your home, they didn't find anything of evidential value there.'

'Is that good news?'

'Well it's not bad; it means we're not looking at anything we didn't already know at this stage. I'll keep you posted and will let the courts know your change of address.'

'Thanks, Lorenzo, I appreciate your help.'

I hung up the phone and set it down on my kitchen worktop and stood there thinking for a moment.

'Fucking hell, you're a cheeky cunt Rich, emailing my solicitor; who does that?' I thought.

This was my solicitor and had nothing to do with Richard; it's not normal to be sending emails to other people's solicitors like that. Richard emailing my solicitor only made himself look guilty and fuck knows what else he was doing behind my back. It was outrageous he would do that; he was putting up the shutters because Richard is a runner when he gets caught out. On another note, I took it from the conversation that when they raided my house, they were looking for further evidence to strengthen their case against me, so when the officers ran up the stairs at court and issued the second EAW it would have been even more damning with a lot more information in it. There was no evidence at mine because I hadn't done anything, that's why my second EAW hadn't changed. I was still in a really shit position, but there were no new skeletons in my closet.

I completed on my house sale for 'The Hayloft' on the 4th of December 2015 and was now living with Lizzy.

Behind that front door at 'The Hayloft', people couldn't see and would never really know just how much I had been breaking down in there, being peeled alive layer by layer. I started thinking a fresh start wasn't a bad idea; maybe that place was cursed for me.

Chapter 31
For Every Action, There's a Reaction

It had been roughly a week since Richard had thrown me out and I knew that the fight between us could destroy our relationship forever. I'm a glutton for punishment and it's in my nature to keep trying with Rich even though I was unsure who Rich was anymore; I wasn't going to give up on him, like he had given up on me. I was sitting alone at The Jester in Ashwell and feeling much calmer. I was having a few pints which made me nostalgic; Richard and I had spent so much time in this pub together.

'I can save this, one step at a time. I can save everything or at least give it a good go,' I thought.

I was sat staring into the fire, I loved the feeling of the heat on my face and watching the flames dancing about while it popped and crackled. I decided to send Richard an email and this is the exact email I sent to him on the 8th of December 2015 at 19.08

Bro

We should neutralise this row sharpish, just gonna spend years fighting. I'm pissed at you and you've let me down but life's too short. What's the fucking point should be me and you all the way! I was ready to take you to the cleaners and do all I could but save the fight for the ones who are worth it. Pride is not something I care about. Won't fix instantly of course but

I more than anyone know what's worth fighting and this ain't it. If you dig your heels in that's fine after all you've done me wrong and I'll carry on fiercely but otherwise happy to fuck off the row

He never acknowledged me or replied.

I heard in the coming days that Richard and Jen were telling everyone that they threw me out because they caught me dealing drugs from their house. It was that simple; there was no mention of Jen driving home drunk or anything about what really happened the night Richard threw me out of his house. This was their cover story and an easy way to camouflage the truth; people hung off Jen's every word, but in reality, she was the devil in disguise. Yes, I took drugs when I was at their house, but I did not sell any drugs. This doesn't make it okay, but they have both used cocaine before and I have been there on occasions when they did it.

I was aware they would now try and bring me down after the text I sent; they would go on a mission to tarnish what reputation I had left. On the surface, Richard and Jen portrayed themselves as the Posh and Becks of Royston. The untouchable couple, and then there was me, an unpredictable firework. Not just an outcast a rejected outcast who wore his heart on his sleeve, a gambler who abused drink and drugs and was no use to anyone anymore. It was going to take some time winning my friends round and make them open their eyes to see the truth.

With regards to Germany, I was still at their mercy, but I hadn't disclosed anything. When dealing in this type of situation, you don't reveal anything until you know exactly what you're up against; you wait until all the cards are on the table. You never reveal your hand early doors; you wait until the last second before deciding if you're going to stick or fold. Richard and what he did would only bring me down, so even though I sent that text I was never going to bring Richard into the situation; I was just venting. Richard speaks first and thinks later, he'd just fuck it all up and I wouldn't have let him anywhere near it; he would have been detrimental to my case. I was still prepared to protect my little brother; I would do whatever I could to protect everyone around me, while trying to save myself and leave that can of worms firmly shut.

In the meantime, Richard still owed me £42,000.00 and I wanted that back. I did have some money left over from my house sale and I was lucky because if Richard would have bit his lip another week and controlled his temper, I'd have given him that money too and he would have had the lot.

'Thank fuck he never got that,' I thought.

It was getting close to Christmas and I tried everything I could to reach him, email, calls and texts. I was becoming more and more frustrated; regardless of any arguing, you owe what you owe and we had unfinished business.

I was sitting on the sofa at Lizzy's when something occurred to me. Pausing for a moment, I thought, 'Fuck I've left that paperwork at Rich and Jen's; I didn't pick it up when he threw me out.' This was the paperwork that they had both signed stating that I still had a financial interest in XS Homes Limited; it was my company the company that I invited both of them to be part of: the company that I created and financed; something Richard and Jen were privileged to be part of and I had stupidly signed it all over to Richard to look after.

I decided to go to his house and see him I didn't know what else to do; I wanted to start trying to put things right and discuss the money that he owed me. After all, he owed me a lot of money. It was early in the evening, but it was so dark. I was driving in the Porsche and I put my foot down; at speed, the car was hugging every corner as I sped through the country lanes on my way to Biggleswade. I was not there for a fight, but was mindful things between Richard and I can get out of hand quickly, so I pulled up and parked the car nearby and walked the rest of the way to his house. Walking up to his front door, the street lights were the only thing lighting up the street. His house was pitch black as I stood there on his doorstep; I could see that none of the lights inside the house were on, but I stepped forward and knocked on his door and then took a step back. I always do this so I'm not on top of you when you open the door and it also gives me enough time to react if you come flying out of the door at me.

I stood there a little apprehensive waiting for some movement from inside the house or for the porch light to flick on, but nothing. I stepped forward and knocked again; I did this three times and waited patiently.

'There's no one in. Fuck it, what am I going to do now?' I said to myself.

I decided to knock on the next-door neighbour's house and the neighbour answered the door.

'Hello, Richard, how's it going mate?' the neighbour said to me.

'Hiya, mate, I'm the other one; it's Christian,' I said to him.

'Hello, Christian, you two don't half look alike; it's impossible to tell the difference,' he replied to me and was laughing.

'Listen, mate, can I ask you a favour; have you got a pen and paper handy? Looks like my bro's not in and I wanted to leave him a note.'

'No problems, mate, wait there a second,' the neighbour said as he left the front door slightly open and walked off into an adjacent room.

The neighbour came back with a pen and a Christmassy bag tag.

'Sorry, mate, I couldn't find any paper; will this do ya?' he asked me.

'Yeah, that should do it mate; that'll be fine,' I said.

'Keep the pen if you need it; I've got plenty of them,' he replied.

'Thanks again, mate, appreciate that,' I said as he closed his front door.

I didn't have much space to write on the tag, but I sat in the car and wrote a message to Rich.

'Listen, Bro, I'm not here for a row. I popped round to discuss my money; we can work this all out, but please get in touch,' and I signed it off with a kiss.

The house was still dead and there was no indication to me that anyone was in at all. I posted the message through the letter box and drove back to Lizzy's. When I got back to Lizzy's, I asked if I could borrow her phone as I was sure Richard had blocked all lines of communication. I simply wrote the same thing that was on the Christmassy bag tag and sent it.

It was about two o'clock in the morning and I was sitting on the sofa at Lizzy's watching TV. I heard her get out of bed and start coming down the stairs; the living room door opened and her face looked tearful. She was still sleepy, but looked so upset; she was holding her mobile phone in her hand and could barely speak.

'What's the matter, babe? What is it?' I asked her; I was immediately concerned.

'I just got this text from your brother,' she said looking at me really worried.

'Give it to me, let me take a look,' I said.

I gazed across the text and certain words jumped out at me.

'Hang on babe, just give me a second; I need to read this properly and take it all in.'

Lizzy stood in the doorway in her nightie; she looked so timid and vulnerable.

I'm sitting there reading this text and it's even worse than I thought at first glance. This is the exact wording from Richard's text message.

Start of Text

I'm sorry; I haven't blocked you. The fact you allowed him to text me and turn up at my house is a fucking disgrace. Tell Chris if he comes to my house again or comes near my wife then I will break more than his fragile little fucking nose. Now, and ask him why…

He was accused of rape by Nadine…

(can supply details on request).

Ask him why he has been with other men and I mean literally.

Ask him why he bought and dealt drugs at my house?

Ask him why he continues to threaten my life. If he continues to put me under duress, I will ensure his 5 years will be 15 years. He has been flagged and I have spoken to the police about his threats to my home or my wife.

Come to my door and intimidate my wife again and I will ensure that this story is over. He has been fully reported and I have been in contact with the police so if you'd quite kindly tell Chris to fuck off that would be appreciated. I am sick of living his lie! X

Bring your A game Christian, you have nothing. Authorities have been noted so bring your bullshit. Come near my home or wife again and it is flagged and I will look to harm, now fuck off little boy! x

Oh, and before I finish, you're a junky and rest assured you little cunt you mean nothing. Sorry Liz this wasn't meant for you to read but for some reason he texted me via your phone. He's a fucking scumbag, Chris don't give me a PS text ever again because nobody cared!!

I know exactly who Nadine's boyfriend is and if he doesn't step up to finish you then I easily will. Come near my wife again or look in her direction then I will fucking kill you. You turn up on my door step again little rapist then you'll need more than a Porsche to speed away. By the way I have role all authorities your intention so I'll see you on 15 you little fraudster. Could have quite easily left it, but you chose to open you little mouth, cunt. You little rapist! X

I was happy to leave it but cross me when there was no reason? Come to my wife's home and bring your Porsche you silly little boy. I have called you out and it's time Liz knew the truth, you cunt! x

<u>End of Text</u>

Okay so I read Richard's text and as I sat there my first thought was: I need to clear things up with Lizzy and make sure she is okay; no girl should ever receive a text like that.

Then I paused for a moment and thought to myself, 'Looking at the state of this text and the time that Richard has sent it, he obviously has got in pissed, but why does he keep referring to me going near his wife?'

I got up off the sofa and walked over to Lizzy to give her a hug.

'Fucking hell, babe, you should never have to see a text like that. Richard is a monster; it could be the worst text I've ever read. Richard is like my mum: he just fires on all cylinders for maximum destruction and he doesn't care who he hurts along the way. He will use everything and anything he can when he's trapped in a corner. I'm embarrassed for him; it's seriously embarrassing and he should be ashamed. I've got nothing to hide from you and, even if it hurts me, I would tell you the truth. The funny thing is that if you cut Richard open like a stick of rock, the word 'LIAR' would run right down the centre of him.'

'What's he talking about? He's text things like you've raped someone,' she said, looking at me straight in the face; Lizzy's face was a combination of emotions. I can't even begin to describe how she looked, but it wasn't nice for me to see her that way.

'Yeah, okay, let me clear that up. It's funny how that has come back to haunt me when he was the one who encouraged me not to tell you about it. I confided in Rich about something that happened to me; maybe I was wrong for not telling you, but I was trying to protect you and now Richard has used it as a weapon against me.'

I proceeded to explain everything to Elizabeth about what had happened with Nadine and how this girl had attempted to extort money from me.

'I'm so sorry that you've had to read that. It isn't right that he did that and you've never done anything against him. Once you break this text down, it's a Richie special: one of his speeches that is just absolute bullshit; there's no truth to any of it. Honestly, what fucks me off is him sending it to you and ignoring me. He's trying to split us up in the hope that you will throw me out and then I'm breaking my bail conditions again.'

Once I'd got over the initial shock of his text, the message itself in its entirety was fucking embarrassing and it was shameful of him to send a text of that nature to Lizzy when he could have text me directly; he deliberately sent it to her for maximum damage.

I knew our relationship after this text was definitely over. I won't let anyone not even my brother text my girlfriend a message like that and now the fight was on. I was positive Richard was going to steal my money and my company. I was already on the back foot because he had my money and my company, and now I had the hard job of trying to get it all back. This whole time, Richard had been using me and living in my shadow and God only knows how far back this goes. I've been duped because this guy who looks like me is not just a shit version of me, he's the ultimate con man.

Olney was a failure and, at this point, Richard was in major debt and still owed me £42,000.00. He couldn't give the property away, let alone sell it, so he had to recoup his losses somewhere and what better way to do it; he could just take it from me.

'Wow, the fucking audacity of Rich sending my girlfriend a text like that, so unnecessary and out of nowhere,' I thought.

This bothered me for a few days, but it wasn't long before I found out what had gone on and the reason why Richard had sent Lizzy that obscure text. I found out from my friends that he sent that text in an uncontrollable pissed up fit of rage because Jen was claiming that she was inside the house on the night that I went round there.

'I can truthfully and honestly say that I had no idea anyone was in and that I genuinely thought the house was empty.'

That night, Richard was at a work Christmas party because he had got himself a job and was now employed as an estate agent. Jen was frantically trying to call Richard on the phone and couldn't reach him, so instead, Jen on that night called a few of the girls that were in our inner circle of friends.

Apparently, she was screaming and crying hysterically down the phone telling them that I was trying to break into their house and that Jen was hiding fearful for her life, while I was trying to smash the door down.

The accusation that Jen made against me was so beyond the truth. Trust me, if I wanted to kick his door in then I would have done and I would have got through it. I never did that and if I had, I would have owned it and admitted it; why would I care? And looking back now, I wish I had kicked their door in.

Let's put it into context, I'm sure anyone who was owed £42,000.00 would at the very least go round to see the person who owed it.

'What about the note I left?' I wondered.

Leaving a note was hardly the actions of a crazed mad man who was trying to break down their door and shout 'Here's Johnny!' like the scene from the film *The Shinning*.

The note I left wasn't horrible and I was left questioning if Rich ever received it. I had my suspicions that Jen destroyed it and seized the opportunity to finally bury mine and Richard's relationship forever. Jen made the whole thing up and it certainly would explain the text that Richard sent to Liz.

I can just imagine it now. Richard staggered in from his Christmas party and Jen throwing herself at his feet the moment he came through the front door, telling him I was trying to break into the house—her laying it on really thick—and telling Richard how terrified she was. And, fuelled up on drink and anger, this prompted Richard to write and send that text. It was not the actions of someone who was rational.

In my view, Jen was now complicit and working as his accomplice. I already thought she was pulling the strings somewhere, but I also had to focus on Germany. I was spending more time fighting Rich than dealing with that.

At the end of the day, I was trying to fix things and I wouldn't have been on his doorstep if he had paid me the money that he owes me, or at the very least, just communicated with me—that's all he had to do.

From the moment that I sent that text message calling Richard out concerning the role that he had played in the Germany situation, the shutters were up and the lengths that he was now prepared to go to try and finish me off were quite incredible, especially for someone who apparently wasn't guilty of anything. Our relationship overnight had turned into a twin Armageddon; it really was the last battle between good and evil before the day of judgement, as the saying goes the truth hurts.

New Year was approaching and it was the first year that we had no invitations anywhere. Lizzy and I spent New Year at home. We tried our best but it was a struggle to even raise a smile; we were cuddled up and in bed together early, holding hands and just watching a movie. Lizzy was trying her best, but she was struggling too; she just didn't show it, but I knew.

January hit me quite hard and I missed not having my brother; he was my best friend. I had to remind myself he's not the brother that I thought he was; he's not even the person that I thought he was. I wanted some peace and quiet in my life and I wanted everything to go away. Dealing with Germany breathing down my neck and Richard, who had most of my money and my business, was a lot to deal with. It had been a really tough five months and I was suffering; I could feel that the depression and the suicidal thoughts and feelings were back; well, they never go away, but now they were growing in strength and I was feeling so anxious all of the time.

To get away, I started staying in hotels all over the place, drinking, taking cocaine and gambling. I decided to catch up with one of my close friends at a wine bar which was out of town; it was quiet and out of the way and he was already sitting by the bar.

'Hello, mate,' I said as he got off his stool to greet me and we hugged.

'All right; I've already got you a drink,' he replied.

There was a bit of small talk and I could tell there was something on his mind.

'Listen, mate, I've got to tell you something; it's not cool and you deserve to know about it.'

'Ah fuck me, mate, what now? What is it? Not sure I can take anymore bad news,' I said to him putting my head in my hands.

'You went for dinner last year, round Kirk and Tasha's; I think it was in September or October… I can't remember.'

'Yeah, I remember it, mate; it was practically the only time I went out after my arrest. I had a nice time—why? What's the matter?' I asked him.

'I think you should know; they did a drugs test in their downstairs toilet after you left.'

'You fucking what? Hang on mate, explain that to me,' I said to him. I was taken aback by what he had just said to me and wanted to understand everything.

'There are apparently these gloves you can get that can show positive for cocaine. Tasha got them off of her sister who works in London; they got them before you went there for dinner,' he told me and he was dead serious.

'Hang on, mate, do you know how bad that sounds? Why would you do that to someone?' I asked him.

'Well they told me that it tested positive. Did you do that?' he asked me, looking at me straight in the face.

'Mate, they had that christening at their house, a couple of weeks before I went round theirs for dinner; it was always going to test positive, regardless. I know loads of people who were at that christening doing coke, so I was fucked either way. They trapped me for what reason; why would they do that to me? I was never passing that test and yes, mate, I know it's not necessarily ideal, but I couldn't even leave my own house; I did do it at theirs, yes,' I told him.

'Mate, you know me and I couldn't give a fuck, but you definitely should know about it,' he replied.

'Yeah, but they never said anything to me; why would you set someone up like that? Especially with what I'm dealing with; I was always going to fail,' I was looking down at the floor just so disappointed with what I was hearing.

'Well, I thought you should know, mate.'

'Yeah, I appreciate that, mate. Hmmm, that might explain why me and Lizzy were not invited anywhere for New Year; they are quite influential. I just can't understand why they would throw me to the wolves like that. I can't get my head round it; we've grown up most of our lives together. Christ, I used to live with them.'

I was really miffed about what I'd just heard and was on the way back to Lizzy's and thought, 'I need to know why you would do that,' so, I grabbed my phone and text Tasha.

'Tasha, do you know how upset I am? Why would you set me up like that? Next time you want to stick on a pair of fucking marigolds just ask me,' I text her and she replied almost instantly.

'Oh my God, Christian, I can't believe anyone has told you that; we were trying to prove everyone else wrong, that's why I did it,' Tasha's text back to me read.

'What, so you told all of our friends and now what? You're all laughing behind my back. Do you know how hard it was for me to walk out of my fucking front door that night? How does telling everyone else this behind my back, help me? Did I do it, yes. Could I cope, No. You set me up; I can't believe you would do this to me,' I replied.

I then received a text from Kirk, her husband he was trying to diffuse things telling me that Tasha was in tears; she was in absolute bits, but I was having none of it and I told him to fuck off. I totally accept that I was in the wrong for doing cocaine in their house, but it was the deception of feeling set up by them that really pissed me off and if my friend hadn't told me about it then I would have never known.

You have to put this into context. Friends ask you round for dinner and the whole time they are colluding amongst themselves and waiting for you to leave their house so that they can go and wipe their fingers over everything and then tell everyone else they caught you doing drugs in their house.

Why would you do that to somebody, and especially do that to someone that was in desperate need of help? There's no need to kick me when I'm already on the floor.

I wasn't aware that some of my friends had been stabbing me in the back—right in plain sight—even friends that were like brothers or sisters to me. You're only as good as your last performance and if they like the show, they'll keep coming back, but one slip and you're booted out. Even after all of this, I still love them both.

When a friend falls, catch them!

Chapter 32
Against All Odds

It was Friday lunchtime on the 15th of January 2016 and I was sitting in the Tesco carpark at Royston waiting for my dealer. I'd been on it and had been missing for a few days; I was in self-destruct mode and wanted to be alone. I collected some supplies and drove to The Hardwick Arms Hotel in Arrington. I'd never stayed at this hotel before; it was only a couple of miles away from Lizzy's house, but far enough away for me to fly under the radar.

Straightening my face, I walked into the reception and booked myself a room for a couple of nights. I was given the key for room number three and I went back to my car to grab my bits. The Hardwick Arms is an old-style pub and has a proper pub feel and smell to it, and a fruit machine and pool table in the back room which are becoming so scarce these days—I found it quite comforting. Walking up the stairs, every single step creaked as I reached the top of the staircase. My room was to the left as I stood there looking at the big brass number three stuck to the centre of the door. I stood there for a moment; I was tired and also feeling tired of life. I took a big sigh as I walked through that door with two bottles of wine, forty Marlborough Lights and seven grams of coke. The door clicked shut behind me and I didn't care if it ever opened again. On the left side of the room, there was a work station with a kettle on it for teas and coffees, a double bed with an en-suite bathroom and a TV. At the end of my bed, by the wall, were two chairs and a round table. It was cosy; I liked it as I placed my bags on the bed. I pulled out a bottle of wine from the carrier bag and poured it into a coffee mug and took a sip. Taking things one step at a time, I started my hotel ritual, setting out all of my bits in certain places and the cocaine at my workstation. I racked up a few lines and had it all set out neatly.

'It's just me and this room,' I thought to myself.

I hadn't planned on gambling for a while and the hotel Wi-Fi was really unpredictable even my 4G kicked me out occasionally, so I sat down and started making notes on my phone for what is now this book. I sat at my work station listening to music for hours, drinking and doing cocaine; only occasionally getting up to look out of the window that was in my en-suite bathroom. I'd lifted up the window and fixed the latch, so I could pop my head out and look down onto the main road. I was smoking out of the window when it had started to turn dark and the hours were just melting away.

I was getting slightly wound up and Richard was playing on my mind; I was replaying things over in my head that had happened, things from the past. I wanted to know just how much of an animal Richard really was. I was jotting down all sorts of useful or useless information and significant moments in my life for my book. I was thinking back to the time that I was recovering from a nose job and Richard took my girlfriend Abby to the pub; it was the time they never came back until the following morning. I'm not sure why I was putting myself through it or why I wanted to revisit things that were painful, but I typed out a text message to someone who would just be straight up with me. I wanted to know if Richard ever really did care about me or had he been using me and doing me wrong the entire time. I text Chelsea, this was his ex-girlfriend—remember: the one that he punched in the face.

I knew if she knew anything, she would tell me the truth, I texted her.

'Chey, hello babe; I hope you're okay? I don't know why I'm bringing this up after all this time, but did Richard sleep with my ex Abby when I was with her and she was living with me?'

'Are you okay babe?' she texted me straight back.

'Yeah, I'm fine, I'm just mulling things over,' I replied.

'I'm worried about you,' she replied.

'Don't be, I'm okay, but I want you to tell me the truth. I'm just thinking back to a few things that don't sit right with me and I just want honest answers,' I texted back.

Chey then texted me back, 'Look, your brother is an arsehole and has only ever cared about himself; I didn't tell you this 'cos I wanted to protect you, but you know if you ask me something directly, I will always tell you the truth. The last time I saw Richard, he turned up at mine drunk and he was tearful, telling me he couldn't believe he'd slept with Abby behind your back. God's truth, and then he started trying it on with me.'

'Why am I not fucking surprised? The guy really is a fucking animal. I don't know why I do it to myself, but that confirms to me what I needed to know; he just takes what he wants. I just can't believe I was so blind not to see it,' I replied.

'I feel bad now, please stay safe babe. I worry about you,' she texted me.

'I'll be fine babe okay. Big kiss,' I texted her back and set my phone down on the side.

'Nothing surprises me anymore when it comes to Rich; he'd kill his own wife for money. I am seriously better off without him,' I said to myself.

I was struggling to keep my eyes open as I walked around the room; I was wearing out the carpet. It was just after midnight when I decided to hit the roulette tables. Turning my phone sideways, I clicked onto my online gambling app. I was so familiar with it and I'd learnt how to flick from one roulette table to another really quickly so I could choose the table that I liked the look of in an instant. Roulette interested me; I'd played it for so long, days at a time for well over a year now, and I know where every single number on the wheel is off the top of my head.

I enjoyed playing it because it took me away from what was really going on in my life; since I'd been under house arrest, it had kept me distracted on so many lonely nights.

I carried out the same routine that I always did; I racked up about seven or so lines of cocaine so I can do it while I play rather than fumble about with a note and a credit card. I needed my hands free as much as possible. I did a couple of lines and I was good to go, I zoned out.

I'd been playing like normal and, previously, the most I'd ever put on one number was around £50.00. The truth is, I'd had enough and wanted to do something big. I was losing everything I had around me, so I felt like I had nothing to lose and I didn't care anymore. It was all or nothing, do or die time so I deposited £10,000.00 into my gambling account.

I was looking at the roulette tables, flicking backwards and forwards, my eyes were scanning all of the numbers from previous spins on the wheel and I saw something, I had a feeling, so I clicked on this particular table and in seconds I selected the biggest chip that you could possibly bet with, it was a yellow chip worth £1,000.00. I placed the largest bet that I could at this table on just one number. The timer was counting down and I only had a few seconds, moving quickly I placed this chip on number 16 red.

It was the first bet that I had ever made this big, the bet itself was a monster; you won't find many people putting £1,000.00 on a straight up bet. Any other bet I made previously, paled massively in comparison. I have never ever done this before or to that extreme, but I was very calm, so calm in fact that I could have walked off and brushed my teeth and come back knowing it would come in and it did. The first ever bet I placed of that size came in and I won £35,000.00.

The next seven hours ahead was a battle as I shrugged off the first win and kept going. I kept going at 16 red and using 19 black as a backup, but always placed £1,000.00 on number 16. I remember passing £125,000.00 and I kept going; I remember passing £176,000.00 and I kept going. It wasn't long before I had £250,000.00 in my account.

On a couple of occasions, my 4G froze and threw me off the roulette table and I had to log back in.

'Fuckkkkkk,' I screamed and, by the time I'd logged back in, 16 red had come in again.

This happened to me three times and that would have won me another £105,000.00.

'Okay, it's happened; shrug it off and keep going,' I thought.

By now, the daylight was screaming at me through the en-suite bathroom window which put me on edge.

'Dig deep, Christian,' I said to myself.

The signal was still playing up and I was now literally hanging out of the bathroom window trying desperately not to lose signal and get thrown off the roulette table again. By now, I was up to £327,000.00; I remember a couple of spins where I saw the ball fly past number 16 and I watched it travel half way round the table before hitting a pocket and then come speeding back in the opposite direction, slamming into number 16 and then bouncing to a stop. My account balance was going up and down and it was exhausting, but I was generally making really good progress and for the entire time I played my turnover was well in excess of 1.2 million pounds; it's hard to tell, but I know it was a lot, perhaps even a lot more than that.

I was up to £387,000.00 and then all of a sudden, I took a few bad knocks and went down to £315,000.00.

'Nice one, Christian, you just threw away a Ferrari,' I shouted at myself.

Losing £72,000.00 really rocked me because as far as I was concerned, I was going to make a million pounds, but that hit me hard and knocked my confidence.

I was still hanging out of the bathroom window at the time when I thought.

'Why am I burning?'

I hadn't realised it, but while I was leaning out of the window my thighs were pushing up against a radiator which had come on in the early hours. I was so submerged in what I was doing I hadn't even noticed that it was white-hot and had burnt my legs.

I battled on and it took me seven hours to win and I now had £409,000.00 which was sitting in my account before the magic started to wear off. I was literally running on empty and

I decided I would stop at exactly £400,000.00. The next nine spins at £1,000.00 a time didn't hit anything. I didn't want to look anymore so I logged out and turned my phone face down and stood there thoughtful; I didn't celebrate like you would expect someone to who has just won that amount of money, but I felt a sense of calmness.

'Okay, Richard, bring it on you motherfucker,' I said to myself.

I didn't have the money to fight him back after what he had taken from me, but that all changed overnight and I now had enough power to fight him back and go after what he took from me.

I walked into that hotel room and I started playing roulette on the 16th of January 2016 on number 16 and I won £400,000.00 not bad for someone who could have left in a body bag.

It wasn't long before I received a phone call from the bookmaker, to congratulate me. The girls voice said to me down the phone 'Number 16 was good to you wasn't it? Congratulations, Christian, what you have done is quite extraordinary; it really is incredible, well done.'

I needed some fresh air so I picked up my cigarettes and went outside. The only thing that I am most proud of is that I did it alone, no one else but me and that room.

'I would have loved to have been a fly on the wall when Richard found out—karma's a Rich,' I thought to myself and I burst out laughing.

I want to be clear that I am in no way glorifying gambling and I seriously wouldn't recommend it unless you're playing purely for fun: it's a slippery slope trust me. I know because I've been on both sides of the fence.

There's a reason all of the numbers added together on a roulette wheel add up to 666, the number of the beast, the devil. The house is the devil and it is always in front unless you win big and stop because the only money you are ever going to get back was yours to begin with, remember that!

Okay, so moving forwards, I had been keeping in contact with Mum and Dad on and off and they were so glad I was back in their lives again. Mum and Dad were just the same as when Richard and I had left them all those years ago; they just looked like older versions of themselves. I'd explained to them what was going on and what Richard was doing.

Mum and Dad asked me over for a drink and I knew that meant a piss up so I put on my worst clothes and went to Therfield. Walking back into 'The House of Horrors' was quite strange; the feud between the neighbours still raged on and the only thing that had changed was the number of dogs they had which was now 38. The dogs were everywhere, trying to nip and pinch at me; they didn't like this new stranger who had disrupted their lair. I walked into the kitchen or what was left of the kitchen and it felt like everywhere I turned there was a dog popping out of somewhere. Mum poured some drinks; she was having a 'wicky and baileys' of course.

'I'll have one of those, Marilyn,' Dad said excitedly.

'No, David, that's my drink; you've got your own,' she cackled.

'So, Mum and Dad, I've won £400,000.00.' Their jaws dropped to the floor and they couldn't comprehend what I'd just said.

'How the hell have you done that? What did Lizzy say?' Dad asked me.

'I won it at roulette. It's funny, Dad, she wasn't that interested or excited at all; she just wants me to be fixed and stop what Richard and Germany are doing to me. She's not that bothered by money and was aware how much stress I must have put my body under to do what I did, so she wasn't that impressed,' I replied.

'What are you going to do with all that money? Take me and your father to Barbados,' Mum said with this silly grin on her face, like she was joking… or was she?

'Mum, I don't even have a passport as the police have got it, so first things first, I've got to try and get my money back from Richard; he had all the power, but I can change that now. It's ridiculous he thinks he can swan off with my money and do the things he's done to me. As much as it hurts me, I'm not interested in a relationship with him anymore. I don't know who he is, plus he's got control of the business that I set up; it's a fucking disaster. I'm going to go to Biggleswade and try and arrange a meeting on neutral ground.'

'I know he's my son, Christian, but why is he such a cunt?' Dad said; you could see it in his face that he was so disappointed in what Richard was doing to me and the man he has become.

'Don't say that, David, he's still your son,' Mum said butting into our conversation.

'Well, Marilyn, he is; look at what he's doing to Christian,' Dad said.

'You used to be so close, I don't understand,' said my mum; she looked so bewildered by it all.

'It's not me that changed, Mum,' I replied.

'Anyway, Christian moving on to a nicer subject: do you fancy another drink?' Dad asked me.

'Yeah, sure, Dad. I'm going to have a look upstairs, been so long since I've been here,' I said.

I had to navigate through the living room while Mum tried

to clear a path for me; like Moses parting the red sea, she waved me through clearing the path with all of the dogs either side of me. The living room had two large chest freezers in it, a sofa and a TV.

Walking upstairs, our bedroom was now a shrine to the dogs that Mum and Dad had lost along the way. There were little oak dog coffins everywhere all stacked up, one on top of the other, each little coffin with a gold plate and the name of the dog that had died was engraved on it including the surname Govan. Mum and Dad's bedroom was empty, no bed, just a room with dog cages. Mum was loitering at the bottom of the stairs waiting for me.

'Mum, where do you and Dad sleep?' I shouted down.

'We're okay, Christian, we both sleep on the sofa in the living room,' she shouted back.

'Fucking hell, Mum, you're not getting any younger—that can't be good for you or Dad sleeping upright on the sofa like that,' I said to her. I didn't like to hear that, but that's what they like to do.

'Behave, Christian; I still look 21. Me and your Dad are fine,' she replied.

The relationship between my mum and dad and I is a strange one because even though my childhood growing up certainly wasn't the best, and that's an understatement, there isn't anything that they wouldn't do for me. I wouldn't say its normal by any stretch of the imagination and they still have their squabbles—and, at times, it is really difficult to understand their approach to things—but they have tried their best to support me through everything that I've been through and everything that I'm still going through. That's my mum and dad and I've just learnt to accept them for who they are.

Chapter 33
Police on Speed Dial

The situation with Germany had gone quiet and the lawyers were thrashing it out, so I took this time to try and resolve the situation with Richard; I just wanted my money back.

I drove to Biggleswade on the 3rd of February 2016; it was dusk when I pulled into the pub carpark. The pub was called the Yorkshire Grey and it was Richard's local. I walked up to the bar and the bartender said to me.

'Hello, Rich, pint of Fosters with a top yeah?'

'That's fine, mate; yeah, thanks,' I replied. I couldn't be bothered to correct him.

Remember my cousin, 'The Fluffer'? Well I took my pint outside and sat on a bench and called him.

'Hey, Cuz, listen. I need you to do me a favour; all I want you to do is call Richard and tell him I'm at the Yorkshire Grey. I'm not here for a row and I just want to sort out the money that he owes me; can you ask him to come and meet me so we can sort this mess out?'

'Hello, Crystal; yeah I'll give him a call and I'll tell him exactly what you've asked me to say. I'll call you back when I've spoken to him,' he said to me.

'Thanks, Cuz, I appreciate that.'

It was only a couple of minutes before my cousin called me back.

'Hey, Cuz, did you reach him?' I asked.

'Yes, I told him where you were and I told him exactly what you asked me to say and he went quiet and then he hung the phone up on me.'

'Hmmm okay, Cuz, I'm gonna dash; I bet he's phoned the police,' I said.

'Why would he do that? He wouldn't do that would he?' my cousin asked me sounding concerned.

'Cuz, I wouldn't put anything past him, but I know when something doesn't feel right. Thanks, anyway, take care,' I said to him and I put the phone down and walked straight into the pub and approached a girl working behind the bar.

'Hiya, sorry to bother you, but can you do me a favour?' I asked her.

'Sure, if I can. How can I help you?' she replied.

'Can you look after my car keys for me? Just put them behind the bar somewhere,' I asked her as I held out my keys.

Taking my keys from me she said, 'Sure, I can do that; I'll just put them here okay?' She said as she pointed to a space behind the bar and set my keys safely out of the way.

'Yeah, great, that's fine; thanks, babe,' I said as I made my way back out of the pub.

I walked back to where I had been sitting and sat down on the bench to finish my drink; I knew it wouldn't be long and it wasn't. In less than five minutes, a police car pulled up in the carpark. I watched them park up and I walked over to the two officers as they were getting out of their car.

'Are you looking for Christian?' I asked the female officer politely.

'Yes, we are. Why, is that you?' the female officer said.

'Yes, that's me, I'm Christian. I figured he would call you,

322

so tell me what's he said,' I asked her and, by now, the male officer had walked round the car and was standing by the female officer's side and they were now both in front of me.

'We've had a report from your brother, Richard, of violent and threatening behaviour towards him by you and that you've been drinking and driving and are on drugs,' the male officer said to me.

'That's not true; I've come here to try and resolve something between us. I've come to this pub so that it wouldn't be threatening,' I told the male officer.

I felt like the officers were expecting to turn up and have a mad man on the loose, but they were pleasantly surprised as I was quite the opposite: I was calm; I was coherent and polite to both of them.

I explained to the officers the situation and they were quite understanding. I told them that he owed me money and I was simply trying to get it back and resolve things, but they advised me that as he was the one that made the complaint, they have to quite literally take his side and that I should stay away from him and if I attempt to go near him, his property or his wife, then I will be arrested. They advised me to try and get my money back through the courts and with that, they both got in their car and left.

I stood there in the carpark and watched them drive away. 'He's a fucking idiot; what a wanker! He clearly has no intention of paying me back and is now using the police as a shield—just another attempt to try and get me silenced and locked away,' I thought to myself.

Richard had sent that text to Lizzy with all of those threats about what he was going to do to me and how he was going to harm me and break my fragile little nose; well, he certainly wasn't living up to all the hype that he had created. He didn't even have the decency to try and work things out or salvage any kind of relationship with me and that's simply because he didn't want to, why would he? He has just netted himself £42,000.00.

I stayed to have a couple more drinks and mull things over. I was cautious the police were probably nearby or watching me from a distance so I left my car at the pub and walked to a nearby hotel.

I was drunk while I sat in that hotel room and I just kept thinking how outrageous it was that he'd used my money for his lavish wedding. It was still sinking in that Richard was definitely going to keep my money and keep the business that I'd signed over to him; the business that he promised to look after while I was dealing with the situation in Germany. By now, he would have destroyed the paperwork that I left at his house. He was going to try and royally fuck me over; Rich had decided to take it all and then it suddenly dawned on me that the next problem I have is my friend who had loaned me £225,000.00 was going to come knocking soon. I was aware that he had been paid back £70,000.00 from XS Homes Limited, but my friend was still owed £155,000.00 which was still in the business. I'd signed over my shares to Richard and I couldn't pay my friend personally as it would be like handing Richard over another £155,000.00.

Sitting at the end of the bed in my hotel room, Richard's voice resonated in my head like it was on a loop, repeating over and over again: Richard saying to me, 'What do you think to this wedding? It's the bollocks,' while we clinked our champagne glasses together.

And

'Your money will be safer with me than him,' referring to James Constantinou.

It was my fucking champagne and as for James Constantinou, who is now worth about 5 million pounds, it was obvious where my money would have been safer.

'Richard will destroy your life, take you for all he can and then simply move on,' I thought.

I hated him, I wanted to hurt him; I wanted the chance to see him face to face.

I will always regret the bad decisions that I made, some huge mistakes trusting Richard; I had allowed him the opportunity to take everything from me by being too trusting. I just never considered that my identical twin brother would do this or could do this to me.

With no choice, I prepared a letter and sent it to Richard stating that if he did not pay me the outstanding £42,000.00 that he owed me then I had no option but to start legal proceedings.

I received an email from Richard and this is the exact email he sent to me on the 10th of February 2016 at 11:19 titled Harassment

Christian,

Under instruction you need to be made aware that your persistent contact with me and my wife is harassment and if you wish to proceed with getting 'what you think you are owed' then you need to go down the correct legal channels to do this.

Your email addresses have been blocked and any future correspondence via any other method other than legal will not be read.

The police and authorities are aware of all events and the

situation is being closely monitored.

Richard Potter.

His email was fucking nonsense. He owed me £42,000.00 and he knew it. He was hiding behind the police and using their precious resources as a constant shield, and his reference concerning the authorities, in an attempt to scare me off, was a joke.

His actions were deplorable and this situation was becoming incredibly frustrating for me. He was just trying to hide behind somebody, anybody, to make it go away. I wasn't going to let it go away, so I persisted with trying to contact him. Owing somebody money, and then deliberately blocking their ability to communicate or discuss it with you, is shameful. They are the actions of someone who intends to steal it from you; I wouldn't have needed to contact him at all, if he had just paid me what I had lent to him.

It was Wednesday the 24th of February 2016 when I walked into the police station at Stevenage to sign in as I did every Wednesday, and as soon as the woman behind the counter looked up at me, I knew something was wrong. I watched this woman become nervous and agitated; she was out of breath as she kept dashing in and out of a side room that was to her left.

'Christian, could you just wait there a moment, please?' she asked me.

'Sure, no problem,' I replied as I went and took a seat on the metal-linked chairs in the reception of the police station.

I waited for the inevitable and within a couple of minutes two officers came rushing out and arrested me. I was being charged with harassment; I was being arrested for making contact with Richard when all I was trying to do was get my money back.

Richard had set me up by sending that email. The law states that you have to warn someone if you feel you are being harassed and after this warning, two unwanted approaches are enough to arrest you for harassment, even two phone calls would do it.

I knew the drill by now and I couldn't have been nicer to the police; I was so familiar with being arrested and put in a cell that I was totally calm about it. One thing I'd learnt is that they will spit you back out when they are ready; you are there for the duration and I wasn't going to let it stress me. I got an opportunity to call Lizzy after I was booked in.

'Lizzy, hey babe; listen, I've been arrested—no drama— I'll get back to you when I can.'

Even Lizzy acted like it was normal.

'Okay, babe, glad you called; otherwise, I would have worried about you just disappearing on me. I was making your dinner too; I'll keep it in the fridge,' she said calmly.

Once I was processed, I was placed in a cell and with the Germany situation still hanging over me it was obvious Richard was still trying his hardest to get me locked away; he was relentless. I wouldn't be harassing him if he did the right thing and gave me my money and my business back. I was becoming desensitised with how the officers tried to put me under pressure, and the stresses of keeping you in the cells for longer than necessary. I meditated in my cell and I used the time to work a way out of the situation I was in.

The criminal was Rich and he was hiding behind the police so I couldn't get at him yet.

I was held in the cells until the eleventh hour when the flap of my cell door opened and a pair of eyes said to me,

'We are going to be transporting you to the police station at Bedfordshire where matters will be dealt with there.'

You're only supposed to be in a cell for 24 hours before you're either released or charged, but I'd spent a number of hours in a cell at Hertfordshire and I was now being taken to Bedfordshire where the clock started again and they had a fresh 24 hours on me. I was taken in a police van to the police station at Bedfordshire and I was processed again; I was asked if I was a suicide risk, or if I had ever considered suicide and I replied to the custody officer at the police station in Bedfordshire, 'I'm okay, but if you're asking me if I have ever suffered suicidal thoughts or feelings then the answer is, yes I have.'

The custody officer then arranged for me to be assessed by a counsellor. The counsellor would speak to me and check my general well-being and make sure that I was fit to be interviewed, but this wouldn't be until they had someone available. It was late at night now so it would be until tomorrow morning at the earliest.

'I'm going to be locked up here till tomorrow night at least,' I thought.

I need to do all I can to ensure that I can cope with this so I asked the officer who was about to take me to my cell.

'Would it be okay if you could give me a couple of blankets please, and those nicotine lozenges you do, and a coffee? When you're ready and if that's okay? Thanks.'

You never sleep properly in the cells and it's all designed to stress you out, but I was feeling stronger today and I was okay. It was around lunchtime when the counsellor was available to see me; the cell door opened and I was taken to an interview room.

'Christian, I have been informed that you are a potential suicide risk; can you tell me a little bit about what's going on with you and how you've been feeling lately?' asked the counsellor as she placed her arms on the table and leant forward to listen to me.

'Well, yeah, sure; it hasn't been easy for me lately and there are times that I have contemplated suicide. I have been diagnosed with severe depression and suffer with severe anxiety, so I am struggling a bit. I have a few situations going on and it has been a tough few months for me, since my arrest back in July. I was arrested and I'm being accused of tax evasion for sixty million euros in Germany. I'm fighting a European Arrest Warrant; I also have a situation with my twin brother which is why I have been arrested now because I'm trying to recover money that he has stolen from me and also a business that he has taken from me. All of this could have bankrupted me. I was accused of rape by some girl who was trying to extort money from me and I've slipped a little and been doing a lot more cocaine and drinking a lot more alcohol,' I tried to explain everything the best I could and I looked at her with a sombre expression.

'Christian, sometimes people can create certain things in their mind to try and deflect from what is really happening to them in their lives. Now, I'm not saying you are doing that, but do you think you could be creating some of these elaborate situations? I mean, you mentioned 60 million euros; it does sound a bit far-fetched doesn't it? It may not really exist even though you believe it, which is why you're feeling this way.'

I sat back in my chair and I didn't mean to, but I laughed.

'I'll tell you what, why don't you go outside and check the database or whatever file it is that you look at concerning me and I'll wait here.'

'Okay, Christian, let me just go and check a few details,' the counsellor said as she pushed her chair back and swiftly left the room.

It must have only been five minutes before she walked back into the interview room.

'Okay, Christian, fair enough; it looks like what you're saying is true, so the reason I am here is to make sure you are fit for interview and look after your well-being, okay?' she said.

After a brief chat, I explained I'm fine I may be a little fragile, but I can cope with an interview and I haven't done anything wrong; it's about time I got out of here. I was taken back to the cell and, later in the afternoon, I was taken to be interviewed by this female officer; I can't remember her name, but I clicked with her and I was upfront during my interview. There wasn't much I could do about it as I had approached Richard more than twice so if they wanted to claim that's harassment then it was.

Richard owed me £42,000.00 and I don't think under those circumstances I'd done nearly enough, and Richard was using the police to stop me getting near him.

'I'm sure there are a lot of people that would kill for a lot less,' I thought.

After my interview, I was returned back to my cell and it wasn't until later that evening when the female officer that I'd been dealing with opened the cell door and asked me,

'Christian, how do you feel if we give you a caution? Are you prepared to accept that?'

'Yep, not a problem, can you get me out of here now?' I replied as I stood up, dropping the blankets that were wrapped around me.

Whilst I was being processed and getting ready to be released, I was with the female officer and her phone rang. I could hear my brother's voice on the other end of the phone. The officer was talking to Richard while I was standing there and she explained to Richard that I was receiving a caution. I strained my ear to listen and I heard Richard say to the officer 'How do we stop Christian telling anyone about what's happened?' he sounded disappointed and I think he thought they were going to lock me up and throw away the key and now he wanted a gagging order against me.

'You can't; we have dealt with the matter and he will be free to go shortly,' the female officer replied. She looked confused and annoyed with Richard's comments.

Astonishing, this joker thought he could hide behind the police and then keep it all a secret to protect his image. It was really late in the evening when I finally got released and I had formally received a caution for harassment.

I called Lizzy as soon as I left the police station and she said to me, 'Your dad's been calling me non-stop; he's been going mad trying to get you out. He's fuming with what's going on.'

'I'll talk to you properly later, babe; I just need to get home and have a shower and dust myself off, again,' I said to her.

Standing outside the police station, I was back in the real world; it was cold and dark as I walked along this pathway heading for anywhere that I could see lights. I could see my breath as I walked; rubbing my hands together, I had no idea where I was. Lizzy was coming to get me and I told her to call me when she was close and I'll be in the nearest pub.

After my arrest I needed some normality in my life, so I started going to the gym a lot more and was deciding whether or not to pull the trigger and instruct a solicitor to tackle the situation with my money. It was becoming the only avenue I had; I was reluctant because I knew that it was going to cost me a lot of money. Nobody wants to go through the courts unless there really is no other option; it's a long and expensive process.

It was the middle of March and if it wasn't me dealing with the police, it was Mum and Dad. I just couldn't catch a fucking break from the drama.

The police and the RSPCA raided Mum and Dad's house on Tuesday the 15th of March at 7.30am and it wasn't until around 9am when I received a frantic call from my mum. My phone rang and when I picked it up, I couldn't make out a word Mum was saying in between her crying and stuttering; she was unable to speak.

'Christian, it's your mum. They are taking the...' Mum started to sob so Dad took over the phone call.

'Hello Christian, it's your dad. We have the police here and the RSPCA; we're okay, but your mum's distressed as they are taking all of the dogs away,' Dad said.

'Okay, Dad, I'll be there in a minute,' I replied.

I had enough to deal with as it was and I hadn't signed up for this when I got back in touch with them, but I had to try and help.

I grabbed a piece of toast and jumped in the Porsche. This car was becoming my best friend; it had travelled everywhere with me and was always there in the middle of the drama. I floored it to Therfield.

As I got into Therfield, I slowed up as I drove past the

cricket field and their house came into view. I could see a number of officers and vehicles everywhere. Pulling up in the car, I got out and walked right into the middle of it. Mum and Dad were being really hostile so I became the negotiator to try and bring some sense to the situation; after all, Mum and Dad could fight all they wanted, but this was happening and there was nothing they could do to stop it.

'Come on, Mum, let them get on with it,' I said putting my arm around her.

'I won't, Christian, they're not taking my dogs; this is all because of that shit head next door,' she shouted.

'Mum, they have a warrant and you'll only end up getting arrested,' I told her.

'I don't care, Christian, they can take me away in a coffin,' she protested.

'Mum, come on, let's go upstairs and talk about this,' I said to her.

Once I got upstairs with Mum and Dad, Mum burst into tears and was inconsolable.

'Please help us, Christian, I don't want to be here anymore; I've had enough,' said my mum and she was barely holding it together.

I made a snap decision there and then.

'Okay, Mum, I'll renovate this house for you. It can't be sold in its current state, but I know enough people to get this place looking brand new and I can get you away from here,' I said to her.

'Would you do that for us, Christian? Me and your father? We could buy a Winnebago and get ourselves a piece of land and get some horses, somewhere nobody knows us,' she replied.

They had clearly been dreaming of this situation, but were financially stuck. Richard and my parents were so alike when it came to money, neither of them had any. I was the only person who could help and of course both Mum and Dad jumped at the chance when I offered it.

'I can do that for you, Mum; you can go down the coast and we can walk along eating ice cream and walking your dogs, whatever you like,' I said to her trying to comfort her and give her some hope that everything will be okay.

Mum was starting to calm down at the promise of a new life, and to be fair this row had been going on for so many years I think everyone needed a break—even the neighbours. All of the dogs were taken, and now they were all out of the way, I could finally get to grips with the state of this house.

'The House of Horrors' was always a property that Richard wanted because he thought there was so much potential as a renovation; I remember he used to say to me, 'If Mum and Dad ever left this to you in their will, we'd go halves wouldn't we? After all, we've both suffered here together.'

This would take some time, but I took on 'The House of Horrors' alone and I purchased Mum and Dad exactly what they had asked for: a huge American-style Winnebago. I bought it on the 24th of March 2016; it was called the Intruder, and trust me this thing was so intrusive. Mum and Dad loved it; it was better than their house. It had a full-sized double bedroom which popped in and out, an en-suite bathroom, a dining room and kitchen—it was about 37-foot-long, pearlescent and bronze in colour with the word Intruder scrolled across the back in blue graffiti-style writing.

As far as I was concerned, the property at The Grove, Abington Road, Litlington belonged to XS Homes Limited and it was mine even though Richard owned it on paper. I parked the Winnebago there as it was the only place big enough to house a vehicle of this size; in the meantime, Mum and Dad were deciding where they were going to move to. They would have to attend court some months later where they would both be fined £9,000.00 each for breaching a noise abatement order, but all of the dogs were returned by the RSPCA as they found no evidence of mistreatment; they hadn't been mistreated. The only problem was my mum had nowhere to keep them so she kept a couple back and the rest of them were rehoused by the RSPCA, but they had a fresh start: a new beginning.

Chapter 34
Face-off

The days were flying past and I still hadn't heard any news regarding Germany. Lorenzo had informed me that there was a hearing and it was imminent, but he wasn't being given a date. He said to me, 'I feel like something is definitely going on, Christian, because I can't get a straight answer from anyone.'

On the 29th of March 2016, I was standing in Lizzy's kitchen making a cup of tea when my phone rang and it was Lorenzo; taking a deep breath, I answered the phone.

'Hey Lorenzo, it's Christian, how's it going?' I was wincing as I asked him, waiting for the bad news.

'Listen, Christian, there will be no need for you to attend any hearing; you've been discharged. You're free—it's over,' he said to me; I could tell by the way he said it, that he had a huge smile on his face.

I couldn't speak for a moment while I processed what I'd just heard.

'Are you still there, Christian?' Lorenzo asked me.

'Yes, Lorenzo, I'm still here; I just can't believe that. Thank you, Lorenzo, thank you for everything.'

'It is Christian; I know it's been hard on you, but it's finally over. Take care of yourself, Christian, I'll keep in touch,' and he put the phone down.

I stood in the kitchen for a moment stunned, 'I've got to tell Liz,' I thought so I picked up the phone and called her straight away.

'Hey babe, I just got a call from Lorenzo; they've discharged me—it's over.'

'Oh, my God, baby; I can't believe this!' she said as her voice started to tremble.

'Mum, it's Christian, he's free. Germany has released him!' she shouted out.

'Okay, babe, I've got to go; I've got to take this all on board. Love you,' I said.

'I'm so happy; okay, I'll speak to you later. Love you too,' she said. As I was putting the phone down, I could still hear her in the background; she was excited and tearful all at once.

I sat down and I sent an email to Lorenzo and this is the exact email I sent to him on the 29th of March 2016 at 12:53 titled: Discharged EAW!

Hi Lorenzo/Rebecca

Further to my conversation with you earlier today it looks like things have finally been resolved. Firstly, I'm incredibly grateful for everything you have all done since my arrest, my life was literally in your hands and today I feel free again. I'm so so happy.

I need to check a couple of things. Rebecca, when I spoke to Lorenzo today and if you get an opportunity to liaise with Lorenzo when you are attending court later today.

The security of £10,000.00 must if it is possible be paid back to me as the funds are mine. I am concerned they will be paid to my brother.

Also is there a document I can be supplied with in order for me to keep a copy with the details of my case being dropped. Just in case I travel and encounter any problems and to keep it for my records.

These matters are quite important to me so if you are able to help, I appreciate it.

Once again thanks for everything X

Christian

I was so thrilled that I couldn't put it into words. I had gone through so much; and like a fish on a hook the line had just snapped and they let me go. I heard through the grapevine, and in the coming months, that I was the only person discharged from the entire case. Further raids had been carried out on other people and the six strangers and the new additions were eventually all sent to prison in Germany; many of them still haven't come back and are imprisoned in Germany right now as I write this in October 2019.

It didn't instantly evaporate all of my demons into thin air, I still carry the scars. I feel, once you suffer such deep bruising from depression, the scars are unfortunately with you for life. I have good and bad days and I still feel so much pain, but it taught me: you have to keep going and never give up because you never know what's around the next corner. I could have lost my life too soon.

Over the next coming days, I tried to track down the £10,000.00 that I had paid as security as part of my bail conditions. On the 12th of April 2016, I received a phone call from Lorenzo. He found out, and advised me, that my case had actually been dropped against me on the 5th of January 2016 and the money had already been paid back to Richard. The money had to be sent back to the account where it had originally come from, and to this day I still don't know how it got so fucked up. I was still signing in at the police station in Stevenage for three months after I had been discharged and I didn't find out I was discharged until the 29th of March 2016. I had suffered unnecessarily for another three months and the entire time it was all over. More importantly, my brother knew this and he never said a word, and he kept my £10,000.00 that I had paid as security as part of my bail conditions. It was shocking, it was so disgraceful that Richard kept my bail money; it had mysteriously appeared back in his bank account in January and he kept it and never said a word. Let me repeat this: I need to make sure you take it on board. Richard stole my bail money for the amount of £10,000.00 and kept it a secret.

This is as bad as it gets; I appreciate we weren't talking at the time, but he didn't let anybody know or pass a message onto me through our friends that circumstances had changed. He couldn't care less if I had lived or died. I could have killed myself in those three months after January and he couldn't give a fuck. He saw £10,000.00 drop into his account and kept the money without saying a word; it doesn't get any eviler than that.

Imagine seeing £10,000.00 drop into your bank account that doesn't belong to you and keeping quiet in the most severe of circumstances and deciding to enjoy that money.

The thought of Richard making the decision to keep that money and thinking to himself: 'Result, I'm going to have that,' repulses me.

He owed me £42,000.00 and now he had taken that £10,000.00. The total he now owed me was £52,000.00 again. If you remember, I originally loaned Richard £55,000.00 back in 2014. He had returned fuck all of my money since then.

Over the next couple of weeks, news of my release had spread across Royston like wildfire. I was thinking about taking Lizzy away so we could spend some proper time together. I was free and could travel again, but in the meantime, I went to help Mum and Dad empty 'The House of Horrors' and get it completely cleared out. I'd spent most of my day up in the attic, climbing over mountains and mountains of junk and toys from my childhood that were piled up to the rooftop. It was an Aladdin's cave of Star Wars toys, Beano and Desperate Dan comics, old electronic gadgets and board games.

It was around seven o' clock in the evening and my mum and dad took me out for a Chinese as a thank you. I was still wearing the same clothes that I'd been working in so I didn't fancy venturing out too far afield, so after the Chinese, we went to a pub in a little village called Bassingbourn. It must have been about ten o' clock at night when my dad's mobile phone started ringing; his phone was looking up at me from the table. As it vibrated and slowly started moving, I had to look twice and I recognised the number immediately; I realised it was my brother calling. Picking up my Dad's phone, I answered it; I hadn't said a word and straight away received a barrage of abuse down the phone.

'You better come and move that fucking Winnebago off my property right now, before I smash it up,' Richard said aggressively.

'Oh, is that fucking right?' I said back to him and he hung up the phone on me straight away.

He had phoned to intimidate and threaten my dad and the last thing he expected was for me to answer the phone.

'Christian, who was that?' Dad asked me.

'You're not going to believe this Dad, but that was Rich; he was obviously expecting you to answer the phone and he started making threats about smashing up the Winnebago. He must be at 'The Grove' in Litlington,' I said while thinking at the same time how fucking brave he was to phone and threaten someone who is nearly seventy years old.

'Fuck this, Dad, I'm calling him,' I said.

Richard had hidden from me for all this time and I saw an opportunity to get hold of him so I called him back. There was an exchange of words down the phone, but basically Richard said to me, 'Come and get me.'

Well, you didn't need to ask me twice and I quickly finished my drink and hurried Mum and Dad out of the pub door. We jumped into their car and made our way to Litlington; it was less than a mile away. Dad wouldn't have stood a chance against Richard, but I would and it was playing on my mind what a bully Richard was, phoning up Dad and trying to intimidate him and obviously not forgetting all of the things that he had done to me.

We were driving along and I was sitting in the back seat talking to Mum and Dad.

'When we pull up, I want you and Dad to stay out of the way, I'll deal with this,' I said to both of them firmly.

As we approached, I could see Richard's black Audi A3 parked up in the lay-by which sits directly opposite the property.

I could see two silhouettes inside the vehicle, I knew it was Rich and Jen. I saw Richard get out his car and as Dad pulled up, him and Mum both got out and started walking towards Richard while I'm stuck in the back seat because the child lock is on. I quickly looked through the windscreen and saw my Dad getting closer to Richard.

'They haven't listened to a fucking word I said,' I thought, I'm going to have to move fast.

Rich can certainly hold his own and if Richard hit Dad, I was worried it could kill him.

'Mummmmm,' I shouted and she heard me and looked back realising I was stuck in the car.

Running back to the car, she released me from my car cage and I got in front of Dad within seconds. Shielding him, I went straight at Rich and he put his hands up and lunged at me. I was fully charged up and filled with so much hatred and pain for what he'd put me through, there was nothing anyone could have done to stop me.

'Bring it, you fucking cunt,' I said as I charged forward and grabbed him round the throat and almost bent him into the shape of a pretzel.

I had hold of Rich and dragged him down the road, as I passed Jen who was still sitting in the passenger's seat watching. She went to open the door to get out and help Rich, so while dragging Richard along I kicked the passenger door shut which trapped Jen back inside the car; I was in control as I took Richard to the ground flinging him round like a rag doll. I was aware Mum and Dad were floating around as they let me get on with it, but by now Jen had managed to get out of the car and I could hear her running up and down the street shouting and screaming, 'This is our house! This is our house!'

I remember thinking, 'Cheeky bitch, neither of you have used any of your own money and it's been funded by Lizzy's dad and my mate, and you think it's yours, you thieving cunts.'

Taking Richard to the ground, I had him in a head lock; I raised my right arm and was just about to punch him in the face and I wouldn't have stopped, but as I raised my right arm, Jen appeared out of nowhere—just in time—and with enough force, she pushed my right arm hard enough to move me backwards enabling Richard just enough leverage to roll over with me. 'The Grove' is surrounded by bushes which act as a fence at the front of the property and as we both went to stand up while holding onto one another, we went completely through the bushes together and landed on the other side. We are now on the ground and in the garden of the property, and the garden was so overgrown and thick with brambles. As we landed on the floor, I head-butted him from the ground up; stunned, he let go of me and ran away.

I was up, and on my feet, and in pursuit, while he's shouting for Jen to start the car. I was on top of him as we crashed into his car; the car crumpled on impact and the wing mirror flew off. I dragged him and used him like a paint roller going over his own car, creating dents as we went. By the time I'd finished with him, both wing mirrors were smashed off and most of his panels were dented. Rich had managed to open his car door and squeezed himself through an inch-wide gap and they sped off swerving down the street. As they roared off around the corner, one way, four police cars came speeding around the corner the other way and pulled up outside 'The Grove.'

Richard probably doesn't even realise what a lucky boy he was that night; he should be forever grateful that his wife pushed my arm—he was in a lot of trouble.

I was now standing there in the middle of the road while the police started to circle me; they were not aggressive and I was very calm, but I knew they had me surrounded, so I lit up a cigarette.

'They got here quick, far too quick,' I thought as I took a drag on my cigarette and blew the smoke out of my mouth and watched it dissipate into the air.

I knew they were going to take me and I was placed under arrested and, interestingly, so was my Dad. We were both taken to Cambridge Parkside Police Station. On the way to the police station, I was thinking about the situation and it dawned on me that Richard had been waiting for us at 'The Grove'. When we pulled up, I deduced that Richard had phoned the police prior to that event even happening, like a murderer being caught before he's actually murdered someone. This was a set-up; Richard had called the police on speed dial and pre-ordered them, but you can't phone the police and say you're about to get assaulted and then hang around at the scene. If you were scared, you would leave. Anyway, that didn't matter to me, the fight was very real and I wish I'd done more, but I definitely showed him who was boss. I was okay with what came at me from here. I was far too familiar at check in and I asked for the usual.

'A bunch of blankets and some nicotine lozenges,' you know the drill.

It wasn't until I was in the cell that I realised I had been bitten on each pec; I had two round circles with an inner bruise in both—these were deep bites. Richard had bitten me; he must have done that gasping for breath when I had him in a head lock.

'Not only does he fight like a girl, he bites like a girl; disgusting pig,' I thought.

It was the usual wait times before I was interviewed, but I was ready and the first thing I said to the investigating officer while under caution was that we were set up.

'It was Richard who called my dad and we wouldn't have even known where he was—if he hadn't done that and it wouldn't have happened. Plus, he's calling you before any crime has been committed; he had time to leave, but he didn't.'

I went through the normal procedures; Richard had sent the police my way three times in two and a half months and it was starting to get tedious. For someone that hated the police, he sure was enjoying using them when it suited. I watched the daylight come and go through the glass squares of my cell; it was the only link to the outside world. Dad and I were released the following day and we walked to the nearest pub and I called Lizzy to pick us up. There were no charges brought against either of us.

Dad phoned Mum to let her know he was okay and during the phone call, the police had been in touch with my Mum as Jen had made a statement accusing my mum of assaulting her. This was nonsense and one thing I do know is that if my Mum wanted to assault someone then she would have done. Jesus, she could kick the arse out of most men and Jen would've ended up in hospital, not parading around on Facebook a day later without a scratch on her, showing off her new hairdo—that's what she did.

The police did not make any charges against me, my mum or my dad, although Rich and Jen were trying their hardest and Rich would stop at nothing to get me put away; he couldn't manage it, but he was trying.

It was laughable to me, 'It was Jen and Rich who were partners in crime; they were the ones enjoying other people's money, while crying wolf,' I thought.

I had to start considering my own safety. Richard had tried so hard to get me locked up or charged with something and so far, all I had was a caution for harassment. It was time to change tact and it wasn't just this problem, but another war was starting to gain momentum in the background when my friend and Lizzy's dad became more aware of what Richard was doing; they were outraged, but were not best pleased with me and some of the poor decisions that I'd made. I hadn't discussed this with Lizzy, let alone anyone else, when I signed XS Homes Limited over to Richard and my friend went ballistic when he found out I'd sold my house which was his personal guarantee. I can honestly say at the time, and I know looking at it now, it looks really bad but my intentions were honourable and I thought that I was doing the right thing. I never imagined my friend would struggle to get his money back; it was unimaginable that this could happen and I thought that his money was safe, but Rich was in control and he was fucking everything up and everyone over. It was clear he had taken the company from me and I would never get it back.

I pulled the trigger and my solicitor sent a 'Notice of Claim' and 'Letter Before Action' titled Mr Christian Govan vs Mr Richard Potter on the 29th of April 2016 to pursue Richard for the £52,000.00 that he owed me. I was left with no choice but to take Richard to court.

On a lighter note, Lizzy and I went to Mykonos together; it was our first holiday since my arrest back in July 2015. It was so amazing to me, walking through the white-cobbled streets of Mykonos—a maze of shops, bars, clubs and restaurants, each alley led to somewhere different and it was easy to get lost. Lizzy and I held hands so as not to lose one another; we laughed and chatted stopping at a cocktail bar once we reached the seafront. We sat their sipping cocktails; I loved the warmth of the sun on my face and an occasional breeze cooled me down as I looked out across the sea watching the sunset. I thought back to staring out of the window in my cell at Wandsworth Prison, and I told myself, 'To always take a second to appreciate the moment.' I had more reasons to celebrate than most, after going through so much pain, I was free and I had won £400,000.00. But more importantly, and I just couldn't see it at the time, but Lizzy was always there protecting me and was always doing the best she could by me, in the background. I am blessed to have her in my life!

I was surprised she had clung on to me for as long as she did, any other girl would have ditched me a long time ago. I still had to deal with Rich and I hated him with a passion, but this story isn't over yet. I will drag Richard through the courts to try and recover my money and I will try to put everything right.

Chapter 35
Partners in Crime

Richard and Jen cut all ties and contact from Royston, they were ghosts. Once I commenced with court proceedings, Richard was not going to come quietly and just hand back all of his spoils; he was going to lie and cheat to keep them with the assistance of his wife, Jennifer Potter.

There were fundamentally only two questions to ask.

Why would Richard not return my shares and put things right for XS Homes Limited?

And

Why would he not return the money that he owed to me?

There is only one possible conclusion or answer: Richard, my identical twin brother, had seized the opportunity to steal it and keep it all for himself.

Richard could have stopped all of this at any moment by just returning everything that didn't belong to him. However, the problem with Richard is he has a huge sense of entitlement.

I heard from various sources on his movements that, without me, he fell apart quite quickly in terms of his success. I may not have been able to get near him, but I was always breathing down his neck without him even realising. After being self-employed, he couldn't make it on his own and since we fell out, Richard got a job as an estate agent—which is quite a fall from grace considering what we achieved together—and since losing that job, he had gone back into the electronics industry as a receptionist for a company in Stevenage. I guess he doesn't have that little something, something after all.

In May 2016 Richard, through my solicitor, made me an offer of £21,750.00 to go away, claiming he had already paid me £28,250.00; this wasn't true. Richard had used all sorts of trickery and it was hard for me to keep up. From creating fictitious paperwork, forging my signature, and making up all sorts of claims and fictitious cash amounts—even adding up every single transaction he could find on his bank statements between us for payments, which were completely separate, like us going to a cinema or a restaurant together—he deducted this off of my money; it was ludicrous. He would stop at nothing to wriggle out of paying me. Richard owed me £52,000.00 and it's as simple as that.

When we formed XS Homes Limited, if you remember, I told Richard I would be taking a finder's fee for the amount of £25,000.00. This was because I had secured the financing which totalled £535,000.00 and this was sent to me in June 2015. As normal with our businesses, Richard had always dealt with all of the paperwork, but now I realise that this gave him the opportunity to do some extremely questionable things.

I rejected Richard's offer and, out of the blue, two months later on the 19th of July 2016, I received correspondence from Richard's solicitor. Richard had created paperwork and signed documents in my name claiming the finder's fee that was given to me was actually a loan from the company. I now had a debt and owed XS Homes Limited £25,000.00. Richard had reversed our agreement and stolen the £25,000.00 given to me as a finder's fee by changing the original paperwork and forging my signature.

My case was being dealt with as a civil matter and the bench mark for a criminal case would be so high that it would be extremely difficult to prove that he had done this. He owned the company and there was nothing I could do to stop him. In Layman's terms, he acted as a debt collector for XS Homes Limited; he was a debt collector for his own company. His solicitors created what is called a Deed of Assignment and it is a legally binding contract between him and XS Homes Limited, and it gave Richard the power to claim and deduct the £25,000.00 from my personal money—the money that he owed me. Therefore, Richard had claimed he had paid me back £28,250.00, which he hadn't. He then offered me £21,750.00 which I rejected, so he tweaked the company paperwork claiming I now owed a debt to the business for £25,000.00. Anyway, it's a minefield, but the end result was that he then made a counterclaim against me and alleged that I now owed him £3,250.00.

'Richard was up to his old tricks, creating fake invoices, creating transactions and forging paperwork. 'Fuck this, I'm going all the way; I will go to court and I will not fail. I will work as hard as I have to for as long as it takes,' I thought and I knew the road ahead was a long one.

It was one court fight and straight into another; this next part of my life was excruciating, it was so painful for me and Lizzy to deal with—all of the lies that poured out of Richard were incredible. Jen was also complicit in helping him; why wouldn't she just shake him and talk some sense into him and put a stop to all of this?

My mental health was suffering and I never fully recovered from the Germany situation; I became very emotional at times. We never got a break or the happy ending that Lizzy and I deserved; the fight with Richard ran alongside the Germany situation. Germany was over, but it was straight into battle with Richard, the person who had created this nightmare to begin with. I was left to try and pick up the pieces while they moved onto their next victims—the next group of people they could con while portraying themselves as the new Posh and Becks of Biggleswade, where nobody knew the truth and devastation that they had left behind them.

'That's probably why Richard changed his surname, to hide, or some foolish attempt to erase any links to me and create distance. It fits in nicely, moving onto another town where no one knows you, ready for the next con,' I thought to myself.

This nightmare dragged on for well over a year and due to Richard's behaviour, he wrecked relationships that I had with people and I lost the friend who originally loaned me £225,000.00—that plays heavily on my mind. Richard refused to give me back my shares for XS Homes Limited and as I said, I couldn't pay my friend personally; everyone's hands were tied. Richard completely destroyed everything while he was also helping himself to tens of thousands of pounds out of the XS Homes Limited bank account.

I wasn't quite the same person after the Germany situation and it had affected me in ways I couldn't explain; I am always filled with self-doubt and questioning if I'm good enough, but I would dig so deep to win this court case. I was spending countless days, hour after hour, preparing for my case against Richard. One thing that occurred to me was that I would be up against him in court and the last time we were in court together, he claimed he 'aced' everything and completely tore me down;

this was my chance at retribution, but I was a recluse yet again having to deal with an ongoing court case and mountains of paperwork.

I was consumed by it and it took over my life. My close friend, Carl, supported me and I hung out when I could with my two other closest friends. I grew really close to both of them and they are my best friends; they are called Chink and Whiff. They helped me through some of my darkest days and are definitely more like brothers to me than my actual brother. I would spend so much time at the weekends going over this disaster, seeking their help and guidance, and then there was Liz who gave me the strength and momentum to carry on— along with her parents, Tom and Kim.

I still struggled and occasionally would have a blow out with drink and drugs; it wasn't as often, but when I did it, I really did it. I was improving all the time, but this court case against Rich had brought on a whole new type of pain to my life and I will never get over how he could do this to me. Stealing money from his identical twin brother: that is a really difficult thing to deal with.

The plot at 'The Grove', as I expected, had got planning permission for two houses and I found out that Richard had tried to dissolve XS Homes Limited and take everything; not just my money, but Lizzy's dad's money and my friends. It was well in excess of half a million pounds, but fortunately Lizzy's dad Tom had a first charge over the property on the site; the property was the only asset within the company and this blocked Rich from the ultimate payday. Richard was left with no choice but to hand the company over to my friend and he would then try recouping his money, but Richard didn't hand it over without dissecting it first and raiding the company bank account of at least £60,000.00, using fake invoices and the Deed of Assignment. Fortunately, but not without a lot of heartache, my friend and Tom both recovered all of their money when the plot finally was sold in April 2017 for £549,500.00. There was a lot of profit in the property since we first bought it back in July 2015; it had made £184,377.00 which salvaged everything for them—but as for me, the person who started it, once I signed it over to Rich, I never saw a penny.

Everyone had suffered so much from the ripple effect Richard created, but with everyone else sorted, that just left me to go at him in court. Richard was well up at this stage probably in the region of £100,000.00, including my money. Richard and his wife were enjoying money that they hadn't earned; why earn it when you can just steal it from everyone else?

The nights that I sat there, in complete despair at the situation… and Lizzy felt my pain. It took a long time, but my circle of friends, who used to be their circle of friends, were finally opening their eyes to what was really going on.

Holding my head in my hands, it was early in the morning and I'd just finished preparing some court documents, I heard Lizzy get out of bed and come downstairs to check on me.

'You okay, baby?' Lizzy asked me.

'Yeah, it's just so painful. This didn't need to happen; all Richard had to do was stop and return everything back the way it was,' I said. I was exasperated, I was fucked.

'I know you're doing everything you can; I meant to mention earlier, babe, I'm struggling to see out of my eye—feels like the room is closing in on me, like a kaleidoscope,' she said while closing one eye and scrunching up her face.

'Really? Let me take a look at you,' I said staring into her face and looking into her big blue eyes; she looked fine to me.

'Let's go and get you checked out; book an appointment at the opticians tomorrow,' I told her.

Lizzy thought she might need glasses, but the opticians referred her to the hospital where she was diagnosed with serous retinopathy caused by stress. This can lead to permanent loss of central vision. Everyone has a breaking point and Lizzy was losing her sight. This was really upsetting for me; I hadn't helped matters—that's for sure—but the ripple effect Richard created had affected everyone in one way or another.

Eventually, a court date was set for the 21st of September 2017 sitting for two days at Bedford County Court.

While I was getting ready to take Richard on, he was in the background trying to make himself judgement-proof and he sold the property at 'Olney' just before we walked into the courtroom; he was hiding all of his assets and making sure everything was all in his wife's name. Richard sold 'Olney' on the 19th of July 2017 for £274,000.00. He had bought it for £250,000.00 three years ago and had borrowed £55,000.00 from me which, as we all know, he claimed that he needed my money to finish the renovation of the property. He shifted the house and sold it at a loss to stop me getting my hands on it if I won in court.

'Honestly, what a fucking shit project Olney was. Richard recouped his losses by stealing from me,' I thought, shaking my head in frustration.

In preparation for the court case, I booked the best hotel that I could find in the area for two nights; I wanted me and Lizzy to be fresh faced and on our best form. I'd called Lizzy to be a witness for me; that's obvious and why wouldn't she be? She was aware of everything; you would think that Richard would have asked his wife to be a witness, but he didn't. Instead, he was calling our accountant to be his one and only witness. This was amusing to me; why would you call your accountant to be a witness for what should be quite a simple debt claim?

The court case was upon us and Lizzy and I were making our way to the hotel. Having a base meant we could relax and be in the best shape to deal with matters, and I'm not a morning person so like to take my time. The hotel was called The Bedford Swan and it was two minutes away from the Bedford County Court. The hotel was beautiful and overlooked the Great Ouse River in Bedford; we got out of the car and headed to the reception.

'I can't believe this day is finally here, babe; I've worked so hard to get to this point,' I said.

'I know darling, how you feeling? You got your folders?' she asked me knowing that I'd probably left them in the car.

'I left them in the car,' I replied.

'Do you think that's wise? What if someone nicks the car?' she said smiling at me.

'Yeah, good point; I'm more worried about my files than your car,' I said as I ran off laughing.

I ran back to the car to grab all of my bits, while Lizzy grabbed the room key.

We got settled in, set our stuff down and went to explore the hotel and go for something to eat. The hotel had a spa, a pool with a Jacuzzi and there were a couple of bars and restaurants inside the hotel. The decor throughout the hotel was beautiful and it had so much character; it was the perfect setting for a wedding venue.

Taking Lizzy's hand, we went for a walk along the river, watching the swans gracefully glide up and down through the water—it was so peaceful.

'Liz, how are you feeling about tomorrow, babe? you nervous?'

'I am a little,' she said.

'It'll be fine and I know you'll be okay; don't get me wrong, it is nerve racking when you get in the stand, but just take a moment, get your breathing right and just answer truthfully,' I told her.

'Imagine if Jen and Rich were staying in the same hotel as us,' she laughed.

'I'm not kidding; I wouldn't be able to control myself. Fucking hell, babe, could you imagine? If he is staying at our hotel then Rich will be turning up at court tomorrow wearing a full body cast and a tie.'

'Do you think Jen will show tomorrow?' she asked me.

'No fucking way, babe; he hasn't called her as a witness 'cos he doesn't trust her not to fuck it up. Remember, they are both lying and Jen would fuck it up under pressure. No way would my brother risk putting her in the stand, and if she isn't a witness, it would be crazy if she was there. You've got to picture it right: she's not a witness, yet she's sitting at the back of the courtroom that's never going to happen, it would look fucking weird.'

'This is Richard we're talking about babe,' she replied.

'Nah, babe, it would be ridiculous,' I said.

It was dark as we walked along under the shelter of the trees that ran along the path way next to the riverside.

'Let's go and get you some food babe. What do you

fancy? I've got to make sure my star witness is looked after,' I said.

'I don't know, babe, you choose. I'm happy with whatever,' she replied.

'Well, it's getting late. I know there is a Wagamama's near to the court; I wouldn't mind checking out where the court is so we know exactly where we are going tomorrow morning,' I said.

'Yeah, cool, let's do that,' she said.

'You brought your swimming cozzie too, we will definitely be in that Jacuzzi tomorrow night; we can relax and go over what's gone on. It's gonna be a tough day,' I said.

After dinner, we went back to the hotel. It was important to me that we both got an early night, so I sorted out all of my things, hung my suit up, put my shirt on a hanger, straightened my shoes and went downstairs for one more cigarette. I had been preparing for this day for so long and I'd given this case all I had.

Standing outside, I was looking up into the sky and it felt weird that my brother was out there somewhere getting ready just like I was.

'How the fuck did it get to this? Me having to take my identical twin brother to court; I'm going to fucking crush you tomorrow,' I thought.

Chapter 36
I Put My Armour On

I hadn't slept that well and my mind had been racing all night; I had been going through all the facts in my case over and over again, on repeat. I needed to prepare my team and get organised. My solicitor was on her way and my barrister was staying in a hotel over the bridge. I kissed Lizzy on the cheek and said, 'Come on, babe, let's go downstairs and have breakfast; not long to go now, just stick on some clothes, we can eat and then come back to our room and get ready.'

Once I got back into the room, I needed to zone out and focus on pulling everything together. Taking my Dolce & Gabbana suit out of the wardrobe, I remember thinking, 'The last time I wore this was at Richard's wedding.'

This suit is the bollocks: it's blue with matching waistcoat and trousers. I wore a baby blue shirt with blue brogues and a burgundy coloured tie, a burgundy coloured pocket square and a matching burgundy belt. I put on my Rolex and looked in the mirror, I was ready for battle.

'If this case could be won just by looks alone then I would win this, hands-down,' I thought.

I had a purple shirt with me ready for the next day which was softer in appearance, but today was business mode: look sharp, attack sharper.

I had to leave earlier than Lizzy to go over the bridge and

see my barrister at his hotel for a team talk and I would come back to get her in a little while. After a brief chat with my barrister, I was on my way back and literally a couple of metres from the entrance to my hotel, the door swung open and a woman came out; directly behind her was Richard and then our accountant—I couldn't believe my eyes who the last person out of the door was: it was Jen. Richard looked me dead in the face with no emotion and I smiled; I wasn't expecting it and thought to myself, 'What the fuck am I smiling for? For fucks sake, control yourself,' my accountant stopped and let the others walk ahead.

'Christian, I'm so sorry it's come to this; it's not you, mate, but your brother insisted I was a witness,' he looked slightly embarrassed as he looked down at the ground.

'Honestly, don't sweat it; you do what you gotta do,' I said and he scuttled off after Rich and Jen.

Picking up my phone, I quickly called Liz.

'Babe, you're not going to fucking believe who's here. Jen's here—I can't fucking believe it.' I was seriously shocked; I just couldn't get my head round it.

'I told you she would be,' she replied.

'Honestly, how bad does that look? Anyway, get your arse down here; we've got to get over to the court,' I said to her.

Lizzy looked sleek in black trousers and a matching black suit jacket; it was strange as we walked into the court together. I walked over to join my team and we stood on one side of the room and Richard and his team stood on the other—it really was good vs evil.

When I arrived, my barrister said to me, 'I nearly grabbed hold of your brother, thinking it was you. I was puzzled how you grew a beard so quickly since I'd only just seen you this morning,' he said and he was smiling.

'Yeah, could you imagine if he sat with you pretending to be me and you told him our plan of attack?' I said and we both laughed.

When we were called into court, I just couldn't believe my eyes as Jen sat there at the back of the courtroom, sniffling away and glugging on a little bottle of water, snotty tissues everywhere. It was baffling; she was not going to be a witness in this case and yet was sitting here watching it.

'No way am I letting this slide. I'm going to capitalize on this,' I thought.

The courtroom was as you would expect, with the judge sitting at the head of the courtroom on a raised platform. We were sat on a table on the left and Richard was sat at a table on the right. There was also a witness box which was positioned in front of our table just to the left.

Things happen a lot faster than you think they would and as soon as the judge entered the room, we all bowed and waited for the judge to be seated and then we took our seats. There was an introduction to the case from both sides and it was agreed in which order the witnesses would take to the stand and before you know it, you're in the stand and over the next two days we thrashed it out. The next two days were going to be exhausting and tiring as we went at it. I was first up in the witness stand and it took me a moment or so to warm up, but I was honest, open and truthful.

There was a distinctive difference between how my team operated and how Richard's team did; it was like night and day. I can only describe it that, collectively, my team were approachable and easy to read, warm and friendly. It was very dark over on Richard's side of the room; Jen's mountain of snotty tissues were growing in size, and there was a deceptive and dark undercurrent swirling around all of them. They were not out to fight fair, but it showed and just fuelled my confidence. Now I'm not going to claim it was easy because it wasn't, I was being accused by Richard's lawyer of all sorts, but I promised myself I will fight with everything I had and I did. Richard's court paperwork claimed that I was a coke addict and a gambling addict, but at the end of the day it was a cheap shot to try and assassinate my character; it had nothing to do with the money that I had loaned to Richard. Once I was running at full steam, I ran rings round Richard's barrister and I could sense the judge had warmed to me. As for Lizzy, Richard's barrister wanted her in and out of the stand as quickly as possible. For damage limitation, he only asked her, 'You're only here because Christian asked you to lie for him, aren't you?' he said abruptly.

'No, that's not true,' she replied.

She was defiant, but softly spoken, that she was here to tell the truth.

'No further questions,' he said to her.

The fact that Lizzy was prepared to get up there and defend me that in itself spoke volumes.

I was so proud of her; she did not fail me and for the short moment she was up there, she showed true grit and determination. She was prepared to go all the way, whether it was two minutes or two days in that stand.

As for Richard, he took that dark deceptive shadow with him into the witness stand, evasive and snarling at every question, the lies just poured out of him; he was quite the showman, but for all the wrong reasons and his demeanour in general was aggressive. He was exactly the same person I saw all those years ago when we went up against HMRC. I think Richard truly believes that saying nothing, and being defensive and obnoxious, is the way to deal with these kinds of situations; he honestly doesn't realise that being evasive and saying nothing when you don't like the question, says it all. He spent so much time being elusive while in the stand and focusing on times that he could refer to me as Mr Govan or the Claimant rather than his brother; it was becoming painful just listening to his voice.

We took a small adjournment for about 15 minutes, but before the judge left the courtroom, she asked the room,

'Who is that girl in the background?' She said, pointing her finger towards the back of the room.

'That's the defendant's wife,' my barrister volleyed back to the judge.

The look on the judge's face said it all as she left through her own door at the back of the courtroom because the judge was aware of all of the witnesses who were going to take the stand and Jen wasn't one of them.

After the adjournment, Richard took to the stand again as he was still being cross-examined and my barrister knew the exact question to ask him.

'Richard, can you tell me who that is sitting over there in the corner of the courtroom?' my barrister asked as he looked over towards Jen.

'That is my wife and she is here to support me,' Richard said, raising his voice and protesting defiantly.

Everyone in the entire courtroom all turned to look across at Jen who was looking rather sheepish, hiding behind a mountain of snot drenched tissues.

'But she's not in the stand, though, is she? If she were here to support you, she would have been a witness in this case; she would know quite a lot about what's gone on, particularly as she owned XS Homes Limited with you,' said my barrister.

The last question before Richard left the stand actually came from the judge directly.

'Richard, can you tell me how much did Christian get paid from XS Homes Limited?'

'NOTHING!' Richard shouted back aggressively at the judge.

'Thank you, there are no further questions; you may stand down,' said the judge.

Richard and Jen didn't hang about and before I even got out of my chair, they were gone. They practically ran over each other trying to get out of the courtroom leaving his barrister and solicitor standing there.

In my opinion, Richard had finally found something he was an expert at: he was an expert at losing court cases. If you want to lose a court case then Richard is your man; unfortunately, I wouldn't know the conclusion just yet as the case was adjourned for a separate hearing for the judge's decision.

We left the court and as soon as we got out of there, I hugged Lizzy and lifted her up off the ground.

'Well done, babe, I'm proud of you,' I said to her, kissing her all over the face.

'I didn't do a lot,' she replied.

'But you were prepared to,' I said to her.

We made our way back to the hotel, we were both pretty exhausted, and I was thinking about what had gone on.

'I wouldn't change a thing and I'm pretty confident we couldn't do anymore. I'm not sure we will beat Rich on that

Deed of Assignment, so he'll probably get that £25,000.00. That's air tight due to his fucking lawyers, but he can have that, we will win the rest,' I said.

It was the 5th of December 2017 and Lizzy and I were travelling to Oxford for the final hearing. Exactly like before, I booked a nice hotel near the court for two nights; I didn't intend to drive straight home after the verdict. We had done the hard part in court and all we had to do now was listen.

Meeting up with my team before we walked into court, I could see Richard in the waiting area and this time he didn't bring his wife.

'Crazy you brought Jen along to the wrong hearing, she should have hidden the first time and be here for this verdict. If she was there to support you then why wasn't she here now?' I thought.

Richard probably didn't want Jen to see his ego get torn apart by the judge.

Sitting in the courtroom, there was a recap from both sides, each barrister chasing after one another and putting their best points forward and then there were further questions from the judge. The judge really made us work for it; I think she enjoyed the tussle. I was watching each team argue each point and I was still quietly confident and I knew what I should win and what money I won't retrieve.

I knew the Deed of Assignment was a problem. It wasn't right, but there was nothing I could do about it and I was pretty sure that the documents forged by Richard and the Deed of Assignment would stand. I can't prove it, but I knew he had committed fraud with those documents and like I said he can do my signature. This could be a criminal matter for another day, but I just wanted back a large chunk of my money, plus my costs.

It was a tense moment when the judge started to read out her judgement; I had my hand under the table and every time I won something, I counted it on my fingers. I listened intently as she reeled off a number of things and I knew quite quickly that I was ahead as Richard was awkwardly melting into his chair.

'Rich looks like the witch in the *Wizard of Oz*; I'm melting, I'm melting,' I thought to myself keeping a straight face.

I was pursuing Richard for £52,000.00; it was unfortunate, but Richard pulled off his scam and won £25,000.00 which I expected—pushing that to the side, I was awarded £37,000.00 including interest, plus all of my costs.

An interim payment for costs for the amount of £25,000.00 was given to me and the rest of my costs would be assessed at a costs hearing, but for today, I won £62,000.00—I was victorious!

Once I totalled everything up with all of my costs included, I had won around £105,000.00.

Richard pulled the cord on his ejection seat and flew out of the courtroom; he didn't want to hear the total damage I had done to him. I was straight faced until it was just me and Lizzy and, once out of sight, I picked her up as we hugged and kissed one another. We had done it: we had won—we were the champion of champions.

'Rich should never fucking tell me to bring my A game or say he aced anything to me ever again; he's a fucking embarrassment,' I said.

'Yes! We can move on baby, I love you,' she replied excitedly.

That should have been the fairy tale ending, I survived everything that was thrown at me and I beat the bad guy, but this villain still had a few more tricks up his sleeve.

I went on a Caribbean cruise with Lizzy and her family over Christmas and New Year, and then in the New Year Lizzy and I went to Thailand. It was time to put it all behind us and try to move on; a fresh start after what we had both been through.

It was the 3rd of January 2018 and as per the court order, Richard was told to make a payment to me for £62,069.05 by no later than 4pm. I remember sitting on the deck of the cruise ship, I was having a cigarette and watching the seagulls pass by as we left the port in Barbados. I was thinking back over everything that had happened to me. It was difficult to recall the more painful stuff; it had been such a long journey and it was the first time I could smile in a long time. I made contact with my solicitor and there was no sign of any money; a few days past, and I was starting to feel uneasy.

'I don't like this; that fucker owes me money. He was prepared to roll the dice and fight me in court and he lost and now he is just ignoring the instructions from the court,' I thought to myself.

Richard had gone underground, so I was left with no choice but to instruct the bailiffs to attend his address. What's fucking crazy to me is that the bailiffs by law have to send you notification that they are coming. How does that protect my rights, giving Richard 7 days' notice that the bailiffs are going to knock on your door? This gave Richard time to hide anything of value. Well, it was worse than that, the day the bailiffs turned up, Richard had sold the house and had moved out; he had vanished. Richard and Jen had totally cleared the house out and it was the new owners that answered the door. Richard and Jen had done a runner and gone into hiding. Fucking hell, I cannot explain how deflated I was and it took me some time to try and locate him. We were now heading towards the end of March when I found out that Richard and Jen had purchased a brand new, 5-bedroom, detached house in Biggleswade for £485,000.00. It was just finished when they came out of hiding and they moved into the property.

This house was solely in Jen's name and they moved into it at the end of March 2018. Richard and Jen had managed to hide until his wife had secured a mortgage for this property and then guess what?

Richard Potter declared himself bankrupt.

Richard couldn't go bankrupt until Jen owned the property, but between them, once they had secured their new house in her name, Richard orchestrated his own bankruptcy straight after.

Richard deliberately manufactured his own bankruptcy to get out of paying me and all the other unsecured debts that he had racked up. All unsecured debts were completely obliterated and when I eventually received a letter from the official receiver, it contained a list of creditors that he owed money too.

Richard went bankrupt to stop himself actually going bankrupt and he made a profit doing it. He ramped up his credit cards and overdrafts in preparation for his bankruptcy. I even heard that after he went bankrupt, Richard tried and failed in getting a restraining order against me.

Richard went bankrupt owing £172,562.44 and looking down at the list of creditors in Lizzy's kitchen, even his own wife was on there for the amount of £48,043.00.

He even had his own wife on the creditors list; this is a bankruptcy trick and if the amount Richard owes to creditors reaches a certain level, then the creditors are informed that it's basically pointless trying to recover any of it and the creditors will never see a penny. Is anyone expected to believe that he ripped his own wife off for forty-eight grand? It was all part of the con.

Richard owes me in excess one hundred and five thousand pounds and he has never and will never pay me a penny.

Chapter 37
Robbing Your Relatives

It was the 28th of January 2019 and I was in bed watching TV with Lizzy, or at least I thought I was, but Lizzy falls asleep as soon as her head hits the pillow. I wish that could happen to me, but I still struggle to sleep these days. I was watching a programme on Channel 5 called *Robbing Your Relatives*. While I lay there, I felt so much empathy for these people who were in similar situations to me. They had their money stolen from them by their family members too. It was heart-breaking, but I didn't feel as alone as I did after watching that programme. There are other people out there, other people like me who have suffered a similar fate, yet each story is so different.

I was lying there and thought, 'Fuck this, I'm going on that programme; I want to share my story. I want to try and prevent other people suffering like I have and all for what? Just for being a brother, a brother that cared and would do anything for you, that's what I am guilty of.'

I want to show the world what a monster Richard really is and finish this story my way, so I rolled over to pick up my phone that was at the side of the bed and at 00.35 I sent an email to RDF Television; they are the company who make the programme *Robbing Your Relatives*. My email briefly explained that Richard my identical twin brother had stolen money from me. I received a phone call that same morning around 11am from RDF Television who were interested in meeting with me, and after my meeting with the series producer, the rest is history. Lizzy and I filmed for two days and we became the main story for Series 2 Episode 1.

I often ask myself, 'Will Richard watch the programme?' and the answer is of course he will; it would be too irresistible for him not to. I am sitting in Lizzy's living room coming to the end of my book and the programme is due to air soon. This book has been a long and rough journey for me; I'm haunted by the darkness of some of it and I thought it would be therapeutic.

Is it fuck! I have had to relieve every single painful moment again like I was actually going through it, like my mind was playing a TV show of my life so far and I've had some very tough moments with it. I definitely would be lying if I said that I haven't shed any tears along the way; I've shed many tears along the way.

I also received a telephone call from the Official Receiver via their mobile phone which I thought was strange. An investigation has been taking place and the Official Receiver who has been dealing with Richard's bankruptcy knows this case like the back of their hand. I was told that in all of the years that they have dealt with these types of matters, they have never dealt with a case like mine before. There is no doubt that Richard went bankrupt to get out of paying me or any of his other creditors. The lengths that he went to, as you have read, are unimaginable, but it's all very real.

The Official Receiver has established from a lot of information that they have gathered, including information provided by me, that Richard did not disclose all of his assets.

In particular, the cash that he received from the sale of Olney; the money from the sale of this property went directly into his wife's bank account in an attempt to hide it. Apparently, Richard 'forgot' to mention it. He will be pursued by the solicitors who act on behalf of the Official Receiver for that money. Unfortunately, by the time this money has been disbursed by the Official Receiver—whose charges alone are £9,000.00, on top of that are all of the solicitor's fees—the creditors and I will end up with nothing.

Funny that all of the money from 'Olney' belongs to me, yet it will be distributed between the Official Receiver and their solicitors. I will find out in three years the amounts clawed back when they release the final report.

Richard also failed to disclose the £15,000.00 Rolex he wears on his wrist which is in his wife's name and untouchable.

During the phone call from the Official Receiver, I was being told that Richard is very cunning, manipulative and incredibly deceitful until I got cut off; however, moments later, I received an email. I think the Official Receiver was struggling to speak to me, they had already told me too much.

I received an email from the Official Receiver and this is the exact email that was sent to me on the 23rd of October 2019 at 14:28

Hi Christian,

Lovely to speak to you. I'm so sorry for what has happened to you.

Best Wishes

You have to remember that there is limited contact between the Official Receiver and a creditor, if any contact at all, but the fact my contact went out of their way to say this much to me speaks volumes and I know my contact was touched and upset by what has happened to me and they only know a fraction of what has really gone on.

The programme *Robbing Your Relatives* finally aired on the 6th of November 2019 and amassed over 850,000 viewers. Think about that: it's Wembley Stadium at full capacity nearly ten times over.

It's the 30th of November 2019, and it's our birthday—today, we are 42.

I came into this world as a twin and one day I will leave this world without one. I thought I had someone in my life that would always be there for me through the good times and the bad, but I found out who Richard really was, who he always has been: a parasite. Since I was born, Richard had been eating away at me gradually from the inside out and when he was finished, he sacrificed me for money; he truly is the enemy with my face.

So, what's next for me? I'm not sure yet, it's been a long and tough journey. I've just finished writing my story which I have been dedicated too for quite some time now. I never once wrote any of my manuscript while I was under the influence of any drugs or alcohol so what you are reading is directly from me with no filters or assistance; it's the truth and it's from the heart.

I wrote this book and I think it's time to move on. A fresh start: a new chapter.

My Final Thought

On a good note, I'm still alive. I got through the Germany situation; I eventually put everything right to the best of my ability and I beat Richard in court. I grabbed the devil by the horns, but you can't beat the devil, he always has an ace up his sleeve.

Richard is the ultimate con man and I have to put my faith in God that, maybe one day, what goes around comes around. My advice is to think long and hard before you lend a family member any money. Just because they are a family member that does not give them free access to the VIP area in your life or your money. Treat them as you would any other business transaction and, to be perfectly frank, be even more secure than that because the heartache and depression that comes with it is not worth it—no amount of money is—so protect yourself.

Family and friends in business can at times be the worst mix as your expectations for them to do right thing by you are higher than they would be if it was anyone else. I would approach them with even more caution than you would a stranger, that way you can't get it wrong. After all, they shouldn't be offended if their intentions are honourable when it comes to you protecting your own money. I found that out the hard way.

Remember, my identical twin brother's famous quote: 'Trust me, your money is safer with me than anyone else.' I emphasise this; he was my identical twin brother and all that other shit about his word was his bond etc. 'If I ever hear that bullshit saying again, I'll scream in your face.'

With regards to anxiety, depression and suicide, let's try and get that straightened out. If you take cocaine to give yourself any sort of chance then you need to stop doing cocaine. Give your mind the ability to get itself stable enough so you can actually function on a normal day. Taking cocaine will eventually lead you straight back to depression and the depression may lead you back to the suicidal thoughts. Let's be frank, it has been proven that cocaine wreaks havoc on your mental health. You will never stop the vicious cycle and, yes, I know I'm a fine one to talk and I'm certainly not perfect, but I will continue to try and my life continues to improve; it's really slow progress, but you will get there.

It's okay not to be okay, but you have to look after your mental health, it's paramount for your own wellbeing. I'm damaged after what has happened to me and my mental health took a kicking, but I'm coping. Although, I hurt at times, I know I will be all right. I will always wear the scars so please just take the time to be considerate of others and how your behaviour could affect someone else; your actions and the affect that it has on others could actually kill someone. Suicide is no joke and many people are taking their lives every single day; sometimes in life, you can do something to someone that can never be undone.

If you broke your arm, we can see that. It's easy to sympathise for someone wearing a cast, or having a broken leg and being pushed about in a wheel chair, but you can't see inside someone's head; you can't see their pain and, trust me, I'd rather break every bone in my body then feel the pain that depression brings. Perhaps there's someone you know, someone that instantly crosses your mind who has had a tough time in life. Just take a moment to send a text and see how they are doing. It could take you all of a matter of seconds, but could literally be the difference between life and death.

If someone is feeling suicidal or has attempted suicide then they are still here with us—that's a chance to help them. Don't ridicule that person or shy away from them. There's no such thing as attention seeking when it comes to suicide. Think about what that person is actually saying; they are saying, 'Will somebody please help me the fuck out? I'm struggling here.'

Always run towards that person, don't run away. Just be human, be kind and fucking love one another!

Lastly, never ever sacrifice someone for your own financial gain; there's more wealth to be found in life than money. Never give up on yourself. All is not lost, you just haven't found what you're looking for yet, but it could be just around the next corner!

Me and my brother as babies with my mum. I have no idea which one is which.

A family photo. Our initials were on the bottom of our shoes so that Mum and Dad didn't muddle us up.

Me and my brother aged 9, I'm on the left trying not to laugh for our school photograph.

Growing up as teenagers we were still made to wear the same clothes. I'm on the left.

Clubbing in Puerto Banus, Marbella, with (L-R) my brother, Elizabeth and me.

Me and my brother aged 37, I would have done anything for my little brother. I'm on the left.

The girl who never gave up on me. Me and Elizabeth together.

Just the girls together, Lizzy and Jen.

Out in London's West End. Me and Richard were teasing a bouncer for being bald. I'm on the left.

The ankle bracelet I had to wear 24/7 after the European Arrest Warrant was executed. I was arrested for tax evasion to the tune of sixty million euros.

At 'The Hayloft' I slept on an inflatable bed so that I could be next to my front door after my house was raided by the police.

Not long after my arrest Richard and Jen flew off on holiday to Ibiza. Something to celebrate?

This is the last ever picture taken of me and my brother together in October 2015. On the outside I was putting on a brave face but inside I was falling apart. I'm on the right.

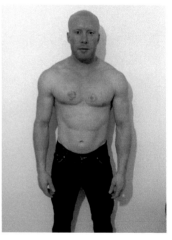

There's no love in these bites that Richard gave me when we fought that night at 'The Grove.'

Group photo, with (L-R) Me, Lizzy, Rich and Jen.

My documentary for Channel 5 'Robbing Your Relatives.'

Mr Christian Thomas GOVAN

Case number: ●●●●●●●●●●●●
Born: 30 November 1977

Extradition Part 1 - Discharged

The extradition proceedings to **Germany** have today been discharged.

Discharge reason:

1. Section 41 - the Part 1 warrant has been withdrawn.

By order of the court

Date: <dateoforder>　　　　　*District Judge (Magistrates' Courts)*　　　　　**Clerk of the Court**

Cases

●●●●●●●●●●●●

Arrested following a certificate issued under section 2 of the Extradition Act 2003 in respect of a Part 1 warrant issued by Germany for Tax Evasion x 266.
In accordance with section 4 of the Extradition Act 2003.

Confirmation that my European Arrest Warrant was formally discharged.

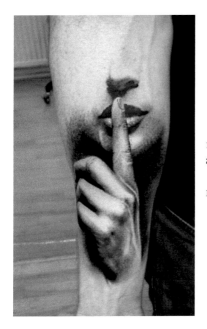

After everything I went through, I got this tattoo, it reminds me to keep fighting and for all those people who doubted me, spoke behind my back and hurt me, if you can't be kind then just shut the fuck up!

Me and my brother were inseparable, we were always together. I'm on the left.

A couple have been fined thousands of pounds after their 38 dogs left neighbours without a decent night's sleep for years.

The ex-council house was stuffed with animals leading to piles of dog faces and a constant noise, which made life hell for their neighbours.

Animals spent hours everyday barking and howling - disturbing neighbours

'The House of Horrors' made an appearance in The Sun newspaper.

Therfield couple plead guilty to noise abatement breach after yapping and barking of 38 dogs troubles neighbours

PUBLISHED: 15:02 28 July 2016 | **UPDATED:** 15:33 28 July 2016

Rebecca Day

David Govan and his wife Marilyn were found guilty of breaching noise abatement orders

A Therfield couple who kept 38 dogs in their ex-council house pleaded guilty to breaching eight counts of a noise abatement notice after the sound of barking consistently disturbed their neighbours.

Mum and Dad made the local and National newspapers. This article was written by The Royston Crow.

My beautiful girls
Elizabeth and Shannon.

The three of us on holiday
together.

Liz, me and Shan partying
in Puerto Banus, Marbella.

First time in my pool on the roof with Lizzy.
New beginnings!

Lizzy sipping champagne on my balcony.

Me and Lizzy celebrating Valentine's Day 2020!

Shannon on my balcony.

Just adding the final touches to my book
on my 42nd birthday.

I decided to fulfil one of my dreams and I now own a new place in Marbella, Spain. My life, even though I find it hard at times and I still struggle, it is improving. I will keep trying and I will keep fighting. It's a fresh start, the next chapter!